DATE DUE			
AUG 4			
MAY 2 1			
NOV 9			
NOV 2 3			

62342
Schoeck

Scientism and Values

The William Volker Fund Series in the Humane Studies

EPISTEMOLOGICAL PROBLEMS OF ECONOMICS
by Ludwig von Mises

THE ECONOMIC POINT OF VIEW
by Israel M. Kirzner

ESSAYS IN EUROPEAN ECONOMIC THOUGHT
Edited by Louise Sommer

SCIENTISM AND VALUES
Edited by Helmut Schoeck and James W. Wiggins

Scientism and Values

Edited by

HELMUT SCHOECK

AND

JAMES W. WIGGINS

D. VAN NOSTRAND COMPANY, INC.
PRINCETON, NEW JERSEY

TORONTO   LONDON

NEW YORK

D. VAN NOSTRAND COMPANY, INC.
120 Alexander St., Princeton, New Jersey (*Principal office*)
24 West 40 Street, New York 18, New York

D. VAN NOSTRAND COMPANY, LTD.
358, Kensington High Street, London, W. 14, England

D. VAN NOSTRAND COMPANY (Canada), LTD.
25 Hollinger Road, Toronto 16, Canada

Library of Congress Catalogue Card No.: 60-16928

Contributors

LUDWIG VON BERTALANFFY, Sloan Visiting Professor, The Menninger Foundation, Topeka, Kansas. His works include *Modern Theories of Development* (1933); *Problems of Life* (1952); and *General Systems: Yearbooks of the Society for General Systems Research* (Ludwig von Bertalanffy and Anatol Rapoport, editors, 1956 *et seqq.*).

WILLIAM T. COUCH, Editor in Chief, *Collier's Encyclopedia*, New York City. He was editor and contributor to *Culture in the South* (1954) and *These Are Our Lives* (1939), and has written articles and reviews for scholarly and literary journals.

PIETER GEYL, Professor Emeritus of Modern History in the University of Utrecht. His works include *The Revolt of the Netherlands* (1932); *Napoleon: For and Against* (1949); and *Debates with Historians* (1955); *The Use and Abuse of History* (1955).

HENRY S. KARIEL is a faculty member at Bennington College, Vermont. Among his recent publications are "Normative Pattern of Eric Fromm's Escape from Freedom," *Journal of Politics* (1957); "Democracy Unlimited: Kurt Lewin's Field Theory," *American Journal of Sociology* (1956); and "Limits of Social Science: Henry Adam's Quest for Order," *American Political Science Review* (1956).

RALPH W. LEWIS, Professor of Biology, Michigan State University. Among his published papers are "Mutants of Neurospora Requiring Succinic Acid or a Biochemically Related Acid for Growth," *American Journal of Botany* (1948); "The Vitamin Nutrition of Alternaria solani," *Phytopathology* (1952); and "An Outline of the Balance Hypothesis of Parasitism," *American Naturalist* (1953).

MURRAY N. ROTHBARD, Ph.D., consulting economist, New York City. Selected publications include "Toward a Reconstruction of Utility and Welfare Economics," in M. Sennholz, ed., *On Freedom and Free Enterprise, Essays in Honor of Ludwig von Mises;* "In Defense of 'Extreme Apriorism,'" *Southern Economic Journal* (1957).

HELMUT SCHOECK, Professor of Sociology, Emory University. His books include *Nietzsches Philosophie des Menschlich-Allzumenschlichen* (1948); *Soziologie-Geschichte ihrer Probleme* (1952); *USA: Motive und Strukturen* (1958); and *Was heisst politisch unmoeglich* (1959).

ROBERT STRAUSZ-HUPÉ, Professor of Political Science and Director of the Foreign Policy Research Institute, University of Pennsylvania. Works include *The Russian-German Riddle* (1940); *The Zone of Indifference* (1952); *Power and Community* (1956); *The Idea of Colonialism* (1958); and *Protracted Conflict* (1959).

ELISEO VIVAS, John Evans Professor of Moral and Intellectual Philosophy, Northwestern University. His publications include *The Moral Life and the Ethical Life* (1950); *Creation and Discovery* (1955), and *D. H. Lawrence: The Failure and the Triumph of Art* (1960).

RICHARD M. WEAVER, Professor of English, University of Chicago. His published works include *Ideas Have Consequences* (1948); *The Ethics of Rhetoric* (1953); and *Composition: A Course in Writing and Rhetoric* (1957).

W. H. WERKMEISTER, Director, School of Philosophy, University of Southern California. His publications include *A Philosophy of Science; The Basis and Structure of Knowledge* (1948); and *A History of Philosophical Ideas in America* (1949).

JAMES W. WIGGINS, Professor and Former Chairman, Department of Sociology and Anthropology, Emory University. Among his publications are *Foreign Aid Re-examined*, coeditor, (1958) and "Society's Interest in the Marital Status," *Journal of Public Law* (1955). He is director of the national study, *A Profile of the Aging: U.S.A.*, to be published in 1961.

Contents

Introduction

Helmut Schoeck

"Scientism" is a term of criticism. In the realm of aesthetic creativity, the critic is usually a revered and accepted professional. But in the field of social science the man who suggests self-criticism and internal systematic doubt of what we are doing often invokes the scorn and wrath of his fellows who feel threatened in smug niches of narrow expertness.[1]

However, though we use the term "scientism" in a slightly pejorative and reproving sense, we do not think of ourselves as antiscientific. Scholars who are critical of scientism do not offer intuitions as the remedy. On the contrary, the word "scientism" conventionally describes a type of scholarly trespassing, of pseudo exactitude, of embracing incongruous models of scientific method and conceptualization. Scientism fosters not only the "fads and foibles" of contemporary sociology, but is also in itself a symptom of an insecure world view, of a negative social philosophy. Certain models of society, certain techniques which this volume evaluates, and for which we suggest the label "scientism," appeal sometimes to insecure individuals and groups because such use of science in human affairs supposedly would allow one to "fix," to freeze the world once and for all.[2]

Moreover, scientistic interpretation of the study of man throws the scholarly grasp of human nature and its volitions open to ideological manipulations when least suspected. Quantities can be as subjective an argument as a stress on qualities. But most people are less aware of this fact. If the public or fellow scholars are unwilling, for prescientific, i.e., ideological reasons, to accept our arguments, statistical data and their expert manipulation will not convince them. Indeed, we can always startle our positivistic friends in the social sciences by asking them to name just one major policy decision or law that came about, against the popular and political preferences for it, on the strength of quantitative data. Can we recapture the proper—i.e., most fertile—balance between elements of measurement, of quality, and of form in the study of social man?

Over a number of years participants in this symposium, and others, have shown, in their individual publications, increasing concern with the harm done to the true study of man, especially as a social being, by a form of scientism that takes various disguises of strict scientificalness. It is not merely neopositivism, which, by the way, has been criticized by a number of able men; it is also more than a cult of quantification. Scientism implies a *cynical* world view—in the original meaning of the word: it is a *doglike* view of man, or shall we say *ratlike?* Man is best understood, so the scientistic expert holds, when seen from the level of a rodent eager to learn the ins and outs of a maze. He can be conditioned to put up with almost anything the few wise designers of the maze have mapped out for him.

And yet a critical attitude toward scientism is not to be confused with an antievolutionary position. On the contrary, we see scientistic sociologists and anthropologists refuse to learn from research on animals because it might challenge their creed of environmental determinism. As A. L. Kroeber observed not long ago,[3] many of his colleagues in America are studiedly ignorant of the work of the ethologists, including such renowned men as Karl von Frisch and Konrad Lorenz, who explore species-specific innate behavior patterns.

Thus, we should ask *just which* aspects of the presocial and nonsocial sciences appeal to those afflicted with scientism? And why are they enthralled and to what effect? The scientistic students of social man have isolated their field from meaningful reality by an arbitrary barrier of methodology. "What we cannot study does not exist—for the time being." This was done partly by reserving the labels "scientific" and "scholarly" *(wissenschaftlich)* for a few approaches to reality which laymen and social scientists conventionally associate with the natural sciences. Scientistic doctrinaires chose to ignore the fact that these few methods were by no means the only approaches used in the natural sciences. Bertalanffy's paper cites striking examples of this naiveté.

Fritz Machlup blames part of this on a semantic confusion and remarks that in German-speaking countries certain excesses of scientism may not have appeared for the simple reason that the word *wissenschaftlich* embraces a larger number of methods and approaches than does "scientific" in the English-speaking world.[4]

And when we examine prenineteenth-century uses of the word *Wissenschaft*—from the Teutonic weight of which the word "science" obtained some additional glamor around the turn of the century—we find that learned men, around 1780, understood *Wissenschaft* primarily to mean "worth knowing" or "worth noticing." When we are critical of a fashionable brand of scientism, we do not intend to belittle the necessity and actual power of the method of obervation. We plead for more courage in observing phenomena, even if the methodologist tells us that his tools are not yet ready for them, or never will be.

We might heed what so eminent an economist as Jacob Viner wrote about his field:[5]

And for some time in the future there will be problems of interest to the economist which will be elusive of the application of the techniques of precise measurement and which will have to be dealt with by methods of inquiry which in the dogmatics of the laboratory scientist have lost their respectability. It is true, however, even of the physical sciences, or at least so I gather from the recent writings of the more articulate physicists, that they are losing some of their late Nineteenth Century preference for naive as against sophisticated metaphysics, and also that until they have devised quantitative methods of dealing with problems they proceed brazenly by means of inferior methods without much apparent injury to their self-esteem.

And even John Maynard Keynes, in his *General Theory of Employment, Interest and Money* (pp. 297 f.), was well aware of a fact that most of his ardent followers seem to have forgotten. He warned:

It is a great fault of symbolic pseudomathematical methods of formalizing a system of economic analysis . . . that they expressly assume strict independence between the factors involved and lose all their cogency and authority if this hypothesis is disallowed; whereas, in ordinary discourse, where we are not blindly manipulating but know all the time what we are doing and what the words mean, we can keep "at the back of our heads" the necessary reserves and qualifications and the adjustments which we shall have to make later on, in a way in which we cannot keep complicated differentials "at the back" of several pages of algebra which assume that they all vanish. Too large a proportion of recent "mathematical" economics are mere concoctions, as imprecise as the initial assumptions they rest on, which allow the author to lose sight of the complexities and interdependencies of the real world in a maze of pretentious and unhelpful symbols.

Adherents of scientism—as far as the study of man is concerned—have turned the meaning of "science" (*Wissenschaft*) into the art of selective "not knowing" and "not noticing." Today's scientistic bias compels students to know the worthless and keeps them from searching for the knowledge of worthwhile bodies of data.[6] In 1953, the student government of Yale University published its rather harsh "Course Critique," a booklet guiding new students to worthwhile courses. According to the specific critique of the course in social psychology, enrolled students seemed to learn little and became impatient because the professor's methodological zeal and rigor kept him from imparting knowledge of what makes human beings really "tick" in social interaction.

We could be amused and simply wait for the eventual passing of this fad. Yet it is not so comfortable a situation. We probably know considerably more about social man, about our systems of social organization, than the fraternity of behavioral scientists and sociometrists allows us to admit. Many of the theoretical achievements, as well as the everyday routine work of the natural sciences, depend on subjective sensory experiences, evaluations, and judgments of a kind that is strictly outlawed as "unscientific" or "unscholarly" in the official social sciences of today.

Especially are we forbidden to use simple declarative, and

sometimes pejorative, terms without which a chemist or anatomist could not even communicate in his profession. If this were because of a humanistic self-consciousness, we could hardly find fault with it, but it becomes ludicrous when the taboo is imposed on the ground that we have to follow the natural sciences.

Under cover of this confusion some social scientists foolishly or mischievously undermine forms of social (political, economic) life the defense of which ought to employ cognitive and evaluative means (and terms) that still constitute the major tools of many natural sciences. If social scientists really knew what natural scientists do, they could hardly derive a mandate for aggressive social reforms from their ambition to be scientists. Natural scientists are often compelled, in certain fields, to let the internal arrangement of their subject matter alone. A scientific grasp of, and approach to, the world around us is by no means synonymous with the wish to change things. There are several disciplines whose masters are committed to, and trained for, the most careful conservation and restoration of past structures. Archaeology, linguistics, medical arts, plant and animal ecology, limnology, to name a few, apply scientific method and care in order to preserve or restore structures and arrangements which came about without benefit of a human planner. For instance, sociology could benefit from the morphological approach used in the life-sciences (e.g., comparative anatomy). Of course, there is no ontological congruity between the objects studied in these fields. What I should like to stress here is the heuristic value of this type of categorization, since I shall show this in detail later.

A famous archaeologist once complained that the advent of photography corrupted the young generation of scholars in his field. They no longer needed to draw what they saw. They simply shot a picture, but in the process of doing this they forgot, or never learned in the first place, how to observe. Drawing with a pencil on white paper some glimpses deep down in a cave was hard schooling. It taught how to see.

Similarly, I am afraid, the arrival and pushing of quantitative methods in the social sciences corrupted young sociologists and social psychologists. They are so proud of the presumed power of statistical tools, of measurement of attitudes, for instance, that they never learn how to observe significant phenomena in their field of study. They learn all about "measuring" attitudes before they can tell one attitude from another by looking at a human being in social action.

This helplessness of our social scientists is shown, for instance, by their failure to come to grips with the phenomenon of aggression. Learned teams have tried to discover what makes human beings aggressive. They have studied international tensions, hostilities, frustrations, and other surface phenomena. It has hardly occurred to them to go beyond the terms "aggression" or "hostility." If they had been as open to such problems as were our students of man in the nineteenth century, it could not have escaped their attention that envy is a much more basic common denominator for various phenomena of "aggression" or "hostility" than "frustration," although a less flattering motive with which to excuse the perfidy of a Hitler or a Castro. The frustration theory nearly allows one to put the blame on the alleged frustrator; in the case of envy, this is a little more difficult.

W. T. Couch has made pertinent comments on this point: the developments we have come to call scientism are probably, in part, responsible for the facility with which social scientists circumvent crucial phenomena of human action that have traditionally formed a link between the empirical observation of man and normative philosophy.

NOTES

1. *See,* for instance, Sylvia Thrupp: "An audience of historians is not enough. Yet will the average sociologist join the audience? Will he be afraid, if he is seen reading a journal of 'Comparative Studies in Society and History,' of being thought unscientific, antiquarian, a deviant in his profession, maladjusted?" "History and Sociology: New Opportunities for Co-operation," *American Journal of Sociology,* LXIII (1957), 14.
   Probably one of the earliest uses of the term scientism in a critical and derogatory vein can be found in Max Scheler, *Die Wissensformen und die Gesellschaft* (Leipzig, 1926), p. 271. Recently one could note an increasing use of the terms "scientism" and "scientistic" in scholarly and scientific writing. Here are a few examples.
   ". . . scientism may be described as an addiction to science. Among the

signs of scientism are the habit of dividing all thought into two categories, up-to-date scientific knowledge and nonsense; the view that the mathematical sciences and the large nuclear laboratory offer the only permissible models for successfully employing the mind or organizing effort. . . . One main source for this attitude is evidently the persuasive success of recent technical work. . . . The danger—and this is the point where scientism enters—is that the fascination with the mechanism of this successful enterprise may change the scientist himself and society around him. For example, the unorthodox, often withdrawn individual, on whom most great scientific advances have depended in the past, does not fit well into the new system. And society will be increasingly faced with the seductive urging of scientism to adopt generally what is regarded —often erroneously—as the pattern of organization of the new science. The crash program . . . the megaton effect are becoming ruling ideas in complex fields such as education, where they may not be applicable." (Gerald Holton, Professor of Physics, Harvard University, in his paper, "Modern Science and the Intellectual Tradition," *Science,* CXXXI [April 22, 1960], 1191.)

Joseph R. Royce, a professor of psychology, writing in the December, 1959, issue of the *American Scientist* (XLVII, 534), offers this definition and warning: ". . . as men . . . we tend to commit ourselves in an ultimate sense to a particular structuring of the value universe. . . . Communists . . . have made this type of commitment to their political views . . . and have thereby made communism their religion. In my opinion, this same attitude can be taken in the name of science, and we may properly refer to this type of religious commitment as scientism. I do not wish to be misunderstood at this critical juncture. As I see it, we should apply the scientific method to any and all problems. . . . However, my point is that the final putting together of the segments of life will always be a highly subjective and individual task . . . which cannot be scientized." Michael Polanyi finds "that modern scientism fetters thought as cruelly as ever the churches had done. It offers no scope for our most vital beliefs and it forces us to disguise them in farcically inadequate terms. Ideologies framed in these terms have enlisted man's highest aspirations in the service of soul-destroying tyrannies." (*Personal Knowledge: Towards a Post-Critical Philosophy* [University of Chicago Press 1958], p. 265.)

And Jacques Barzun, surveying the jargon of several of our "leaders of social science," speaks of the "enormous harm [that] has been done by heedless scientism to language, first, and through it to everyone's mind." (*The House of Intellect* [New York: Harper, 1959], p. 230.

2. Kai T. Erikson, *Psychiatry,* XX (August 1957), 271 f., has shown how the scientistic models of certain psychiatrists tend to lure patients into an unrealistic attitude toward treatment.
3. A. L. Kroeber, "On Human Nature," *Southwestern Journal of Anthropology,* XI (1955), 196 f., 200, 204.
4. Fritz Machlup, "The Inferiority Complex of the Social Sciences," *On Freedom and Free Enterprise, Essays in Honor of Ludwig von Mises,*

edited by Mary Sennholz (Princeton: D. Van Nostrand Company, 1956), p. 165.

5. J. Viner, *The Long View and the Short* (1958), pp. 42 f., reprinted from an article in *American Economic Review, Supplement*, XVIII (March, 1928).

6. *See,* for instance, William C. Boyd, "Has Statistics Retarded the Progress of Physical Anthropology?" *American Journal of Physical Anthropology*, XVI, No. 4 (December, 1958), 483: ". . . the use of statistical methods in physical anthropology, although no doubt useful . . . has in the past retarded the progress of the discipline, by leading to a false feeling of security in the uncritical accumulation of great masses of measurements and by discouraging attempts at physiological and genetic analysis of human traits." If this can be said about *physical* anthropology, should we not heed such warning even more for the social and cultural dimensions of man?

1

Social Science and the Problem of Value

W. H. WERKMEISTER

The purpose of this paper is to consider social science and the problem of value within the over-all framework of "scientism and the study of man." By "scientism" I mean here a boundary transgression or a misuse of otherwise legitimate procedures and attitudes of science.

To put the problem into clearer perspective, it may be well to consider briefly what is meant here by science and the "enterprise of science." To a large extent, of course, this is a matter of method. But that the material success and the prestige of modern natural science have aggravated the problem—if they have not actually created it—goes without saying.

It may be well for our purposes to distinguish two interrelated aims of science: description and explanation. By description is meant a simple enumerative account of the observable features and qualities of things and events, whereas explanation is an attempt to account for the facts and to show why they are what they are. Ultimately all scientific explanation involves some law or laws in terms of which the explanation is accomplished.

This enterprise of science, however, depends on and involves a number of discernible aspects, mostly of a methodological nature. Thus, the first step in any scientific enterprise must be

1

the collection and description of facts, the precise statement of what is the case. Observation and measurement are here indispensable. But it is at this level, too, that experimentation plays its part. The purposes for which experiments may be devised are multiple. They may be simply a part of the procedure of determining the case; but they may also be designed as tests for hypotheses or for the verification or disproof of laws. That experimentation implies its own set of assumptions of a logical and ontological nature may be remarked only in passing.

Facts ascertained by observation and/or by experimentation become the basis for inductive generalizations and, ultimately, for the construction of explanatory hypotheses. Such hypotheses—although they are essentially imaginative constructions of logical schema from which laws descriptive of the observed facts can be derived by logical transformations—must be logically possible (i.e., they must be self-consistent) and must have predictive significance.

Now, the history of science is quite clear on one point: facts were discovered, isolated, and described in various fields of investigation; and explanatory hypotheses were developed correspondingly. Thus, there was the field of classical mechanics and the field of electrodynamics, and there was also the quite separate field of chemistry. Each field was developed independently, and in each field explanatory hypotheses made possible the derivation of specific laws descriptive of the observed facts. That all the facts were, in essence, the results of measurements and were statable in purely quantitative terms was but a result of certain assumptions underlying the enterprise in all fields of investigation.

But when facts were discovered which legitimately belonged to more than one field of investigation—to classical mechanics, for example, as well as to electrodynamics—it was found necessary to construct a theory (Einstein's theory of relativity) whose definitions and postulates made possible the logical derivation of laws in both fields. And, similarly, new definitions and assumptions, entailing the law of quantum mechanical resonance, led to the integration of the whole realm of physics and the realm of chemistry as well. There emerged, in other words, the ideal of an integrated and closed system of science encompassing all of physical existence. This actual achievement in the natural sciences of an all-encompassing integrative theory had its unmistakable effects in other areas of knowledge as well. The dream was born that some day—and in the not too distant future—the same methods and procedures so successfully applied in the natural sciences would, via the biological and behavioral "sciences," encompass the whole of reality and would make everything—man included—amenable to scientific interpretation and understanding. From the point of view of the integration of all knowledge this was unquestionably an ideal worth striving for.

This ideal of an integrated science, however, was keyed to two crucial assumptions. One of these assumptions, formulated by Galileo and actually employed in the natural sciences, was that only quantities or facts reducible to quantities could be admitted as real in science. The other—perhaps only a corollary of the first—was that only material objects and their interactions could be regarded as legitimate objects of science. The ideal of an integrated universal science would therefore inevitably entail a naturalistic reductionism and the elimination of all value concepts from the realm of science. Values, however, are part and parcel of human existence—of an existence, that is, which is essentially purposive activity and a matter of manifold valuations. In view of the value-permeated character of human existence, a special problem arises for all who advocate a total unity and integration of science. It is this: Can man and his deliberate and purposive actions be subordinated to a value-free conception of reality, and can the human world be integrated with physical nature into an all-comprehensive scientific view of the world? To put it in still other terms: Can the reality of man, permeated with values as it is, be fully understood in terms of value-free concepts and theories? The problem would not arise, however, were it not for a number of influential persons in the field of the social sciences who ardently believe that it can be done and who work toward the realization of this goal. Still, the problem of value looms

large in the human world and cannot be brushed aside easily.
If only the advocates of the reduction of social studies to the level
of a natural science (could get around the problem of values,) they
would have clear sailing. The problem of values, therefore, occupies a key position in this quest for an all-encompassing science.

An examination of the learned journals in the various fields
of the social sciences soon reveals, however, that it is not always
clear just what is meant by "the problem of value," or whether
any particular author regards it as one problem or as many.
There is evidence, on the contrary, that different authors mean
different things when, overtly or by implication, they are concerned with values; that their perspectives differ; and that their
aims are at variance.

I submit that "the problem of value" occurs in the social
sciences in at least three basic forms; that these three forms must
be strictly separated if we are to solve "the" problem at all; and
that each form, in its own way, is ultimately related to an all-
inclusive value theory, the broad outlines of which I hope to
indicate in a moment. And I submit, more specifically, that in
dealing with "the problem of value" in the present context we
must speak of (a) the value *of* the social sciences, (b) values *in*
the social sciences, and (c) values *for* the social sciences.

                                I

(a) The question of the value *of* the social sciences constitutes
no particular problem. Knowledge obtained in any field of inquiry
is of value to us—including the knowledge obtained in the social
sciences; and it is of value to us in a twofold sense. It is of value
(i) because knowledge of any kind satisfies man's innate curiosity;
and it is of value (ii) because knowledge and understanding are
of crucial importance as the basis for rational decisions and reasonable actions.

As to (i), little need be said here. We must realize, however,
that man's innate curiosity—his desire to know—is the driving
force behind much of our basic research. The personal satisfac-

tions derived or derivable from the enterprise known as science are, for many of us, sufficient to ascribe value to a science. Let us not underestimate the significance of this side of our work.

As far as (ii) is concerned, the value of the social sciences transcends, of course, all merely subjective valuations. We have to deal here with the pragmatic and empirically demonstrable value of the social sciences—with their value in the service of man's aspirations, intentions, and hopes, including his aspiration to understand himself and to control his environment. It is noteworthy, however, that this pragmatic value of science—of the social sciences as well as of the physical and the biological sciences—is but the value of a means to an end, and that scientific knowledge, being a means only, is neither the end pursued nor a substitute for the decisions and actions which determine the end. Value relations of quite a different nature enter the picture here.

It is true, of course, that any knowledge we have or can obtain concerning the facts relevant to a decision is of value. A rational and reasonable decision is impossible without such knowledge. But the knowledge upon which the decision is based concerns not only the actualities prevailing at the time of the decision; it concerns all foreseeable consequences of the decision as well. And the key to decision-making is not the knowledge provided by the sciences; it is the value commitments of a civilized humanity. These commitments, and not the sciences, determine ultimately what our ends and goals shall be. The various sciences may determine the appropriateness of the means of attaining a desired end; they may enable us to estimate the probability of achieving that end and to determine the cost of achieving it in terms of a predictable loss of other values; and in this sense they may materially contribute to our selection and revision of the ends to be pursued. Nevertheless, science as science—and this includes the social sciences—does not define the ideals or value norms that constitute the over-all framework of valuations within which we make our decisions concerning ends and goals in relation to which the facts of science are themselves appraised in regard to their instrumental value.

II

(b) The problem of values *in* science also occurs in a twofold sense. It occurs (i) in so far as valuations and value commitments are part of the facts which the social scientist studies; and it occurs (ii) as a question concerning the explanatory categories needed in the social sciences.

The concern of the social scientist with values in sense (i) is again obvious. After all, human beings are end-pursuing creatures. The ends pursued are evaluated, individually and socially, and these evaluations—their origins, changes, and manifold interrelations—are part of the facts, of the very subject matter which the social scientist studies and interprets. As subject matter of the social sciences, values constitute no particular problem—although it is true, of course, that even in this sense the problem of values *in* science does not exist for the physicist or the chemist.

The second case (ii) in which the problem of values in the social sciences arises requires more extended discussion, for it is crucial to the very nature of science as science. I shall deal with it in some detail in the latter part of this paper. For the present it suffices to say that, in the social sciences, values may function as explanatory categories—as universals, that is, in terms of which social phenomena must be understood; and that the structuralization and interrelation of value categories provides the only rationale for an understanding of the structuralization of a society or a culture.

III

(c) The third basic form of our problem is the problem of values *for* the social sciences. It arises because the investigator himself makes, and must make, certain value commitments— both as a person and as a scientist. His commitments as a person reflect in general the value pattern of his own "community" and of the social group and the institutions of which he is a member. As a scientist, however, he is committed also to the specific value framework within which alone scientists operate. And it is this framework in particular that I have in mind when I speak of values *for* science.

However, not all valuations contained in that framework are of equal importance for science. By and large, we may speak of two groups of valuations, each having its own particular significance for science. There are (i) the over-all value commitments and valuations of any given culture or period in history with respect to science in general; and there are (ii) specific value commitments which an investigator must make if he is to be classed as a scientist at all.

As far as (i) is concerned, the record of history speaks for itself. The over-all valuations and value commitments—the "value climate"—in contemporary America are much more favorable to the sciences than were the value commitments of medieval Europe; and the post-Sputnik emphasis upon science in the United States indicates a still further shift in the over-all value framework within which science exists and has its being. A reappraisal of science is taking place in our own culture. What effect this will have upon science itself and upon the humanities only the future can tell. Even so, the value pattern of our American culture also sets limits to scientific enterprise—e.g., by delimiting the extent to which social experiments may be attempted. In addition, however, every scientist makes personal value commitments which also have a bearing upon his work. His own valuations determine not only his choice of a field of research, but the specific problems with which he is concerned and the manner in which he pursues them. It would be a mistake to overlook these facts when we speak of values for science. Nevertheless, values and valuations of this type do not affect the character or nature of science itself. They are therefore only loosely connected with our problem.

The specific value commitments and valuations referred to under (ii) are of a different nature and are of crucial importance *for* science. Moreover, they are inescapable; for the moment we accept scientific rather than nonscientific procedures of investigation, we must also accept that complexus of valuations summed up in the term "standards of research."

Exactitude and punctilious care in the compilation of data, in-tegrity and intellectual honesty, sound reasoning, imagination to see alternative possibilities of interpretation, courage to follow an argument to its logical conclusion, and a willingness to abandon cherished ideas in the light of new evidence—these are but some of the qualifications and valuations indispensable to the enterprise of science. Their significance for science is obvious.

There is one value commitment, however, which, though as-sumed in all scientific enterprise, is of particular importance for the social scientist. This is the commitment to objectivity in the evaluation and interpretation of facts.

The problem is related to, but not identical with, Max Weber's thesis of "ethical neutrality" as a prerequisite for the social scien-tist. What Max Weber demanded was essentially that the social scientist refrain from passing moral judgment on the facts he studies. The various Kinsey reports would in this sense measure up to Max Weber's demand; and, in an obvious sense, the require-ment of "ethical neutrality" is fundamental and must be fulfilled. In this same obvious sense, however, the requirement of "ethical neutrality" is not identical with the demand for objectivity which I have in mind. Under certain conditions the two demands may even be in conflict with each other.

In a superficial sense the demand for objectivity means that, as a scientist, one is to be guided only by facts and by logically sound inferences from these facts. Actually, however, the problem cuts deeper and cannot be dealt with so simply; for the so-called facts do not always exist well defined and in pristine purity. Even in the physical sciences a certain degree of abstraction from con-text, of isolation, is required if individual facts are to be obtained. In the social sciences this process of delimiting the "facts," of isolating them from overarching contexts, is even more important, and also more difficult. In all of the sciences the selection and the demarcation of facts are determined by the basic assumptions which define the problem to be investigated and delimit its scope, and by valuations which guide the investigator at every step in the course of his investigation. Because of the relative sim-plicity and the completely value-free character of his subject matter, the physical scientist here has an advantage which the social scientist does not have; for the latter is himself an integral part of the culture in which he lives, and shares in a large measure the value commitments prevalent in his society; and the normative ideas of his own culture (conceptions of human rights, of private enterprise, and the like) and his own value orientations (be they conservative or liberal, static, dynamic, or anything else) may affect his research from its inception to its conclusion, including his delimitation, collection, and interpretation of "facts." And, as a rule, the investigator himself may not even be aware of the influence which these valuations and value commitments have upon his work. The problem of objectivity, therefore, is one of the most difficult which the social scientist has to face. I have dealt with it in another context and shall not discuss it further at this time.[1]

IV

Because we appreciate the value *of* science, we are inescapably committed to values *for* science. But only as explanatory categories are values of crucial significance *in* science. And to this problem of values *in* science I shall now return.

In order to see our problem in its full significance and proper perspective, let us remind ourselves for a moment of the fundamental change in concept formation and the ideal of explanation which was essential to the emergence and development of science during the sixteenth and seventeenth centuries.

During the Middle Ages and for centuries thereafter, every explanation of natural events was given in teleological and value-loaded terms. Every object and event was assumed to have a purpose, a value-determined place in the world. Man might not understand in any given case what the purpose or value of some particular thing was, but a purpose and value it had—if its purpose was only to "glorify God." In the Aristotelian scheme of explanations, which included "material," "formal," "efficient," and "final" causes, only an understanding of the "final" cause—of the purpose, that is, for the sake of which a thing exists or a change takes place—can provide a full explanation of the facts. But this is merely another way of saying that in the Aristotelian scheme of things, which prevailed prior to the development of modern science, value terms were indispensable as explanatory categories. To understand things and events meant to understand them in terms of the values which they embody or which they tend to realize. Even the Copernican view of the universe was still charged with value; for did not Copernicus argue that it was better to have the stars at rest rather than the earth since they are nobler and more divine?

(It was Galileo who first enunciated the principle which became basic for the physical sciences—the principle, namely, that in science nothing is to be admitted as real which is not itself a quantity or is not reducible to a quantity.) Here for the first time the ideal of a science was envisioned in which value terms and teleological conceptions were no longer acceptable as explanatory categories. And from the time of Newton on, all interpretations of the mechanistic processes in nature were given in terms of "efficient" causation only. "Formal" and "final" causes had no longer a legitimate place in science as such.

We need not trace here the history of the gradual acceptance of this new idea in the physical sciences. Nor need we discuss the problems confronting the biologist in his efforts to free his own science from value concepts and teleological categories of explanation. Our concern is with the social scientist; and for him the problem of value terms as explanatory categories is a complex and difficult one. It is unavoidable, too; it arises in the social realm irrespective of any commitment or noncommitment to Aristotelian presuppositions, simply because, consciously or unconsciously, human beings pursue ends which they value, and their valuations and value commitments determine their behavior.) If the social scientist does not take this fact into account, then human behavior, in so far as it is purposive, remains inexplicable, much of our social action remains unaccounted for, and the social sciences cannot advance beyond the elementary stage of mere description.

It may be argued, of course, that even in the area of the social studies the employment of value terms as explanatory categories should be avoided; that unless this is done, social studies cannot attain the status of a science. Even so advanced a social science as mathematical economics, however, is based upon value assumptions, namely, that all goods to be exchanged involve some factor of production; that, if no effort were required to produce the goods, the buyer would not be willing to pay for them; and that every producer of goods seeks to maximize his profits and that he acts rationally toward that end. The corollary principles of marginal utility to the consumer and of marginal return to the producer but emphasize the reference to valuations and value commitments inherent in economic theory. Mathematical economics, therefore, does not show that it is possible to avoid value terms as explanatory categories in the social sciences, but only that social studies can be scientific despite the fact that all explanations are ultimately given in value terms, and that this can be achieved by including value terms in the basic assumptions which are foundational to the whole science.

The point I am driving at—and I shall elaborate my argument later on—may be made in another way. Man is by nature gregarious, valuing positively whatever satisfies his affiliative needs. The whole structure of social living is therefore—and from the very beginning—value-oriented; and it is stratified in conformity with value conceptions. Ruth Benedict's *Patterns of Culture* provides but one of the many proofs of this fact. The social group as a whole functions as a "community" only when its members have at least some basic value commitment in common and when, collectively and individually, they are intent on realizing or maintaining those values. It is in this sense that we can speak of a "community" of scholars, although the individuals who are members of this "community" live thousands of miles apart and speak different languages. And it is in this sense also that we may witness the complete disintegration of a "community" even though all members are next-door neighbors within a city block.

When the collective behavior in a group, a tribe, or a nation (functioning as a community) becomes clearly defined, standardized, and patterned, then "institutions" emerge as the socially recognized or acknowledged embodiments of co-operative efforts on behalf of approved but less comprehensive values. So understood, social organization is but the outward manifestation of more specific hierarchical or co-ordinate value commitments. Changes in these value commitments—either in the values themselves or in the character of the commitments—will inevitably result in modifications of the institutions involved and, thus, of the structural pattern of the whole social group or the "community." It is obvious, I believe, that the social scientist may well be concerned with the emergence, the function, and the development of institutions, with their mutual interrelations and their relations to the individual, and with their change, persistence, cultural lag, disorganization, and reorganization. But it is equally obvious, it seems to me, that no matter what aspect or phase of the social institutions is under study, the social scientist cannot avoid using value terms in his explanation of the facts; for it is a socially approved complexus of values which, in the first place, constitutes the very core around which an institution develops; and it is a modification of that complexus of values or of its approval which entails the structural changes in the institution itself. Thus, whether he wants to or not, the social scientist cannot escape the problem of value *in* science in its profoundest and epistemologically most significant meaning.

One word of caution, however, is now in order. The value terms which the social scientist employs as explanatory categories should not be expressions of his own valuations, predilections, or biases, but should be the basic value commitments inherent in the phenomena to be explained and should be obtained through a most scrupulous examination and analysis of the facts themselves. That is to say, the value premises of social theory should state what *has been* or *is being* valued within the social group under investigation, not what *should be valued* in the opinion of the investigator. Value terms, if they are to be useful at all as explanatory categories, must be indigenous to the subject matter itself.

V

In the preceding sections reference has been made again and again to "valuations," "values," and "value commitments." It is now necessary to clarify this terminology and to explain precisely what is meant.

Let it be understood from the beginning that no reference to a Platonic realm of value essences is here intended. Nor shall I hold that "values" in themselves are entities which factually exist in the world of things. My position is now —as it always has been, and with respect to the world of things no less than with respect to "values"—that the only basis we have for asserting anything (be it true or false) is our own first-person experience—the experience to which I can refer as my experience and which, when you analyze your own experience, you identify as *yours.* It is the experience which is simply *there,* in all its self-revelatory factuality, when we discuss or analyze anything. That this experience is bipolar, including a subject-pole and an object-pole which, in their conjunction, constitute "my" (or "your") "awareness" of "something," is but an analytic truth. Interpretation of the subject-pole leads to our conception of the "empirical subject," the "self," the "person"; and analysis and interpretation of the object-pole leads to our conception of "things," "events," "other persons," and, ultimately, the "world" as the sum total of all there is.

It must be noted, however, that from the very first all first-person experience has a "felt" quality about it which also requires analysis, and in which are rooted our "felt-value" experiences and our "valuations."

In its most primitive form this "value" quality is recognized as a felt pleasantness or a felt unpleasantness of the experience or of the "something" which is being experienced. But such is the complexity of human experience that, at a more clearly defined level of reaction to a "world" around us, the gratification of appetites, the assuagement of affiliative needs, the satisfactions of the mind, and the sense of harmony and self-fulfillment (which is happiness) are also "felt" as "values"; whereas, in general, the negative in each case is "felt" as a "disvalue." We are here confronted with a "hierarchical order" of felt qualities which, despite many infractions and temporal inversions, tends toward an equilibrating harmony and constitutes the experiential basis of all our valuations and value ascriptions—our "engagement" as a person in the experience itself providing in each case the criterion of the "order of rank" of the values.

Moreover, such is the "felt" quality of our experience that it encompasses at once the object, event, or situation which occasions the "felt" experience. And this fact is the basis upon which we ascribe "value" to the objects, events, and situations themselves. "Values," therefore, do not exist in the world around us. But things and events *have* value because, as warranted by the "felt" quality of our experience, we ascribe value to them.

Beyond the objects, events, and situations which immediately occasion a "felt value" experience, we ascribe "value" also to all things, events, and activities which, being causally related to the former, contribute indirectly to the experience; and to those objects, events, and situations which we anticipate as occasioning a "felt value" experience. That realization may fall short of anticipation and that a present experience may have to be judged within the perspective of future events and "felt values" significantly implies that value experience is not atomistic and that the context of this experience itself provides an empirical basis for revaluing any particular value ascription.

It is not necessary to discuss in detail the many and complex problems which here confront the philosopher and which have made progress in value theory so difficult. It is sufficient to point out that the approach here suggested—starting with the intrinsic "value" of certain "felt" qualities of experience and leading to the ascribed "values" of objects, events, and situations, and an interpretation of their "order of rank"—avoids the *cul de sac* of emotivism and subjectivism no less than that of Platonic realism. At every step in our analysis we can find empirical warranty for our assertions, and from the most ephemeral "valuations" we can advance to the most stable, from instantaneous "felt" responses to "valuations" in the long run and on objective grounds. Value theory itself is now not only meaningful, but empirically testable.

VI

In referring to the complexity of "felt values," I spoke of a "hierarchy" and an "order of rank" of these values. Although I indicated at the time that in actual experiential situations there might occur infractions and inversions of such an order, it is now necessary to augment my earlier references in still another way.

The key to what I have to say lies in the fact that "felt value" experiences cluster around certain "core values" which are associated with distinct facets of human existence. Aside from the primitive level of simple sensory pleasures—such as the agreeableness of the taste of a cherry, the pleasing quality of an azure sky—there are "felt values" which cluster around the basic gratification of an appetite, and the cluster of "values" varies with the appetite involved in any particular situation (e.g., hunger or sex). There is a cluster of "values" associated with the "felt value" quality of well-being; and, surely, this cluster of values, except for certain marginal cases, differs essentially from those centering around an appetite. There is, furthermore, the whole scale of "felt values" associated with the assuagement of affiliative needs; and there are yet different clusters of "felt values" associated with intellectual satisfactions and aesthetic enjoyments, with the joys of creation and the experienced sense of self-fulfillment or happiness. And there are the infinitely manifold and variegated value ascriptions—of means and of ends—which reflect our "felt values" in a world of facts.

My thesis is that these clusters of "felt values" and of ascriptive valuations are relatively stable in basic orientation; that many of them—even in their interrelations—constitute the value basis for social institutions; and that, therefore, the "core values" of the various clusters, and their augmentations and modifications, constitute explanatory categories indispensable to the social scientist.

One additional point must be considered, however, before we return to the problem of value as an explanatory category in the social sciences. There are two levels of value clusters which are of particular significance for us. One is the cluster of felt and ascribed values associated with man's affiliative needs; the other is the cluster of felt and ascribed values associated with the sense of fulfillment. The former encompasses the whole range of values pertaining to "communal" relations of individuals in actual societies. The latter consists of the ideal projections of self and community "images," constituting patterns of culture which include most, if not all, of the other value clusters. That the transition between the two levels is fluid is obvious. Nevertheless, only the latter is the projection of some ideal of a "cultured humanity," infusing the rest of man's valuations with their ultimate significance and with their relative importance. The degree of harmony (or disharmony) between the actualities of any given society, on the one hand, and the valuations inherent in its ideal projections, on the other, is in itself of greatest significance for an understanding of that society. The United Nations, in ideal conception and actual functioning, is but one obvious illustration of what I mean.

VII

To some students of human behavior, in all its complexity, the institution is the real isolate of culture. And if this is so, then the valuations and value ascriptions embodied in institutions are the key to a real understanding of man's communal living and to the cultural pattern which dominates it.

A "community" or "society," so I have said earlier, is possible only because, explicitly or implicitly, its members accept certain value commitments as binding for them. Mere spatial togetherness is not sufficient. Persistent value commitments are foundational to, and more or less clearly defined in, all institutions; and in and through its institutions a society is structuralized—the structure reflecting a "hierarchy" of valuations. That there are "overlappings" of institutions merely confirms the fact that things and events may be valued from different perspectives. In so far as individuals are members of the same institution, there exists among them a "hierarchy" of tasks and functions, reflecting the complexities of the conditions under which the major value commitment is to be realized; and in so far as individuals are members of different institutions, conflicts in institutional obligations become value conflicts for them. A stable society, therefore, is one in which the value commitments embodied in its institutions reflect all basic valuations of its members and are harmoniously adjusted—a society, in brief, which provides for the highest self-fulfillment. And it is in this sense, too, that throughout history institutions have helped mold men by stabilizing their highest valuations and making them socially effective.

It goes without saying, of course, that institutions, once established as means to certain ends, may, in time, be perverted into ends in themselves. Such a shift, however, reflects but a shift in valuation and must be understood as such. But institutions may also be modified, expanded, or shifted to a place of new importance in any given society because members of that society have caught a new vision and have made new value commitments. The relation of the individual to any particular institution, therefore, is always one of mutual interaction: the institution embodying valuations of the past; the individual reflecting those valuations in the mirror of his own experience and his own insights. The dialectic of this interaction is, thus, the dialectic of two sources or perspectives of valuation. Individuals are to a large extent creatures of the valuations embodied in the institutions of their society; but, in turn, these institutions and, in fact, the whole of society reflect the effective valuations of individuals.

In brief, the logical structure of a society contains as foundational a set of interrelated valuations. Commitment to these valuations is basic to the unity and the institutional pattern of that society. Changes in individual valuations effect changes in that pattern, and changes in the institutions, being dependent on values, affect, in turn, the value commitments of individuals. And in this context I see no possibility of escaping values and value references as explanatory categories.

VIII

I said a moment ago that in and through its institutions a society is structuralized. I now want to enlarge on that statement.

Since each institution is the embodiment of a complexus of valuations centering around some basic value, the structuralization of any given society as a whole is ultimately a matter of the distribution of value emphases—that is, it is a question of what is the dominant valuation and what are its stratifications. And here the social scientist faces the problem of discerning in the society which he studies, not his own valuations, but the valuations and value commitments indigenous to that society itself. The problem has no easy solution; but unless it is solved, not only "in principle" for societies in general, but for every particular society under investigation, the investigator's work remains incomplete with respect to that society. It is evident, however, that, even so, a "value schematism," valid for any society, may also be of significance—in the sense, namely, that it provides a "model" by comparison with which (as an ideal case) actual societies or institutions within a society may be better understood, even if only in their deviations from the "model." And any investigation designed to disclose the valuations and value commitments within a given society is therefore a contribution to sociological knowledge. It is at this point, incidentally, that interest in value as an explanatory category in the social sciences is intimately interwoven with value as factual subject matter for the social sciences. It is clear, however, that reference to value in the latter sense is but auxiliary to value as an explanatory category.

It is true, of course, that many of our basic valuations are subconscious commitments which we make because they are part and parcel of the society into which we were born and in which we attained maturity. Nevertheless, as in our individual lives, so in our social existence, there comes a time—at least for some of us—when we demand a rational justification for our value commitments and our distribution of value emphases. And it is at such times—at times, that is, when we come to a clearer understanding of our own value commitments—that we also approach society and its institutions with a new understanding; that we see most clearly that institutions are but socially approved means for the realization of socially approved key values or "ends." And we realize also that the devotion of men to the institutions they serve is in direct proportion to their own commitments to the values embodied in the various institutions which, together, stratify their society. A basic change in these commitments—be it a shift in emphasis or the projection of new goals—inevitably entails a change in that devotion. The whole range of institutional changes is thus clearly dependent upon changes in valuations which, individually conceived, are, in time, socially approved—where "approval" means a value commitment. And it is this very fact that makes value terms indispensable as explanatory categories in the social sciences.

IX

I now return briefly and in conclusion to the matter of boundary transgressions and abuses of legitimate science and to distortions of, and interferences with, the whole scientific enterprise, which I regard as the very essence of scientism and to which I referred in the opening paragraph of my paper.

Corresponding to the three aspects of the value problem—the value *of* science, value *in* science, and value *for* science—I distinguish three areas in which scientism may be encountered. It lies in the nature of things, however, that the abuses and distortions encountered in one area may overlap other areas as well, or may even entail scientism in all areas together. Where matters are fluid, as they are in this case, it can be only a distortion of facts if we insist upon too rigid separation. Nevertheless, the distinctions I have in mind will clarify the picture and may well be useful in erasing some of its worst features. At least we shall then know that the term "scientism" is itself a somewhat ambiguous abstraction.

That exact and dependable knowledge in any area of investigation has immense value—in itself (as providing a better under-

standing of the world we live in) and in its practical aspects
(as providing a basis for policy decision)—need not be stressed
again. This legitimate value *of* science is distorted, however, when
Science—with the capital "S"—is enthroned as an Authority in
whose presence we are expected to genuflect and whose mere
mention in connection with a product or a cause is meant to
persuade us of the latter's excellence. This type of distortion of
the value *of* science culminates quite logically in the conception
of a "technocracy" as the ideal of societal living.

Scientism—and scientism of a radical and profoundly significant type—arises with the problem of values *in* science. As I
have repeatedly stressed in this paper, it is in the nature of
science to be concerned ultimately with the quantitative and
material aspects of reality only. Physics and chemistry legitimately
restrict themselves to this sphere. That there are aspects even of
human society which are amenable to quantitative analysis need
not be denied. Scientism here means that only value-free concepts
are to be employed in the interpretation of the human situation,
and that man himself is to be reduced—via a behavioristic
psychology—to a purely physicochemical complexus of interrelated processes amenable to a complete explanation in terms of
the value-free concepts and categories of the natural sciences. In
other words, scientism here emerges as a reductionistic naturalism
which denies in principle that there are irreducible values or that
values, if they do exist, have any significance whatever. The picture of man which here emerges, and which is inherent in the
scientistic boundary transgressions that would extend the value-
free concepts of the natural sciences to encompass the whole of
knowledge, is frightening indeed in its distortions of man. But it
becomes even more so if now it is combined—as quite naturally
it is—with the projection of a technocracy as the ideal of a human
society.

The third type of scientism arises in connection with the problem of values *for* science—in connection, that is, with the value
framework within which science itself operates. As I pointed out
earlier, this framework involves, on the one hand, that complexus
of values and valuations usually referred to as "standards of re-

search." But it involves, on the other hand, also personal and societal biases and ideological prejudices. Scientism here means the intrusion of ideological biases and personal prejudices— usually in a more or less subtle way—into the enterprise of science itself. The problem here is most acute as a quest for objectivity. Even if we grant—as I think we must—that *ultimate* or absolute objectivity is beyond human reach, still the effort must at least be made to state clearly our presuppositions and indicate our basic valuations, and not to let prejudice and ideological concern distort our findings as scientists or as philosophers, as the case may be.

NOTE

1. "Theory Construction and the Problem of Objectivity," in *Symposium on Sociological Theory*, Llewellyn Gross, editor (Evanston: Row, Peterson and Company, 1959).

2

Objectivity and Social Science

W. T. Couch

The thesis of this paper is that the idea widely prevailing among social scientists that the social scientist knows how to proceed impartially, that he knows how to counteract or get rid of bias in his work, is an illusion.

I

The problem of impartiality, as everyone knows who has concerned himself seriously with the idea, is a part of the problem of objectivity. Objectivity, it might seem, has to do with objects. But the term "object" has been applied to everything from the universe, and the stars and chairs and dogs and mathematics and logic that are in it, to the completely private and wholly subjective notions of individual persons. Everything that has existed, whether its existence has been private or public, has constituted an object if existence is taken as the definition of objectivity. But this definition is obviously unsatisfactory. It leaves no room for distinguishing between objectivity and subjectivity. Now, if we persist with sufficient zeal in the effort to get a satisfactory definition, we shall discover that we are not the first to have this interest. Plato had it. And Aristotle. And St. Augustine and Thomas Aquinas and Descartes and Locke and Hume and Kant and Hegel and Kierkegaard and a host of others.

The problem of objectivity is indistinguishable from the problem of reality. It involves such questions as: What is the universe made of? Where did this something come from? Has it always existed or was it created? What is change, does anything new come into existence with it, and how does change occur? What is permanence, and could there be any change unless there were permanence? What are past and future, and how much do we know of what we are talking about when we talk about them?

In addition to questions of being and of the sources and nature and purposes of being, objectivity involves two other classes of questions. One of these has to do with the problem of correct method in dealing with any question. This is the field of logic. The third has to do with the question how we know anything. This is the field of epistemology.

We are not bringing any new knowledge into the world when we say these things. They are, or ought to be, well known, and there would be no excuse for taking time to talk about them here if all of the important assumptions of modern scholarship and science were practiced as well as preached. One of the most important of these assumptions is that learning is a co-operative effort, that the field in which labor is needed is so large and diverse that division and specialization are required, and that work in one field may safely be used as a foundation for work in another. It will be shown here that there is room for grave doubt about the last clause in this assumption.

In the field of epistemology, the questions that may be asked may be regarded as comprising three classes. One has to do with extension and motion and figure and number, generally referred to as the primary qualities of objects. One has to do with color and odor and sound and taste and tactile impressions, generally referred to as the secondary qualities of objects. And one has to do with all such matters as fairness, impartiality, justice, and goodness, which are commonly referred to as values. But what value is, whether it is a quality or a relation or something else; whether it is a simple, unanalyzable, indefinable, nonnatural something; whether it is created by interest and conferred by interest on objects—all are questions of extreme controversy.

The status of value is far less certain and far more obscure than the status of objects. The status of objects, if we accept modern science, is so uncertain and obscure as to render worse than worthless any term such as "objectivity" that depends on this status for its meaning. If knowledge of objects is knowledge only of extension, motion, figure and number, as was assumed when the foundations of modern science were laid; if sense impressions are all contributed by the subject; and if, as George Berkeley [1] pointed out, objects can be seen only because they are colored, it follows, if anything follows, that the status of both minds and objects in science is such as to raise the question whether rational discourse is possible. Berkeley failed to take into account the consideration that if objects existed only in minds, as he held, one could close and open his eyes without having any effect whatever on the visibility of objects. And if there is any such process as proof that involves the world—as distinguished from proof that has to do only with words that have no necessary connection with the world —then the fact that when one closes one's eyes objects disappear is proof that objects exist outside of human minds.

It would be fatuous to assume that because Berkeley did not take these considerations into account, he was unaware of them. His attention was focused on the more important consideration that modern science was undermining the foundations of rational discourse. His object was to keep modern science and at the same time restore the foundations.

Berkeley insisted on the one implication, assuming the validity of the work of Copernicus, Galileo, Descartes, and Newton, that was necessary to save man from a situation in which it would appear to be warranted to say that something both is and is not at the same time and in the same way, and that two persons may see something truly and yet see it as something totally different. Berkeley's insistence that modern science necessarily implies a mind that contains everything, that maintains everything in existence, that sees everything truly as it is, is, among other things, a way of insisting that rationality is available for the government of the universe and that the effort of man to understand and participate in this rationality and govern himself by it is not utterly hopeless. Berkeley held, as everyone has had to hold who has proceeded rationally, that man cannot create rationality out of nothing. If it is to be available to him at all, it must be made available to him by some power not his own.

It is impossible to accept modern science and at the same time save objectivity in any sense that distinguishes it from subjectivity unless Berkeley's implication is accepted.

Modern science, all of us know or ought to know, has not accepted Berkeley's implication. It has swallowed camels in the way of implications and, with the exception of a very few thinkers like Alfred North Whitehead, has refused to have anything to do with this gnat. Whitehead saw clearly that Berkeley's implication was necessary to save rationality as well as objectivity, and, being devoted to both, he did not hesitate to accept it. But on this point Whitehead is not generally accepted. Modern science, as a consequence, remains in the bog of subjectivity into which Copernicus and Galileo and Descartes led it. Modern phenomenology has not solved this problem. If the bias which pervades modern science is to be eliminated, it is necessary to hold that "what Hume gave to Kant as a problem Kant handed back unchanged as the solution." [2] The followers of Kant—and not to follow Kant is to be in a negligible minority—have either buried the problem or evaded it. In this situation, the use of the term "objectivity" or equivalent language is indulgence in a practice for which primitive people who have no chance to know better could be excused, but for which the modern social scientist has no excuse. Dorothy Emmett, in her *Nature of Metaphysical Thinking*,[3] correctly characterizes this practice: "If we confine ourselves to a purely phenomenalist account of perception, any assumption concerning an external world would be an animistic projection, since on this view sense data are subjective states."

Now, hopelessly confused as is the problem of objectivity in the sense of the real existence of the external world, the problem of value is incomparably more confused.

No one doubts that objects, whatever their status in existence, have primary qualities. No one doubts that there are correlates of such linguistic expressions as "chair," "table," "this person," etc., even though the questions how the correlates exist and how it is that this existence is public and there can be communication about it are in a state of extreme confusion. No one doubts that there are correlates of such linguistic expressions as "yellow," "stench," "buzzing," "sweet," "soft." Despite all confusion, it is possible to point, or seem to point, to objects that exemplify, or seem to exemplify, primary and secondary qualities, and scientific means and standards are available for determining the relations of these qualities to objects, whether the objects are in minds or in the external world or in both or are distributed among and between the two or have some other unknown and perhaps unthinkable status.

The situation is entirely different in regard to the question of value. Here there is doubt about the existence of correlates. It is possible, as we have seen, to verify statements about objects such as chairs and tables in so far as these statements involve primary and secondary qualities. But what of such statements as "This is good" or "This is bad"? "The question really at issue," wrote G. E. Moore more than a quarter century ago in his essay on the "Nature of Moral Philosophy,"

is the question whether when we judge (whether truly or falsely) that an action is a duty or a state of things good, *all* that we are thinking about the action or the state of things in question is simply and solely that we ourselves or others have or tend to have a certain feeling towards it when we contemplate or think of it. . . . If this view be true. . . . when I say "That was wrong" I am merely saying, "That sort of action excites indignation in me, when I see it"—and when you say "No; it was not wrong," you are merely saying, "It does not excite indignation in *me,* when I see it." . . .

"If this view be true," concludes Moore, "then there is absolutely no such thing as a difference in opinion on moral questions." [4]

David Hume stated the same problem when he wrote in his *Treatise on Human Nature:*

Take any action allowed to be vicious: wilful murder, for instance. Examine it in all lights and see if you can find that matter of fact, or real existence, which you call *vice*. In whichever way you take it, you find only certain passions, motives, volitions and thoughts. There is no other matter of fact in the case. The vice entirely escapes you, as long as you consider the object. You never can find it, till you turn your reflexion into your own breast, and find a sentiment of disapprobation, which arises in you, towards this action. Here is a matter of fact; but 'tis the object of feeling, not of reason. It lies in yourself, not in the object. So that when you pronounce any action or character to be vicious, you mean nothing, but that from the constitution of your nature *you* have a feeling or sentiment of blame from the contemplation of it. Vice and virtue, therefore, may be compar'd to sounds, colours, heat and cold, which, according to modern philosophy, are not qualities in objects, but perceptions in the mind.[5]

In another passage Hume makes it clear that according to this same modern philosophy, vice and virtue cannot consist in relations any more than they can in qualities of objects. But if they do not consist in either qualities or relations, the question arises whether they exist at all. The thing that John Donne saw when over three hundred years ago he looked at the direction modern science was taking and wrote:

> 'Tis all in pieces, all coherence gone
> All just supply and all relation. . . .
> Sight is the noblest sense of any one,
> Yet sight hath only colour to feed on,
> And colour is decaid; summer's robe growes
> Duskie, and like an oft dyed garment showes.
> Our blushing red, which used in cheeks to spred
> Is inward sunk, and only our soules are red [6]

the modern social scientist has not yet seen in spite of his concern with physical science as a model of what all science should be.

The view that color and odor and sound and taste and tactile qualities are all in the subject, none in the object, if any, that somehow gives rise to them, is ancient. Montaigne summarizes this view in a classic statement at the end of his famous "Apology for

Raimond Sebond." But this view was only beginning to have scientific significance in Montaigne's time. The only important opposing view, that of Aristotle, was still dominant when Montaigne was writing. The Aristotelian view is the only systematically objective one that the world has had. The basis for displacing it with the subjective view of modern science was being laid during the hundred years before and after Montaigne wrote his essays.

The position of physical science in the twentieth century is completely in line with the trend started by Copernicus and Descartes, Galileo and Newton. Alfred North Whitehead summarizes this position:

. . . the mind in apprehending also experiences sensations which, properly speaking, are qualities of the mind alone. These sensations are projected by the mind so as to clothe appropriate bodies in external nature. Thus the bodies are perceived as with qualities which in reality do not belong to them, qualities which in fact are purely the offspring of the mind. Thus nature gets credit which in truth should be reserved for ourselves; the rose for its scent: the nightingale for his song: and the sun for his radiance. The poets are entirely mistaken. They should address their lyrics to themselves, and should turn them into odes of self-congratulation on the excellency of the human mind. Nature is a dull affair, soundless, scentless, colorless; merely the hurrying of material, endlessly, meaninglessly.[7]

"However you disguise it," says Whitehead, "this is the practical outcome of the characteristic scientific philosophy which closed the seventeenth century." And, he says,

It is still reigning. Every university in the world organizes itself in accordance with it. No alternative system of organizing the pursuit of truth has been suggested. It is not only reigning, but it is without rival.

"And yet," adds Whitehead, "it is quite unbelievable." [8]

Whether it is believable or not, one thing is certain. This statement of Whitehead's shows what an animistic hash the objectivity is that the social sciences get from the physical sciences. It shows the physical world with nothing whatever in it that could even remotely be imagined as a correlate for fairness and impartiality, justice or injustice, good or evil, nothing that even suggests value.

The point here for our purposes is that if all moral questions are illusory, if the feelings that people have about such matters as justice and good and evil and right and wrong have no correlates, if the nature of things is such that there cannot be any moral correlates either in states of affairs or states of mind, it is obvious that the pretension of the social scientist to objectivity as fairness or impartiality or justice is merely testimony concerning the state of his feelings, and, so far as the states beyond his feelings are concerned, his claim is wholly illusory. The social scientist lives in a world in which conflicts of world-wide proportions are occurring over what people imagine to be justice. He has made important contributions to the idea that these conflicts are really about justice. But when he is asked what this justice is, he is unable to say anything that is distinguishable from the appeal of the demagogue to the mob. And this is not all.

One of the chief accomplishments of the social scientist during the last century or so has been to help undermine the notion that ideas of good and evil, better and worse are more than mere vagrant feelings. The charge that the social scientist wants to have a piece of moral objectivity, and that he has been preaching that there is no moral objectivity to have a piece of and that there cannot be any, is serious, and I now turn to evidence bearing on this charge.

II

The discussion that follows will seem to the reader petty unless he remembers that we are concerned here with problems of more than ordinary importance and that one of the first questions we have to ask of a piece of writing that is presented to the world as a contribution to knowledge is: Does the author know what he is talking about? Has he succeeded in understanding what he says? Has he solved the problem of reasoning, of communicating with himself?

Ruth Benedict's *Patterns of Culture* [8] has been one of the most popular books to come from the field of the social sciences during the last quarter century. In addition to being extremely popular, as evidenced by more than a dozen printings in cheap editions— each of which could hardly have been less than 100,000 copies— it has received the accolade from leading social scientists. We take it as an example because of its distinction in these respects.

On page 2 of *Patterns of Culture,* Miss Benedict says, "No man ever looks at the world with pristine eyes." Now, "no man," is a great many people; in fact, it is everybody; and "ever" is a long time. In the sentence which follows Miss Benedict makes a typical statement of the principle of social causation, the principle that says that we are what we are because of the society into which we are born. Miss Benedict does not take into account the fact that if social scientists succeed in getting outside of social causation, this fact has to be explained; and, if they do not, her book is merely an example of the fact that some societies produce people who, as a consequence of social causation and for no other reason, busy themselves with the "study" of other societies, and otherwise these studies are meaningless. It could be a matter of some significance to know that some people in some societies do get outside of social causation and, as a consequence, may be able to see the world and man as they really are. If this happens, to know how it happens could be a step to some real knowledge in social science.

Miss Benedict tells the reader on page 1 that "To the anthropologist, our customs and those of a New Guinea tribe are two possible schemes for dealing with a common problem. . . ." It is hardly possible for us to doubt this, and we wonder why Miss Benedict says it. At first it appears she is telling us we have no real reasons for thinking one way of doing things is any better than another. It does not take us long to see that she does not know what she is saying when she says this. For it can hardly be open to dispute that on a rational basis it makes all the difference between science and not science how things are done. If this were not the case, there would be no reason for having anthropologists, much less for taking them seriously. All of us know better than to be taken in by the argument that one way of doing carpentering or plumbing or electrical work is just as good as another. The support that we give to schools and colleges, to the cultivation of knowledge and skill in all fields, stands as testimony to our belief that there are better and worse ways of doing things.

Why does Miss Benedict feel it necessary to write as if she equates primitive ways with civilized ways? Does she really intend to maintain this equation? If she does, it is impossible to understand her repeated arguments for a "rational social order" based on what she calls a "realistic social faith." Why, if Miss Benedict really believes that the "patterns of life which mankind has created for itself" are "equally valid" and should all be tolerated, as she says at the end of her book, does she speak on page 4 of her first chapter of "battles we may fairly count as won"? The truth is, and Miss Benedict makes this as clear as it is possible to make anything, she is writing to help destroy what she regards as prejudice in the United States and to establish what she regards as a "rational social order." Now when Miss Benedict does this, she is simply doing what all the rest of us do, trying to maintain what we think is the best way of doing things. But whatever Miss Benedict's purpose, we cannot accept her view that no people in the world have developed better ways of doing things and at the same time accept the view that some people have developed better ways.

Now, if we cannot agree on the principle used in our last sentence, if we do not understand it and are not able or willing to use it on our own arguments as well as on Miss Benedict's, in our opinion we are incapable of understanding anything and will remain incapable until we have mastered it. Until this principle is understood, it is a waste of time and worse to discuss anthropology or anything else but this principle.

Immediately after telling the reader that "To the anthropologist, our customs and those of a New Guinea tribe are two possible social schemes for dealing with a common problem," Miss Benedict goes on, "and in so far as he remains an anthropologist he is bound to avoid any weighting of one in favour of the other." This is the principle of objectivity in method. Does Miss Benedict know what she is saying when she says this? "The study of custom," Miss Benedict tells us on page 3, "can be profitable only after certain preliminary propositions have been accepted, and some of these propositions have been violently opposed. In the first place any scientific study requires that there be no preferential weighting of one or another of the items it selects for its consideration." This is the same principle of objectivity again. It is repeated at least a half dozen times in the first chapter, and, in our opinion, it deserves emphasis; but again, we have to ask, does Miss Benedict know what she is saying when she says this? Does she really mean that the anthropologist ought always to proceed in such a manner that he cannot see and condemn the evils in societies such as Hitler's National Socialism or Stalin's or Khrushchev's Communism? Does she really mean to advocate no "preferential weighting" against such things in societies as concentration camps? If she does, then so far as we are concerned, she is using something labelled anthropology to cultivate something worse than barbarism. If she does not mean this, how do we explain what she says, and the fact that she says it over and over?

It happens that we are convinced that objectivity as fairness and impartiality is essential to the proper development of social science, but we doubt whether our words, or the word "objectivity," or such sentences as those that Miss Benedict utters in its place, have any magical powers. Resolutions and ritual observances involving the repetition of formulas that are not clearly understood seem highly inappropriate to the sciences. But perhaps we are wrong and Miss Benedict does somewhere elaborate on the meaning of this principle to which she appeals, or perhaps some other social scientist has done so; but we have searched and we have not found any anywhere. We have found plenty of statements such as those Miss Benedict utters, and all of them are virtual equivalents of the definition given in Fairchild's *Dictionary of Sociology* that objectivity is "The ability to detach oneself from situations in which one is personally involved, and to view the facts on the basis of evidence and reason rather than prejudice and emotion, without bias or preconception, in their true setting."

It is evident, if we examine this definition, that objectivity contains some problems. One of these is the meanings of words in the definition such as "fact," and "reason," and "prejudice," and "bias," and "emotion," and "preconception." Shall we rely on our untested conceptions of the meanings of these terms—a practice that has been condemned in scientific procedure for hundreds of years—or shall we try to find and use scientific meanings?

Take, for instance, the terms "prejudice" and "bias." If we assume that it is possible to be unprejudiced and unbiased, we still have some problems. We still have to demonstrate that this state of mind is not equivalent to that which Kant [10] called "indifferent-ism—the mother in all sciences of chaos and night." We have to show that it is possible for some people to get outside of social causation, and this has not been shown. We have to deal with such arguments as that of Ralph Barton Perry that

It is characteristic of living mind to be for some things and against others. This polarity is not reducible to that between "yes" and "no" in the logical or purely cognitive sense, because one can say "yes" with reluctance or be glad to say "no." To be "for" or "against" is to view with favor or disfavor; it is a bias of the subject toward or away from.[11]

Perry does not say it is characteristic of some living minds to be objective, or to be able to achieve objectivity, and of other living minds to be for some things and against others. He says simply that "it is characteristic of living mind to be for some things and against others." If this is true, and if its application is universal, and it contains no modifier saying that it isn't, bias is not only universal, but there is no way of getting rid of it. In this case, objectivity as absence of bias is a meaningless concept. And if we are allowed the assumption that social scientists are people, this applies to them as well as to others.

Finally, we need to know what happens to a feeling when we detach it from ourselves for the purpose of examining it. If moral feelings have no existence except in human breasts, as in Hume's argument and as in modern science, it is obvious the logical positivists are right and we are talking about nothing when we talk about detached moral feelings.

III

Let us resume our examination of Miss Benedict as scientist. On page 9 Miss Benedict tells the reader that "A very little acquaintance with other conventions, and a knowledge of how various these may be, would do much to promote a rational social order." Notice how in this statement on page 9 "a very little acquaintance" is all that is necessary to take care of the argument for social causation introduced on page 2 with the statement that "no man ever looks at the world with pristine eyes." However, let this pass, and let us say immediately that we too are interested in the idea of a "rational social order," but by this time we are beginning to wonder whether we are supposed to accept these words as words of magic and to assume that if we repeat them often enough they will bring us what we want.

The effort to discover what a "rational social order" would be did not start with modern social science. It is, in our view, anything but evidence of rationality in social science that it should be necessary to elaborate on this question. Miss Benedict could have learned from many easily available sources that the question of a rational social order is ancient. Let us take one of the many possible early sources, the play *Antigone* by Sophocles, and show how it poses the problem that Miss Benedict seems to think is solved by three words. Here is an abbreviated outline of the play:

Antigone's brothers, Eteocles and Polyneices, have killed each other in a battle before the gates of Thebes. Polyneices had invaded his homeland with an armed force. Creon, after the death of Eteocles and Polyneices, was next in succession to the kingship and his first action as king was to issue a proclamation:

Eteocles, who died as a man should die, fighting for his country, is to be buried with full military honors, with all the ceremony that is usual when the greatest heroes die; but his brother Polyneices, who broke his exile to come back with fire and sword against his native city and the shrines of his fathers' gods, whose one idea was to spill the blood of his blood and sell his own people into slavery—Polyneices, I say, is to have no burial: no man is to touch him or say the least prayer for him; he shall lie on the plain, unburied; and the birds and the scavenging dogs can do with him whatever they like.[12]

Creon is moved by feeling in conjunction with and guided by a notion of law. Antigone is moved by the same. The difference between Creon and Antigone that is relevant for our discussion is in their notions of law. Creon as king in his proclamation makes law. He does not make explicit something already in custom and habit or the nature of things. He does not discover. He invents, creates. Antigone says Creon's proclamation "was not God's proclamation. That final justice that rules the world below makes no such laws." Antigone takes the position that the higher law says, regardless of what Polyneices has done, he should be given decent burial. Antigone is asserting what the evidence in the play says Sophocles regarded as the objectivity of justice. Creon is denying the objectivity and asserting the subjectivity of justice. Now the important point for our discussion is that it is impossible to make sense and hold both positions at the same time. Miss Benedict holds both positions. There are no grounds, she tells us, for holding that the ways of one society are better than those of another. At the same time she says there are grounds for holding that the ways of one society are better than those of another. And what are these grounds? Miss Benedict's notions of a rational social order. Which, unless she shows that they are objective, may be merely Miss Benedict's notions. She gives no evidence whatever that she recognizes that there is a problem here.

One more example from the first few pages of the first chapter of *Patterns of Culture*. On page 1, Miss Benedict tells the reader that "custom has not commonly been regarded as a thing of any great moment." Since Miss Benedict's work is presented to the public as that of a scientist, and since scientists are supposed to pay scrupulous attention to facts, it is necessary to say that this statement of Miss Benedict's is not true. She leaves out a large body of important facts. Only one sample of many that are possible will be given here.

One of the most important collections of the various customs of different peoples was made over two thousands years ago by Herodotus, the first historian whose works the modern world has inherited. Now it happens, as everyone interested in custom ought to know, that Herodotus not only gave the world an extensive account of the customs of different peoples of his time and preceding times, but he also told a story about burial customs that has long been famous, has been told and retold many times, and illustrates the great problem of custom as well as any story that could be told. The story is worth repeating here.

Darius, after he had got the kingdom of Persia, so Herodotus [13] tells us,

called into his presence certain Greeks who were at hand, and asked— "What he should pay them to eat the bodies of their fathers when they died?" To which they answered that there was no sum that would tempt them to do such a thing. He then sent for certain Indians, of the race called Callatians, men who eat their fathers, and asked them, while the Greeks stood by, and knew by the help of an interpreter all that was said—"What he should give them to burn the bodies of their fathers at their decease?" The Indians exclaimed aloud, and bade him forbear such language.

It is not recorded either by Herodotus or anyone else that as a consequence of this experiment by Darius any progress was made toward the establishment of a rational social order. It would be possible, however, to interpret the work of Miss Benedict and many of her colleagues in the social sciences as illustrating the great principle discovered by Herodotus in his study of custom: "I have no doubt whatever," says Herodotus,

that Cambyses was completely out of his mind; it is the only possible explanation of his assault upon, and mockery of, everything which ancient law and custom have made sacred in Egypt. If anyone, no matter who, were given the opportunity of choosing from amongst all the nations the set of beliefs which he thought best, he would inevitably, after careful consideration of their relative merits, choose that of his own country. Everyone without exception believes in his own native customs, and that being so, it is unlikely that anyone but a madman would mock at such things. There is abundant evidence that this is the universal feeling about the ancient customs of one's country.[14]

It is necessary only to make a few substitutions such as that of "science" for "nation" or "country" to see how closely this statement made more than two thousand years ago fits the modern case. Most of us today worship science. There has never been a time when so many people—communists and anticommunists, national socialists and antinational socialists—were joined in one worship and so convinced that the thing they worship is the thing that will bring everybody the good things of life and therefore ought to be worshipped.

Herodotus, it is clear, would have understood how it is that the problem of Antigone and Creon, which we have outlined above, is a perennial problem and how this problem arises out of the nature of society and the effort to create a rational social order, with or without the aid of social science.

Now we cannot say that for a person to communicate with himself or others he must have complete understanding of a subject, for it is possible that every subject in the world is connected with every other, and complete understanding or objectivity in this case would call for knowing the whole truth about the world and everything in it. But we can say and we can know as certainly as we can know anything that we can't say something in one sentence and deny it in another and make sense. If what we have said is true, Miss Benedict does not make sense of a rational kind. The kind of sense that she makes is of the irrational propagandistic kind, a kind bound to lead away from rather than toward the rational social order which Miss Benedict professes to want and that all of us ought to want and work for.

IV

We do not have the space here to report and discuss in any detail the allegations of social scientists concerning methods of eliminating or counteracting bias in their work. The dodges are numerous; but the most frequent procedure is either to use the term "objectivity" or equivalents to invoke the thing that is wanted. The assertion is never made in so many words that the social scientist can call spirits from the vasty deep who will see to it that his procedure is fair and impartial, but the pretension is there nevertheless; and no one asks seriously, will they come merely because they are called? The best discussion of the problem that is available is probably Max Weber's, but it seems not to have occurred to Weber or any of his followers that social science is no better equipped to take value into account than it is to drop it out, that it is necessary to know what value is before you can do either, that the great achievement of economic theory lies precisely in its leaving the question of value to wholly subjective processes. Weber says that "all evaluative ideas are subjective." [15] "It is simply naive to believe," he says, "although there are many specialists who even now do, that it is possible to establish and demonstrate as scientifically valid 'a principle' for practical social science from which the norms for the solution of practical problems can be unambiguously derived." [16] That Weber went far toward recognizing the difficulty of the problem is clear. "The possible," he said, "is often reached only by striving to attain the impossible that lies beyond it." [17] He was obviously searching for a combination of empiricism and theory, and we cannot escape the conviction that he was right in doing so. "The earliest intentionally rational therapy," he said,

involved the almost complete rejection of the cure of empirical symptoms by empirically tested herbs and potions in favor of the exorcism of (what was thought to be) the "real" (magical, daemonic) cause of the ailment. Formally, it had exactly the same highly rational structure as many of the most important developments in modern theory. But we do not look on these priestly magical therapies as progress . . .[18]

And so Weber advises the social scientist to recognize that in dealing with social problems he cannot escape the problem of value, that he cannot know what he is doing unless he recognizes values and deliberately and openly gives them place in theoretical systems or ideal types which he can then use somewhat as the physical scientist uses his mathematical formulas. But just how the social scientist can take into account something that he is unable to show in existence, Weber does not say. Yet what he does say, and he says it clearly (if in accepting implications we do not strain at gnats while we swallow camels), is that the social scientist has no basis for his science but beliefs; and Weber's theory thus has the highly significant consequence of making social science a function of belief.

It is not possible in a necessarily brief discussion to dispose of all the puerile arguments on the subject of objectivity as fairness and impartiality, but we ought not to overlook the prescription, so blandly and so often given, that all we have to do is guide ourselves by the relevant facts and logically sound inferences from facts. If this were as easy to do as it is to say, Miss Benedict would not have made the elementary logical blunders that we have shown she did make in her *Patterns of Culture,* and if it were easy to recognize these blunders social science would long ago have become a more rational discipline. The failures of social science are human failures. Let us now consider whether our understanding of what a fact is, is any better than our understanding of the first principle in logic.

V

It would be possible to interpret the case of Antigone as that of an overwrought young woman whose "higher law" was a mere projection of her fantasy and who, because she lacked the advice of the modern psychoanalyst or psychiatrist, did not know any better than to risk her life in an unnecessary conflict with authority over a meaningless burial custom. Polyneices was dead. What difference did it make what was done with his body? In a rational social order, presumably, no one would be so foolish as to risk his life to support one method of disposing of a dead body rather than another. Antigone and Creon made the mistake of not being born in a rational social order. In such an order facts of this

nature would be looked on indifferently. But there are some facts
that if allowed to exist might threaten the existence of a rational
social order. Could a rational social order exist if no one was willing to risk his life to keep such facts from coming into existence?
It is necessary in any reasonable examination of the problem of
objectivity to consider the possibility that both Antigone and
Creon were trying to discover the meanings of the facts that they
had before them and struggling to do what they felt necessary to
establish and maintain a rational social order.

But, it might be said, this is an ancient example and we have
not faced in it the question of the meaning of fact. We have to
face this problem, so let us take a few samples of what has been
said in the last fifty years or so on the question what facts are. We
shall start with William James. James does not give us a definition,
but he speaks of facts as hard, stubborn, irreducible. "The tough-
minded," he says,

are the men whose Alpha and Omega are facts. Behind the bare
phenomenal facts . . . there is nothing. When a rationalist insists that
behind the facts there is the ground of facts, the *possibility* of facts,
the tougher empiricists accuse him of taking the mere name and
nature of a fact and clapping it behind the fact as duplicate entity
to make it possible . . .[19]

If we examine this statement seriously, we see that James refuses to try to account for facts before their appearance and after
their appearance. James was doing essentially the same thing that
men do now when they repeat the proposition of Descartes,[20] "I
think; therefore, I am," without considering that this formula,
when used as an article of faith today, cries for expansion into the
question: There was a time when I did not think; therefore if I
believe what I am told about myself and the world, I was not.
Now, I think; therefore, I am. I am approaching a state when
again, if I believe what I am told, I shall not think; therefore I
shall not be. But this is something coming from nothing and going
into nothing. This is a miracle. And I am told not to believe in
miracles. Is there anything that I can believe that makes sense?

James saw his world as consisting of facts that, so far as his explanations were concerned, appeared out of nothing and disappeared into nothing.

At the time that James was writing, F. H. Bradley was also writing about facts from a totally different point of view. Bradley said, "By fact I mean either an event, or else what is directly experienced. Any aspect of direct experience, or again of an event, can itself be loosely styled a fact or event, so far as you consider it a qualifying adjective of one . . ." [21] "And," goes on Bradley, this fact or event "must happen in a soul; for where else could it exist?" [22] Bradley does exactly what James objects to. He claps the fact into a soul to give the fact, as the condition of its appearance, a place to exist before and after it is seen as a fact.

According to Alfred North Whitehead, fact depends on point of view.

Galileo said that the earth moves and that the sun is fixed; the Inquisition said that the earth is fixed and the sun moves; and Newtonian astronomers, adopting an absolute theory of space, said that both the sun and earth move. But now we say that any one of these statements is equally true, provided that you have fixed your sense of "rest" and "motion" in the way required by the statement adopted. At the date of Galileo's controversy with the Inquisition, Galileo's way of stating the facts was, beyond question, the fruitful procedure for scientific research. But in itself it was not more true than the formulation of the Inquisition. . . . Yet this question of the motions of the earth and the sun expresses a real fact in the universe; and all sides had got hold of important truths concerning it.[23]

And so it is in modern science: precisely the same fact is a fact or is not a fact, depending on where you stand, and there is no ground that can be taken and on which what is fact for one is fact for all. There is no truth; only truths.

Let us now jump to definitions of recent years. "What, then, are facts?" ask Cohen and Nagel.[24] "Are they, as is sometimes asserted, hypotheses for which evidence is considerable?" And they say, "Whether a proposition shall be called a fact or a hypothesis depends on the state of our evidence." It also depends, they might have added, on the state of opinion on inductive proof. If the present opinion that all the evidence has to be in continues, on this basis we shall not know what a fact is until Gabriel blows his trumpet. Cohen and Nagel, let us remind ourselves, are writing about logic and scientific method. Their definition is the one most popular today in scientific circles. It is substantially the same as that of the logical positivists. Theirs is that "all propositions which have factual content are empirical hypotheses. . . ." [25] Another popular definition is that "a fact is an empirically verifiable statement about phenomena in terms of a conceptual scheme." [26] This may be criticized on the grounds that time does not stop and keep phenomena lying around conveniently for statements about them to be verified. The phenomenon, like murder, is something that happens, and once it has happened it is part of the past and you can't bring the murdered person back to life and have the murderer do the job all over again in order to verify statements that may have been made about the first occurrence. As a final sample we shall mention those schools of thought to which facts are configurations of particles, or of energized particles, or of particles of energy, and to which scientific knowledge is mathematical equations correlating such configurations.

It occurs to us at this point, and the thought will not be repressed, that the problem of objectivity now calls for the question: Do any of these particles of energy have wings, and are some of the wings white and others black? And then the thought comes, are wings really necessary? And how many of these particles of energy can dance on the point of a needle?

Now, in all seriousness, it is not necessary to reject this last explanation of fact in the name of sanity. Plato was very close to it, whether we follow Jowett in the view that Plato said, "The definition of being is simply power," or Cornford, who translates (Sophist 247E): "I am proposing as a mark to distinguish real things that they are nothing but power." The difference between Plato and the modern social scientist is that Plato's theory of facts was systematic, relatively complete, and remarkably consistent. The same is true of Aristotle. The best we can get from the social scientist today is such exhortations as to distinguish between what is and what ought to be and to keep the two separate and distinct, and then, after his exhortations, he gives evidence that he does not know what he is talking about.

The position of the social scientist who talks about objectivity and facts today is indistinguishable from that of the hunter who is telling his friends of his adventures.[27] One of the most exciting, he says, is the occasion when he was completely surrounded by wild animals. "How did you escape?" his friends ask. "I didn't," he replies. "They ate me up." And he continues talking and his friends continue listening without showing any interest whatever in the question how someone who has been eaten up can continue talking.

VI

We have now shown what we started out to show, namely, that the assertion of the social scientist that he knows how to proceed impartially, that he knows the meaning of objectivity as fairness and is able to apply this meaning in his work, is an illusion. It remains only to suggest that the effects of this illusion are as destructive in society as the action of a man who has lost his mind and believes that he can walk out of an airplane that is in flight and step safely on solid earth.

So far as this writer has been able to discover, very few social scientists are aware that there is a problem of objectivity, that this problem poses a test of rationality in its most crucial form, and that this problem has not been solved by modern science and philosophy because of a deep and ineradicable bias in both against the one implication that is necessary to save rationality as well as objectivity. It is not possible here to explore further the charge that rationality has been lost along with objectivity. We shall take space only to mention areas of tremendous importance in which modern social science, instead of proceeding rationally and helping to create the order and the understanding and the acceptance of order that are possible and most desirable in the interests of the general welfare, has given tremendous impetus to proceeding irrationally and to the consequent increase of all the impulses and conditions in society that are opposed to the general welfare. It should not be necessary to say here that the pretension of social science to stand for and to cultivate the general welfare is not a self-vindicating one. It is held here that the power of the social scientist in modern society is even greater than that of the physical scientist. The power of the social scientist is the decisive power. He, more than anyone else, created the state of mind in the United States that led the people of this country to accept a policy that, during the second of this century's world wars, turned a large part of the world over to communism and resulted in the situation under which, after the war, free society had to retreat or face a third world war. He, more than anyone else, created the state of mind that prior to and during the Second World War denied the possibility of any choices in the world other than those between fascism and communism. He was completely unaware that his talk about justice was empty and illusory and that in engaging in such talk he was stirring up and adding to the destructive conflicts that he said he wanted to allay.

We shall now call on two distinguished social scientists to illustrate this problem. Robert M. MacIver illustrates it with crystal clarity in his *Web of Government* as well as in other writings. We shall refer here to only two passages of many that need examination. First, let us document the statement made above concerning the attitude of the social scientist toward communism during World War II: ". . . the successors of the Versailles statesmen," writes MacIver, "dream vain comfortable policies of appeasement, wishfully thinking that the growing fury can be diverted from themselves toward Soviet Russia, the portentous revolutionary state they stupidly imagine to be the real menace." [28] This attitude was general among social scientists during World War II. A few, like Joseph Schumpeter, saw the truth in spite of the blinkers that modern science had put on them; but what they saw has never been passed on effectively to the general public, so deep is the prejudice that has been built up against the truth in this matter. It might be argued in extenuation for MacIver and the majority of his colleagues that the leaders of the country in all walks of life, and not merely the social scientists, held this attitude. But it has to be said that if the social scientist does not know better in regard to questions that involve his science, as this question does, then his science is a snare and a delusion.

Secondly, we shall document the statement that the social scientist in talking about justice not only does not know what he is talking about, but is stirring up and adding to destuctive conflict. "Every society," says MacIver,[28] "is held together by a myth system, a complex of dominating thought-forms that determines and sustains all its activities. All social relations, the very texture of human society, are myth-born and myth-sustained. . . . When we speak here of myth," he says,

we imply nothing concerning the grounds of belief, so far as belief claims to interpret reality. We use the word in an entirely neutral sense. Whether its content be revelation or superstition, insight or prejudice, is not here in question. We need a term that abjures all reference to truth or falsity.

It follows that every society to preserve itself has to preserve its myth. MacIver eliminates the only possibility of mediation between myths when he says that in using the term "myth" he "abjures all reference to truth or falsity." Under these conditions, the role of the social scientist is necessarily limited to that of supporting and strengthening the myth of the society to which he belongs. The fact that MacIver devotes much of his writing to searching for a basis for mediation between the myths of different societies does not alter the fact that he himself specifies conditions that eliminate the only possible basis for such mediation.

MacIver's case is particularly instructive because his work is far superior to most work in the social sciences. If he makes his own way to the bog of subjectivity and falls in and stays in and does not know where he is, it cannot reasonably be expected that other and lesser minds can do better.

We now come to the second of our social scientists that we have picked for illustrative purposes. We shall now take a brief look at Gunnar Myrdal and his *American Dilemma*. First, let us observe that this work would not have been written without the support of the Carnegie Corporation, one of the country's wealthiest foundations. The Carnegie Corporation gave Myrdal a commission to produce a "wholly objective and dispassionate" [30] study. Myrdal accepted the Carnegie Corporation's commission, but produced a work in which he says correctly that objectivity achieved in the conventional ways, that is by rituals involving assertions and resolutions, is not trustworthy.[31] Myrdal, flouting his commission —which certainly deserved to be flouted—argues that it is the duty of the social scientist to serve the ends chosen by the society of which he is a member; he assumes that the United States is one society; and he argues that the United States has chosen equality as one of its ends. The difficulty with Myrdal's argument is that in the context of modern science, a context which Myrdal accepts, an appeal for equality is an appeal to power. Most of us want equality, and the meaning that we give to equality is all the power that we have the power to get. We work for or against equality as we think it works for or against getting power for us. Modern science has made power and only power the supreme and the only reality. All else is illusion. Freedom, equality, justice are in its scheme only means of deception, and necessarily so. It would be necessary to change the foundations of modern science in order to have any other possibility. The social scientist in this view does not necessarily engage in deception by intention. His use of deception may be a consequence of his ignorance, or it may be a consequence of his willingness to play a Machiavellian part.

It should not be surprising, when we have some understanding of this problem, that in the two most destructive periods in the history of mankind, the periods of the two world wars of the twentieth century, modern social scientists generally supported the ends of their own societies and in doing so supported the destruction. The perennial enactment within and among societies of the parts played by Antigone and Creon goes on and on, and the meaning of the parts is utterly lost.

In summary, our argument reaches further than proof that the social scientist's idea that he knows how to proceed impartially is an illusion. It raises the question whether there is any illusion in modern society more destructive than this one. It takes no great wisdom to see that if there is no genuine knowledge in the world on moral questions, the social scientist makes a bad situation worse when he supports the claims of various groups to what they imagine are their rights without first finding a sound basis for rights. The effect of such support is obviously to intensify strife within and among societies.

NOTES

1. The gist of Berkeley's argument is in the first few pages of his *Principles of Human Knowledge.* This work will be unintelligible to anyone unfamiliar with the foundations of modern science. Everybody knows, or ought to know, that these were laid by Copernicus, Galileo, Descartes, Newton—to name only a few of the leaders. What everybody does not know—and everybody here includes most of the people working in the sciences—is that when the foundations of modern science were laid, no place was provided for anything objective as distinguished from subjective.
2. William Temple, *Nature, Man and God* (Macmillan, 1934, 1949), p. 74.
3. (Macmillan, 1945, 1949), p. 64.
4. *Philosophical Studies* (Humanities Press, 1951), p. 330.
5. Book III, Part I, Section I. The position taken by Herodotus is often adopted in contemporary discussion without any recognition of the fact that it was taken by him and by many others after him. Here, for instance, is a passage from Dewey: "All that is needed is acceptance of the view that moral subject matter is also spatially and temporally qualified." (*Reconstruction in Philosophy,* New American Library Mentor Book, Introduction, p. 13.) But, of course, this is not "all that is needed." And so Dewey says further (p. 27): "Nothing is more intellectually futile (as well as practically impossible) than to suppose harmony and order can be achieved except as new ends and standards, new moral principles, are first developed with a reasonable degree of clarity and system." Obviously ends, standards, and moral principles that are not so spatially and temporally qualified as to make a reasonable measure of harmony and order impossible are what is needed. It is not clear that there is in the world today any more knowledge of how to meet this need than there was in the days of Herodotus and Sophocles. Dewey certainly added nothing to this knowledge. His philosophy is, as Bertrand Russell said, a power philosophy.
6. From the "First Anniversary."
7. *Science and the Modern World* (Macmillan, 1925, 1948), p. 80.
8. *Ibid.*
9. Page references are to the New American Library Edition.

10. From the Preface to the first edition of *The Critique of Pure Reason.*
11. *The General Theory of Value* (Harvard, 1926, 1954), p. 115.
12. The edition from which this is quoted is a superb example of the art of translating and editing at its best. It is *Greek Plays in Modern Translation,* edited by Dudley Fitts (Dial Press, 1947).
13. Book III, ch. 37.
14. Book III, ch. 38.
15. Edward A. Shils and Henry A. Finch, eds., *Max Weber on the Methodology of the Social Sciences* (Glencoe: The Free Press, 1949), p. 83.
16. *Ibid.,* p. 56.
17. *Ibid.,* p. 24.
18. *Ibid.,* p. 34.
19. *Pragmatism* (Longmans, 1943), p. 263.
20. *Discourse on Method,* Part IV.
21. *Appearance and Reality* (Oxford, 1940), p. 280.
22. *Ibid.,* p. 282.
23. *Science and the Modern World,* p. 263.
24. Morris Cohen and Ernest Nagel, *Introduction to Logic and Scientific Method* (Harcourt, Brace, 1934), pp. 217 f.
25. A. J. Ayer, *Language, Truth and Logic* (Dover, n.d.), p. 41.
26. L. J. Henderson, cited in Talcott Parsons, *Structure of Social Action* (McGraw-Hill, 1937), p. 41.
27. Morris Lazerowitz, *The Structure of Metaphysics* (Humanities Press, 1955), p. 4. Lazerowitz uses the hunter story to illustrate what he characterizes as "a likeness between many philosophical views and grotesque fiction." The application of the story is far more general than Lazerowitz suggests. The quotation that we have given from Whitehead on the subjectivity of modern science is not only literally true of modern science, but very few people in either modern science or philosophy realize how deep the modern world is in the bog of subjectivity.
28. (Macmillan, 1947), p. 111.
29. Page 4.
30. Author's Preface (Harper, 1944).
31. Appendix II, "A Methodological Note on Facts and Valuations in Social Science." Myrdal's argument in this note is sorely in need of extensive analysis. His superficiality is of a different type from that of Miss Benedict. He uses "science" to conjure with, just as Miss Benedict does. But unlike Miss Benedict, he sees the need for ethics in social science. Yet here also he conjures. His ethics, by his own account, has no more relation to reality than do these marks on this paper. His "ethics" is entirely arbitrary. It is, of course, within the power of man to adopt an arbitrary "ethics," but it is not within his power to escape the consequences. We see Myrdal's superficiality only when we see that modern science has made the idea of objectivity wholly animistic and that arguments such as that of Myrdal can be used to justify Nazism just as well as what Myrdal argues for as the "American Creed." It is just about the worst thing that could happen for the less fortunate people of the United States and the rest of the world that the study of the

problems of freedom and equality and justice should be conducted so regularly at the superficial level at which Myrdal was content to make his study. It is not possible to express a more severe criticism of social science than to say that social scientists generally are content to work at such superficial levels and seem unaware that there are any deeper levels at which work needs to be done.

3

Science and the Studies of Man

ELISEO VIVAS

I

These notes intend to show that the disciplines fashionably called at present "the behavioral sciences" are not scientific in the sense that the physical and the biological sciences are scientific. It is in the latter sense, in the sense we employ it in speaking of the exact, the natural sciences, that I shall use the term "science." The so-called behavioral sciences I shall refer to as the disciplines or studies of man. It is a pity that we cannot call them collectively "anthropology," thus providing ourselves with a much needed term to refer to all the disciplines whose subject matter is *anthropos* and the institutions that actualize and secure his values.[1]

But since I do not hold that the only valid knowledge is the scientific, but believe that there is philosophical knowledge of a substantive nature and that there is moral and religious knowledge and, in a qualified sense, even aesthetic knowledge, it is not my intention to disparage the studies of man. These disciplines attain truth of their kind and have worth irrespective of whether or not they employ the methods of the sciences.

Although in view of the *Zeitgeist* it would be naive to expect the differences between the studies of man and the sciences to be acknowledged, nevertheless it is important to be clear about them because the studies of man, when they are thought of as scientific, tend to develop a number of objectionable symptoms. Their language tends to become gobbledygook.[2] The matter accepted as the object of inquiry tends to be confined to those aspects of man and his activities that can be handled quantitatively or at least objectively. This would not necessarily be productive of harm were not the assumption widely and uncritically accepted that the real is only that which can be brought to the attention of the scientist. This assumption is operative in academic psychology with harmful consequences. We are told by men superbly equipped mentally that man has no mind. The psychologist initially understands what the statement means. Mind is not an entity in the sense in which the liver or the lungs are entities. But soon the statement is taken out of its context to mean that man's minding is a process that can be understood adequately by analogy with complex "thinking" machines. The upshot is that subjective experience, what Santayana called "the inward landscape," is first denied existence as a valid object of inquiry and finally denied existence *tout court*. Those who accept these denials do not stop to think what effects they have on scholarly thought. Consider, for instance, that neither Freud nor Rhine (whatever the ultimate judgment concerning the validity of his speculations or experiments) could have even started on his work had he taken the behaviorists seriously.[3]

Along with the acceptance of these denials comes the habit of looking upon man as we look upon the other animals, simultaneously failing to realize the consequences of our change of attitude. But we cannot maintain our self-respect if implicit in our approach to ourselves and others lies the conviction that man is only that which science says he is. And one of the consequences of a loss of self-respect is that the fiber of actual living is coarsened.[4]

Other objectionable symptoms appear when we overlook the difference between the studies of man and the sciences. A false and sometimes an utterly absurd quantification is introduced into subject matter that is not quantifiable. The triviality and the egregious absurdity of the results thus obtained do not daunt the man bent on such specious feats, since he does not take the slightest pains to inquire what makes one subject matter quantifiable and another not. This question, apparently, is not one that can be sensibly asked, since, not being quantifiable, it is not itself a scientific question. It must be, therefore, what misologists refer to as a "philosophic" question—by which is meant one that no sensible man would bother his head about.

Still another objectionable symptom appears when we overlook the difference between science and the studies of man: the latter become irrelevant to the human situation, since they are taken to be value-free, pure. As a result a number of consequences follow. The distinction made by Aristotle between the theoretical and the practical sciences is erased, and the studies of man become irrelevant to the human situation, which presumably they were initiated to elucidate. When it is acknowledged that they can be applied in the way that the pure sciences can be applied, a factitious problem appears, viz., the relation between fact and value, between the pure science and the valuable ends that they are applied to secure. The ends are taken to be external to the science and therefore considered arbitrary and unattainable by rational suasion.

In moral philosophy and in the philosophy of religion, the consequences of erasing the distinction between the theoretical and the practical sciences are even worse. Philosophers of a positivist and those of a linguistic orientation insist that their task is to carry on a philosophical analysis and not to "preach" or "moralize." The latter is considered demeaning, although sometimes the need for it is verbally conceded. The immediate result of this doctrine is a kind of institutionalized schizophrenia, according to which the philosophic analysis of moral decisions is kept in one compartment of the mind, hermetically sealed and inviolate, while the actual life of the philosopher goes its way untouched by what he knows or professes to know about morality. At a time when we could use the maximum of intelligence in solving our practical problems and still not have enough, philosophers take pride in demonstrating, on the basis of an antiquated psychology and simplistic dichotomies, that moral conflicts cannot, ultimately, be resolved rationally. If this were truly the case, one could not adduce the disadvantages of this view as reasons for not accepting it. But one would expect that responsible human beings would explore the alternatives in a wholehearted way and not be complacent about what they take to be the truth, when it is so obviously one that cannot improve our desperate practical situation.

II

To show that the disciplines of man are not sciences, all one needs to do is to point to the fact that while the physical and the biological sciences are each *one* science, or a constellation of disciplines more or less interdependent in respect to subject matter and in the process of reduction to one science through the extension and simplification of their laws, this is not the case with the studies of man. There is no such thing as Marxist physics as distinct from capitalist physics. Pontecorvo can defect to Russia, but the knowledge of physics he takes with him was developed in the Western world. This is true also of biology. When Lisenko, for reasons external to the science of genetics, proposes theories that are in harmony with his political beliefs, there are means of showing that his results are false—if, indeed, they are, which is something experts decide. But this does not hold for the disciplines of man. Among them we do not find a science or several sciences, but innumerable schools at bitter war with one another, aiming, as it seems to the outsider, for total victory and the unconditional surrender of the loser. At best these factions lack any kind of relationship with one another; at worst, and not infrequently, they actually contradict one another.

Take psychology. The work of the Gestalt psychologists has not been integrated with that of Hull and of Tolman and of Lashley and Eysenck and the hundreds of schools of psychology that make up the chaotic domain of that discipline. When we turn to depth psychology the factionalism is even more obvious, the partisanship among the various schools more rife and more embittered, and the possibility of integration seems less likely. Recently a psychologist named Ruth Monroe published a book entitled *Schools of Psychoanalytic Thought, An Exposition, Critique, and Attempt at Integration*.[5] The one thing we can say in favor of this work, without fear of contradiction, is that Dr. Monroe's amiable modesty is not false, for all she succeeded in doing was to make the attempt at integration. We have not yet heard that as the result of her attempt Freudians and Jungians have united with Adlerians and with the followers of Rank and of Sullivan and of Horney and of Fromm and the other schools in a grand ecumenical fellowship of integrated love and intellectual cooperation.

This is also true of sociology and of anthropology. Malinowski has his school, and so has Radcliffe-Brown and Kroeber and any one else who is any one and some who are not.

In 1931, Radcliffe-Brown wrote:

It is impossible to reconcile the different theories with one another, or even to discover principles of method about which there is general agreement. To say nothing of theories of the derivation of culture from a lost Atlantis or a lost Pacific continent, we are offered a choice between the Egyptian theory championed in its latest form by Professor Elliot Smith, or the theory of culture cycles of Graebner, or the somewhat different theory of Father Schmidt, or that of Frobenius, and I know not how many more. Each school goes its own way, building up its own hypothetical structure, not attempting to seek out points on which agreement can be reached with others. The procedure is often that of disciples of a cult rather than that of students of a science.[6]

And a little later Linton referred to the same situation. Falling back on the youthfulness of the science, he tells us that anthropology is "unsure of its objectives" and that "this has resulted in the development of a number of different schools." Although these statements are over twenty years old, they apply to the contemporary situation.[7]

Obviously, where there are schools and no effective means of mediating among them and of integrating the results, there is no *one* science, and where there is no one science, there is, properly speaking, no science. If it is any comfort to the students of man, we can say that their disciplines constitute a protoscience, an *Urnaturwissenschaft,* out of which, it is hoped, a science will come in the fullness of time. Against hope there can be no argument.

But at the moment we must admit that the presence of these factions and divisions is clear proof that conflicting differences of opinion—for we cannot call them scientific hypotheses—cannot be subjected to the same kind of verification and invalidation to which scientists submit their hypotheses.

I do not mean to assert that some aspects of man and of his institutions are not susceptible of scientific treatment or of something that makes the brave effort—all the more admirable because it is so pitifully unsuccessful—to approximate the rigorous techniques and procedures of the sciences. There is a great difference, for instance, between Hobbes' or Hume's psychology and some areas of contemporary psychology. And there is a great difference between the accounts of primitive peoples brought back by missionaries prior to the development of anthropology and the studies of contemporary anthropologists. It is easy, on the other hand, to exaggerate the difference between us and our prescientific ancestors, and the reason is that we think of our studies of man as scientific and of theirs as not scientific. But in quite a responsible sense the *Historia general* of Fr. de Sahagún has been called a rigorous linguistic and ethnographic account of early sixteenth-century Mexico.[8] Still, when one has said the most that can be said for the scientific status of contemporary studies of man, the difference between them and the sciences remains. What aspects of man and of his activities can be treated in a manner approaching that of the sciences and what aspects cannot is a question that cannot be answered in an a priori manner; it is a strictly empirical, casuistic question. But it is not a question that I expect to hear asked seriously in my lifetime by students of man. There are not many men in any generation who have the courage to challenge the *Zeitgeist*. When scientific status is uncritically claimed for the studies of man, the result is what, following Hayek, is known as "scientism." And scientism is endemic in our culture—or so, for the moment, it seems to be.

But scientism is not yet absolutely pandemic, and a number of students of man can be cited who are fully aware that their disciplines are not scientific in the sense in which I am using the term in these notes. Let me cite two instances among the several that have come to my attention. In an article entitled "Social Scientist: Man Between," Robert Redfield, with the wisdom and modesty those who enjoyed the privilege of his friendship expected of him, acknowledged the differences between the social scientist and the student of the humanities.[9] In psychology, Abraham Maslow has courageously and, in my outsider's opinion, successfully tried to inquire into phenomena in which the imitation of the methods of the physicist is simply inconceivable.

When I say that physics and biology are sciences, I do not mean that in any given science at a given time there are not stubborn, unresolved problems about which scientists are in doubt. These problems no doubt exist, and they are no doubt the source of disagreements. But these disagreements seem to arise for the most part, at least in the Western regions of the science, so to speak, where the explorers are opening the land and no settlement has yet taken place. Nor do they seem to be the source of the kinds of schools or factions that we find in the studies of man.

I am aware that in biology there are unresolved problems that seem to be cause for factionalism and cannot be said to be frontier problems: there is a minority that holds that teleology and vitalism are unresolved problems—if they are two, and not essentially one. The outsider is in no position to judge the merits of the solutions proposed for these problems when they are formulated within the domain of biology. All he can do is suspend judgment on the ground that if these problems have been resolved successfully, it is difficult to see why reputable scientists continue to reject the solutions offered. May not the reason be that these stubborn problems are philosophic, and not scientific, and seem to arise from causes similar to those to which the factionalism of the disciplines of man can be traced, viz., the effort to deal with biological subject matter in the way in which the physicist deals with his? However that may be, when allowance is made for these disagreements, it still can be said in fairness that the factionalism that is the normal condition in the studies of man does not exist in anything like the same degree in biology.[10]

The preceding argument should carry conviction, although it is external to the disciplines themselves. When it is advanced, students of man make two replies. With Linton they plead the youth of their studies. When one remembers the rapidity of the development of classical mechanics from Galileo to Newton, all this old excuse does is to remind one of Oscar Wilde's epigram about the United States: "America's youth is its oldest tradition." The second reply is that what gives a discipline its status as a science is the use of the scientific method, and since the studies of man use this method, they are sciences. It is fair to reply to them that it is a strange kind of subject matter that, when treated scientifically, produces no better results, in terms of agreement, than philosophers produce. It is also fair to add that it is a question whether in some of the disciplines of man scientific method in any but the most rudimentary sense can be said to be applicable. Indeed, it might not be useless to ask whether *"the* scientific method" (as distinct from a variety of generalized techniques, procedures, and manners of observation and correlation) is not the most successful canard palmed off by philosophers on philosophically naive scientists— but let me hasten to add that I would not dare ask this question, for only madmen dare outrage the pieties of their fellow beings.

We must consider another difficulty that prevents the studies of man from achieving the status of a science. The difficulty is not encountered by all the studies of man; it is encountered only by those that must reckon with value.

Let us first note the obvious fact that the student of man cannot always exclude value from his discipline. The social scientist (whether anthropologist or sociologist), the political theorist, the depth psychologist, and the student of personality turn their work into sheer triviality if they ignore the values of men. I know that Freud asserted that the psychoanalyst is not interested in the morals of his patient. But I take it that it is generally recognized today that this is one point on which Freud was in error. For there seems to be a close link between neuroses and morality, as Freud himself clearly saw. I have not forgotten that since Spinoza's day many philosophers have professed to be able to observe moral phenomena scientifically—by which they mean, as the physicist observes falling bodies. Hume alleged that his method was that of the physicist and called on philosophers to follow his lead. And in our day, as I have noted above, numerous moral philosophers—particularly the positivists, those known as analytic philosophers, and the *soit-disant* "metamoralists"—make the same assertion. I do not deny that some observers are more objective than others. But the problem is not as simple as those who allege that values can be observed objectively seem to think it is.

One fact that complicates the objective observation of values is that the student has no means of observing values but that which is employed by anyone at any time, be he Tom, Dick, or Harry. When Fortune characterizes Dobu culture, Ruth Bunzel observes the Zuñi, and Margaret Mead the Arapesh, they observe the values that give these cultures their distinctive qualities in the very way in which we observe one man's honesty or another's vanity. When Miss Mead's observations are criticized, as they were by Thurnwald, because they were hurriedly gathered, she elaborates her method and takes photographs and thus seeks to show that her observations are valid. In other words, the anthropologist may employ highly elaborate methods in order to make sure that he has interviewed a representative number of members of the community he studies and that he has not, in haste, attributed to it traits that are not there. But ultimately the judgment, "The Pueblos are Apollonian," is grounded on the same procedures of observation that enable me to say that John is honest and Dick is vain. Photographs, adequate sampling, statistics, psychographs, personality tests, and the rest of the apparatus the anthropologist employs to avoid misreading the value traits he observes seek to validate the grasping of a value or complex of values. But this must first be grasped, nor can the observer grasp it in any other way than you or I grasp it. If another anthropologist had disagreed with Fortune —as I understand one did—about Dobu, the discussion would have to be carried on in precisely the same terms we would carry it on if you were to disagree with me about Tom's honesty. You would point out certain actions of Tom that you have observed. These are purely behavioral observations. You might say that he invariably returns money loaned to him, even when the lender forgets about the loan, and that you saw him return money to a cashier who had "shortchanged" herself. And I would have to agree with you, or I would have to cite other actions of Tom which, I would assert, override your judgment. This is to say that when we discern value, we point to it, and when someone else does not discern it where we point, we give the physical features to which, as I am wont to put it, value is "anchored."

It should be noted, however, that value is not identical with the physical traits to which it is anchored. And the reason for this is that two men can agree thoroughly on the physical traits of an object and disagree on its value. I doubt whether D. H. Lawrence and Hemingway would have disagreed about what actually goes on in a bullfight: what the picador and torero and the horse and the bull did, how they behaved. But we know how deeply these two writers disagree about the moral and aesthetic values of bull-fighting.

It is true that the physicist also starts with objects and events of ordinary experience, which is to say, with observations that can be made either with the naked senses or with instruments that are extensions of these. In this respect he cannot be said to differ from the student of man. But sooner or later he finds ways of going beyond the initially observable data and of correlating his subject matter with scales and other instruments of measurement. How he does this beyond elementary physics I do not exactly know except in the vaguest way. But that he does it I believe I know. It is necessary to bear this in mind, for it points to the difference between the objectivity of the scientist and that which the student of man can achieve. Scientific data, even when not quantifiable, are thoroughly public, are objective in the sense that there need be no question concerning their presence within the purview of observation. The values observed by the student of man cannot be freed from inherent vagueness. When we speak of the Apollonian character of a culture, we cannot be certain that all of us are talking about the same thing—even if, after reading Miss Benedict, we backtrack and read Nietzsche also.[11]

These considerations are not intended to deny that there are cases in which value can be correlated with objective, value-free data—money or work done or some other physical event or feature of things objectively observable—but the limitations of such correlations are too obvious to need going into them. Again, we may be able to discover a man's or a group's values by means of psychological tests. But aside from the fact that the reliability of these tests is at the moment a controversial matter (for in principle they need not be unreliable), their radical defect, from the standpoint of our discussion, is that they cannot dispense with the definition of the value and its observation and its relation to behavioral traits expressed in the answers to the tests. We cannot judge the presence of a value without apprehending it to be present, and we cannot apprehend it except through the act of intuition through which it makes itself present to us as an intelligible object. From the standpoint of the kind of objectivity which is represented by the judgments that make up the sciences, the study of value is, so to speak, born with an original sin that no methodological baptism seems to be able to absolve it from. Let me add, however, although only in passing, that this does not make value judgments hopelessly subjective, mere expressions of affective responses which in principle are beyond rational suasion. They can achieve, and often do, a remarkable degree of objectivity. But what kind of objectivity is achieved and what degree and by what means are not questions that I can address myself to in this paper.

This does not exhaust our difficulty. The preceding remarks refer to the difference between the objects of science and the objects with which the student of man is concerned. But there is another difference, and that is located in the nature of the observers. This difference is pointed out by Robert Redfield in the paper referred to above. I shall let Redfield speak for himself: The difference between what I call a scientist and a student of man, lies, for one thing, in the fact that the latter observes values, and he

. . . enters imaginatively into the minds of the value-carrying human beings he studies. To understand another's value, I exercise my own valuing nature. Moreover, I come to see that this valuing of mine, as I work, is a part of my problem of observation and analysis. It has to be thought about and controlled. The social scientist no longer sees himself as a special kind of machine studying other things conceived as machines, but as a human being bringing to his study value judgments of which he may take account in accomplishing his work. Today one hears, without a sense of shock, one anthropologist say to another, "a value-free anthropology is an illusion." [12]

This is well said. All of it is true. But as regards Redfield's picture of how the student of man sees himself, one may be allowed to express doubts. Redfield was no man to fall into imprudent exaggerations. Nor can I match my superficial and scanty knowledge of anthropologists with Redfield's. But his statement leaves me wondering whether he was pointing to a fact or expressing a hope. For I have heard anthropologists claim for their discipline the status of a science. And I have also heard sociologists make the same claim. And to my dismay, it has come to my attention that students of politics, whom until recently I had ignorantly taken to be free from scientism, are introducing into their discipline the methods and the procedures the employment of which turns a discipline into scientism.

But if Redfield's statement describes correctly the attitude of anthropologists toward their discipline, something follows, the importance of which cannot be exaggerated: We are in a position to return, if not to the identical distinction, at least to a distinction similar to that made by German philosophers between the sciences of nature and those of the spirit. If and when and to the extent that this distinction becomes accepted, scientism will be dead.

But these are not the only obstacles that prevent us from giving the studies of man the status of a science. Were we able to apprehend values with the same degree of objectivity that we apprehend the traits observed in the objects of the sciences, and were the student of man capable of keeping his own valuations out of the subject matter observed, and were we able to make invariant correlations of an adequate nature between values and physical structures, our observation of the values espoused by an individual and a group would have, as regards susceptibility to scientific treatment, one inherent and ineradicable limitation. In principle prediction is impossible about values to be espoused in the future. Only on a simplistic assumption of a thoroughgoing cultural or some other kind of determinism could prediction be depended upon. Having said this much, I shall drop the point, for a full elucidation of it would plunge us into the difficult problem of freedom, and from such a plunge we cannot be sure to return.

Another obstacle that prevents us from giving the studies of man the status of a science—or perhaps another formulation of the point just stated—is that some predictions in the field of these studies can be nullified or realized by the operative force of the prediction upon the matter which is the subject of study. Thus, the prediction that the stock market will fall tomorrow could lead to its fall—if stockholders took the prediction seriously. And the announcement that a given neighborhood will turn into slums could lead, if taken seriously by the inhabitants of the neighbourhood, to just the condition predicted.

Before we drop this subject, it is advisable to make two remarks. The first is that I am not asserting unqualified freedom, as some philosophers seem to assert. Such an assertion, were it true, would make impossible the development of character, the development of neuroses, and the art of mental healing, and even human living. The institutions of society are possible because, within limits, men can be relied on, and they can be relied on because their behavior can be conditioned.

The second remark is that the qualification I have just made as regards freedom may seem unimportant to anthropologists who study custom-bound societies and who approach their data in an ahistorical manner. In such societies men do not seem to be free. Their values do not seem to change. Predictions about the Aruntas are possible—if the pictures we have of them are true. But the number of groups as static as the Aruntas is not great in the world and is diminishing rapidly; alas, we are running out of primitives, as we ran out of dodos.

In dynamic societies in which freedom is operative in moral judgments, prediction is not possible. We can know what men have done; we cannot always know what they will do. For when a man asks the question seriously, *What ought I to do?* to the extent that the perplexity that gave rise to the question is radical and to the extent that the man confronted with it is a serious moral agent, the resolution of his perplexity is unpredictable.

The upshot of these considerations is that the studies of man cannot be considered "scientific" in the sense in which I am using the word in this paper.

III

The claim that man can be studied scientifically is based on one assumption, among others, that should be examined critically. I refer to the conviction, widely shared by students of man and by philosophers, that the hypothesis of organic evolution accounts for the origin of man and of his cultural institutions. How this conviction came to be widely accepted by educated people after Darwin and what results it led to in the studies of man it is not necessary to review here. Nor do we need to review the arguments Boas employed to put a stop to the freewheeling of evolutionary anthropologists. What we need to consider is that anthropologists are embarrassed by the problem of human origins.

In 1949, S. F. Nadel asserted that "a search for origins which is purely speculative and unsupported by genuine historical evidence can be dismissed out of hand." In support of this statement Nadel quotes Radcliffe-Brown. On the other hand, in his Presidential Address to the American Anthropological Association, Hallowell raised the question about human origins and attempted to answer it.[13] We do not need to examine Hallowell's answer. All we need do is to point out that it is a purely speculative effort founded on definitions, generalizations, and inferences, all of which assume that man must have evolved from an earlier form of life. Anthropologists and students of man in general give their readers the impression that they know, in the sense in which the scientist knows, that man is an animal and that his cultural institutions are the product of evolution. This conviction appears to many educated men today to be an irrefragable truth, so well established as to require no further proof. And this is, indeed, the case as regards the manner in which it is accepted: if truth were decided by the

majority vote of those who concern themselves with such questions
—the educated—this statement would be as indisputably a truth
as any we have.

It is this conviction that I propose to analyze in this section. But
before we turn to our problem let me reiterate that biological evolution is not in question. It takes an utterly ignorant man or a
hard fundamentalist impervious to evidence to reject the evolutionary hypothesis. However, we do not know how man developed
his capacity to think and to rear his institutions. And until we
have answers to these questions, there is a break between animal
evolution and the process of human history as we know it. This
break can be bridged only by means of speculations that, were
they offered by a theologian or a religious man, would be hooted
at by genuine scientists and by scientistic scientists.

In order to examine this question in concrete terms I shall use
two illustrations of extrapolations from biological to cultural evolution. The first illustration I take from a book written for the
general reader by an anthropologist whom I take to have achieved
distinction in his profession, judging by the position he occupies.
Mr. Carleton S. Coon, we are informed by the jacket of his book,
is a professor of anthropology and curator of ethnology at the University of Pennsylvania. He tells us that:

More than twenty million years ago, long before the first appearance
of man on earth, his remote tree-living ancestors took their first step
in a human direction. Somewhere in the tropical regions of the earth,
probably in Africa, a band of large monkeys lived in a forest. Every
morning at daybreak they awoke, and the males began calling to their
families to follow them to the feeding grounds. There they spent most
of the day, picking fruit, peeling and eating it, and robbing birds'
nests of their eggs and their fledglings. As time went on, however,
the fruit became scarcer, and when the monkeys tried to move to
another part of the forest they found their way blocked. Every way
that they turned they came to the edge of the trees, and all about
them was grass. They were trapped. As the fruit and fledglings failed
them, they had no choice but to climb down to the ground.

In their frantic search for food they learned to lift up stones to collect insects and grubs, and to dig ground squirrels and moles out of their burrows. As the monkeys acquired a taste for meat, they came to relish the flesh of antelope and other large hoofed animals that grazed on the plain, though these were hard to catch. They also soon learned to watch out for lions and other beasts of prey with which they had begun to compete for the meat. Life on the ground was as dangerous as it was exciting. In the trees they had feared only falling and the snake.

Although some of these monkeys may have found their way back to the shrinking border of the forest, others stayed on the ground, where they continued to run about on all fours, lifting stones, picking berries, and nibbling on buds and shoots. They still do. They are the baboons and Barbary apes. Others learned to stand on their hind limbs and to walk or run erect when they needed to use their hands. After a while, however, the climate changed once more and the forest crept back over the plain. Some of the descendants of the monkeys that had learned to walk upright went back to the forest, where they became the ancestors of apes. Only those upright ones that stayed out in the open grew to be men.

It cannot therefore be said that man is descended from apes, but rather that apes are descended from ground-living primates that almost became men. There is sound evidence of this. We know that all animals repeat, during their embryonic life, the general history of their ancestors, from the form of a single-celled animal onward. The human embryo at various stages has gill-slits and a tail. The embryo of a chimpanzee at one stage has a foot resembling that of man in that its great toe points forward for walking rather than backward for grasping. Only as it approaches its birth size does its foot acquire the appearance of a hand. At no stage of its development does the human foot resemble that of an adult ape. The chimpanzee embryo has hair on its head like that of a man, and human-style eyebrows.[14]

It is true that Mr. Coon is not unaware that the evidence on which he bases his remarkably fanciful "reconstruction" is inadequate. On page 43 he states that the Early and Middle Pleistocene bones on which he bases his reconstruction are few and their exact date is dubious. Nevertheless, he is confident about the reconstruction, for, although early man's bones are scarce, "the product of his handiwork is abundant," and the tools give him confidence, for they tell him the same story he has read from the bones.

It should be noted that Mr. Coon's scientific reconstruction constitutes an astonishing achievement. Take, for example, a problem that has troubled philosophers for quite some time and that linguists have wrestled with until they seem finally to have given it up as hopeless—the question of the origin of language. For Mr. Coon the problem is easy. He tells us that by chirpings and roaring animals communicate with one another. But there is, of course, a difference between the vocabulary of the gibbons, who have "been shown to possess at least nine sets of sounds with specific meanings," and human language. The gibbons, we are told, utter simple imperatives, "Keep away from my wife!" or "Let us go get some fruit!" whereas human languages "include much larger vocabularies and more complex ideas expressed in units known as words. Not only do we speak and hear words, but we produce them silently when we think." And then he proceeds to tell us how human speech began:

The earliest forms of human speech must have begun when man's brain had no more intellectual capacity than that of the gibbon, capable only of a few commands and warnings, and limited entirely to immediate interpersonal relations. Qualities of objects of various classes, such as safe and dangerous, large and small; ways of referring to other persons, such as husband and wife, father and son, in their absence; and methods of expressing the idea that a given action had been finished, rather than left incomplete—these mechanisms of expression must have followed, with the eventual addition of further abstractions.[15]

By avoiding the difficulties that make the problem an insoluble one for philosophers, Mr. Coon's account is considerably simplified. For philosophers insist that we must draw a distinction between signs and symbols. It does not take a gibbon to give and respond to signs. All animals do. But, so far as we can tell, man is the only animal that employs symbols. And the difference is radical and indispensable if we are to understand what is meant by thinking and communicating and what is the problem of the origin of language.

Mr. Coon has many other wonderful stories to tell us. Thus, he gives us a picture of the social and intellectual life of Upper Paleolithic men, the Late Ice Age Hunters, although so far as I have been able to find out, these men left us no books, newspapers, clay tablets, or any records from which such pictures could have been drawn, nor does Mr. Coon mention any they might have left.[16] They did leave us their wonderful paintings, and these give evidence of equality, if not superiority, in skill to the artists of today. But from them what can we infer? Not much, and that only in very general terms. Thus, we may assume that animals endowed with such aesthetic sensibility were fully developed human beings and must have had systems of morality and probably all the other forms of cultural life that we find in men today. Yet if we believe this, and I do not doubt it, it is because we cannot imagine that such aesthetic sensibility as the cave painters gave evidence of could have existed by itself, unaccompanied by the other kinds of sensibility that accompany it in the case of the human beings we know and are. But this is all we can infer; nothing more. Particularly nothing about what manner of animals were the "ancestors" of the cave painters. We do not know how Mr. Coon's ape or Hürzeler's little animal became a human being—which is to say, a being capable of employing symbols and developing a culture. That human beings somehow appeared we know, for here we are and seem to have been here for quite some time. But Mr. Coon, who seems to believe his own fairy tales, does not realize that the problem cannot be solved on the evidence we have. The missing link, of which I used to hear in my childhood, and which gave so much comfort to believers in special creation, is still missing, and while it cannot legitimately give comfort to fundamentalists any more than Piltdown man can, it should disturb the dogmatic slumbers of the evolutionists—and I take it that it does, at least occasionally, as Hallowell's presidential address evinces.

The problem, needless to point out, is an extremely complex one. For it is not only a question of factual evidence, but of basic definition of terms. We do not yet know with any reasonable confidence what makes a being human. The impasse is radical and substantive, and not a merely verbal one, because until we know how we came about, we cannot draw the line between our earlier ancestry, if we had such ancestry, Mr. Coon's "half-brained man," his "full-brained man," and Hürzeler's Oreopithecus.[17]

That the cave painters were fully human we can reasonably hold. But it should be noticed that, if challenged, the conviction can be defended only by a purely speculative, a philosophic, and not a scientific, argument. For it is based on our inability to imagine aesthetic sensibility unaccompanied by other modes of sensibility—moral, religious, and cognitive. And our inability could be disposed of as Dr. Johnson disposed of the young man who said to him, "Sir, I do not understand." Replied the formidable Doctor: "Sir, I cannot give you understanding." If we cannot imagine, no one can give us imagination. In point of fact, however, there is nothing absurd or self-contradictory in the concept of an animal that gives evidence of aesthetic sensibility and skill and who does not use symbols and has no capacity for moral or religious response. There are Australian birds that are said to "adorn" their nests. We could interpret their activity as protoaesthetic sensibility and skill. But could we infer from their elaborate preparations for mating that these birds have a capacity for moral response? In any case, from the marvelous paintings of the caves of France and Spain and the others nothing but the most general deductions can be made.

How does Mr. Coon find it possible to give us his detailed account of the social and intellectual life of men who left us no records? He makes inferences from contemporary primitives and from monkeys: Australians studied and photographed by Mountford, African pigmies, some peoples living in modern times—Australians, Negritos, and Andamans—who use fire but do not know how to make it, and from the behavior of chimpanzees and gibbons—these are the bases of Mr. Coon's remarkable "reconstruction."[18] Prior to reading Mr. Coon I had been under the impression that anthropologists had given up the practice of deducing the culture of early man from that of contemporary primitives and from chimpanzees and gibbons; but obviously I was in error. However, the arguments interdicting such practice seem to me to be conclusive. And since they are well known, I do not need to review them here.

The abundant and detailed knowledge Mr. Coon succeeds in gathering by these means about Upper Paleolithic man is quite remarkable, and I would offer other specimens of it were I not in fear of abusing the reader's patience and were not Mr. Coon's book easily accessible. I shall confine my remarks in this respect to pointing out that Mr. Coon knows even about the motivations of these early people. Thus, he knows why they painted. This is a question on which aestheticians since Plato and Aristotle have not been able to agree. But for Mr. Coon the problem is one that can be settled in passing: "One great solace in the face of disturbance is art."[19] These full-brained men did not have the advantages that we, now living, have. In the face of disturbance all they could do was paint or look at paintings, whereas for us the Metropolitan or the National Gallery has become obsolescent. Here lies the genuine value of scientific progress. When disturbed we take tranquilizers. It is much less trouble.

Mr. Coon also knows about the religion of Upper Paleolithic man:

The Late Ice Age religious institutions likewise exceeded political boundaries, as it should in any healthy society. Ancestral heroes who hovered over the band were shared by other bands that met at ceremonial times. Cult heroes responsible for the landscape and its animal life were likewise shared, as were the combined capacities of the old men teaching the young.[20]

These are not the only problems that Mr. Coon resolves. Philosophers have quarreled about the nature of religion for some time, and they have been very perplexed, since William James' day, by the difficulty of giving an adequate definition of it in view of the varieties of what, *prima facie*, seem to be religious experience. But for Mr. Coon these difficulties do not exist. He tells us: "Religion is the sum total of behavior concerned with restoring equilibrium to the individual or the group after disturbance." [21]

"But," I hear one of my readers ask, "what harm can there be in Mr. Coon's fictional 'reconstructions'? For he is not trying to palm off his fairy tales on his fellow scientists. He is writing for the general reader, who is not a specialist." The answer is that there is no harm whatever. For we know that when a religious fundamentalist teaches that his myths are literal truths, he is spreading error and darkness; but when a scientist passes off fiction as science, he spreads truth and light. Mr. Coon is interested in the truth, for he is a scientist, whereas the fundamentalist is interested only in acquiring equilibrium after a disturbance—and there is an obvious difference. Perhaps. But I cannot rid myself of the feeling that we have a right to expect responsibility from a scientist, whereas from a fundamentalist all we can expect is his fundamentalism.

It must be acknowledged that when specialists write for themselves, and not for the general reader, they do not write fiction. Their assertions are sober and cautious. But the same faith that can be detected in Mr. Coon animates them. To show that this is the case, I turn to my second illustration, from an article by G. S. Carter:

Man is an animal, and, however greatly his present state differs from that of the rest of the animal kingdom, we must accept that he arose from sub-human ancestors by a process of evolution. And, since the life of those ancestors must have been very like that of other animals, the process by which he evolved must have been similar to that which other animals undergo. If so, it is clear that some consideration of the general theory of evolution is required before the special case of the evolution of man can be discussed.[22]

This statement sounds unexceptionable on first reading. And it cannot be said to be fiction. It is merely a deduction. If man is an animal, he must have arisen from subhuman ancestors by a process of evolution. In what other way could he have arisen?

This would seem to be self-evident. But the reason is that we readily supply the implicit premise of Mr. Carter's enthymeme, to the effect that whatever happens must happen by natural means. This assumption is not a scientific proposition, but a philosophical one.

That this implicit premise is an unsupported assumption can be noticed when we look with care at another paragraph of Mr. Carter's article. He tells us:

We must now consider how far man's evolution since he arose from his primate ancestors can be interpreted as governed by the same controls as those we have seen to govern the evolution of other animals. There can be no doubt that his evolution has been in many ways most unusual, and it is to be expected that unusual factors may have taken part in its control. But man is an animal, and he arose from animals much less unusual than he himself is. Also, his genotype is similar in its organization to those of other animals, and there should be no great difference in type between the variations that form the raw material of evolution in him and his animal ancestors. His ecology, at least in the earlier stages of his evolution, must have arisen by modification of that of the Primates from which he arose. Changes in ecology undoubtedly occurred in the course of his evolution and must have largely influenced its course, but he must have arisen from a primate life, probably arboreal, very like that of many of our modern Primates. I shall assume, for the sake of the argument, that he early gave up his arboreal life, coming to live an omnivorous life on the ground; that at first he lived in small groups not much larger than the family; and that the size of his communities was enlarged only later when he began to develop a social life.[23]

What is of interest in this paragraph is the style in which it is couched. "There can be no doubt . . ." we are told, and "there should be no great difference in type," and "he must have arisen," and "changes in ecology undoubtedly occurred." And finally: "I shall assume." As a student of philosophy, I find myself utterly at home in this kind of reasoning, for it is the rhetoric philosophers use when, as is so frequently the case, they want to per-

suade their readers and have little more than their own belief
in their doctrines to help them achieve their end. If "there can
be no doubt" of something or other, why are we not given the
evidence that makes it indubitable? And if man "must have
arisen" in a particular way and not in another, why are we not
given the facts in the case? And if changes in ecology "undoubtedly
occurred," why are we not forced to accept the proposition that
they occurred by being confronted with the evidence? And why is
it necessary to "assume" for the sake of the argument what ought
to be the conclusion of an empirical demonstration that has to
be accepted whether we like it or not? The reason Mr. Carter
uses the persuasive form of address rather than an argument based
on evidence is that he cannot point to the causal process by which
an animal that was the primate ancestor of man finally became a
human being. Or, changing the expression, Mr. Carter has to
cross from the subhuman to the human, and, lacking factual step-
ping stones, he pole-vaults by means of his sturdy and trusted
conviction that the change could have come about only by natural
means.

How does Mr. Carter know the truth of this proposition? He
cannot profess to have examined all the processes operative in the
universe or even a representative number of the kinds of processes
that are known about, nor can anyone else have done this for him.
Neither he nor anyone knows by what means man acquired his
distinctive powers and developed his institutions. It would seem,
therefore, that before we can hold that man is nothing but an
animal, we shall have to establish by scientific means that whatever
happens can happen only by natural means. But how could the
latter statement be established scientifically? However it is established, until it is, we shall have to be content to call it a philosophical statement. This is all it is. It is, indeed, the most succinct
means of expressing a *Weltanschauung* known as "naturalism"
and widely accepted by contemporary men. To ask, therefore, the
question, "How does Mr. Carter know this statement?" is to
initiate an inquiry into the validity of naturalism. And to this
inquiry we must now turn.

IV

Let me begin with two prefatory remarks. The first is that naturalism is not a school of thought in the sense that idealism or phenomenology is. It is a conviction about the universe that is elaborated in diverse ways. "Orthodox" naturalism, so to speak, adds to the proposition that nothing happens except by natural means another proposition, namely, that the only way to know what happens is to bring it within the purview of science. This second proposition has been elaborated with great care by positivists and instrumentalists who are committed to belief in "the unity of science." There are, however, naturalists who do not accept the doctrine of the unity of science.

The second prefatory remark is this: It is widely held today that naturalism is one of the indispensable foundations of science. I heard an academic psychologist recently assert, with a warmth one does not expect of a scientist, that psychology is possible only on a naturalistic foundation. However widespread this belief may be, it is false. Scientific activity of the most rigorous kind is consistent with an indeterminate number of philosophical convictions. The business of the scientist is to discover the invariant relations operative in the domain of his competence. What is to be found beyond the purview of scientific inquiry he need not make any assumptions about. He does not even need to believe, as has been alleged, that nature is through and through governed by the order that is expressed in scientific laws. When he espouses naturalism, his views do not have the authority that his scientific hypotheses have. When scientists speak of mathematics or geometry as the alphabet of nature, as the men of the seventeenth century did, they speak as philosophers; they do not speak as scientists. A scientist can say, with Kant, that nature is the realm of law. But if he does, he must stop there, and he does not even have the right, *qua* scientist, to say that what we ordinarily call nature, the spatiotemporal world, is completely governed by law. Of course, in his inquiries he discovers laws—these are what he is searching for. But whether the spatiotemporal world is through and through law-bound or whether this is the only world or realm of being that there is, are questions to which he may turn as a philosopher, but which his scientific method is not designed to answer.

When we examine naturalism critically, we find the arguments offered in its favor puzzling. Among the difficulties that naturalism must face are the lacunae in the scientific account of evolution, the missing links that Mr. Coon has so elegantly and courageously supplied us with. We do not know how man appeared on earth, we do not know how he came by his capacity for the employment of symbolic processes, we know nothing of the beginning of culture; we do not know about his first intimation, his first dim awareness of himself and of others, his first apprehension of beauty, his first fit of remorse, his first response to something he ended by calling "God." Until we know how these and other distinctive modes of human experience came about, naturalism is a purely speculative conviction.

Some naturalists avoid this difficulty by employing the term "emergence" to cover up the critical point at which the lacunae are found. This is a mere verbal dodge. But one naturalist, at least, discerning the dodge for what it is, interdicts its use. He writes:

. . . even some professed naturalists sometimes appear to promote the confusion when they make a fetish of continuity. Naturalists usually stress the emergence of novel forms in physical and biological evolution, thereby emphasizing the fact that human traits are not identical with the traits from which they emerge. Nevertheless, some distinguished contemporary naturalists also insist, occasionally with overtones of anxiety, that there is a "continuity" between the typically human on the one hand and the physical and biological on the other.[24]

Elsewhere our philosopher assures us that naturalism is not based on anything analogous to religious faith. And somewhere else he is emphatic in his assertion that his philosophy is "supported by compelling empirical evidence," rather than being "dicta based on dogmatic preference."[25]

We must examine with care the problems generated by these avowals and disavowals.

But before turning to the substance of our philosopher's argument, I invite the reader to consider its form. I think we owe our philosopher thanks for the linguistic lesson that he has taught us in passing. The phrases "compelling empirical evidence" and "dicta based on dogmatic preference" are descriptive, neutral, utterly value-free, and therefore appropriate for scientific discourse.

However, isn't there something slightly unscientific in the manner in which our philosopher dismisses the beliefs of those with whom he disagrees? His opponents accept their beliefs on the ground of *preference*. Our philosopher knows *their* motivations. And, of course, *his* own conviction has been gained the hard way, by gathering empirical evidence irrespective of his own preferences. Indeed, he has no preference except to go where the evidence leads. If this argument were put forth by anyone else than a scientific philosopher, I would suggest that what he was doing was psychoanalyzing the opposition—a game that we all can play.

Let us consider next the dichotomy with which our scientific philosopher operates: On the one hand, we have a doctrine supported by empirical evidence and, on the other, mere dicta based on dogmatic preference. No third alternative is conceivable. Truth on the one side and error on the other. It is as simple as that. But is it? The question of the "evidence" on which even the most dogmatic of us and the most depraved victim of his own preference holds his beliefs cannot be resolved by rigging up a simplistic dichotomy. And to attempt to resolve it in this manner is to display an ungenerous intolerance based on God knows what kind of preference. Other philosophers arrive at their convictions in much the same manner and for much the same kind of psychological reasons as naturalists arrive at their views, by means of much the same kind of evidence, and the differences between them, if they can be settled at all, cannot be settled by means of simplistic dichotomies.

The disagreement is, in the last analysis, one about the nature of experience and the quality of life that one philosophy makes possible and another does not. The noun "experience," the verb "to experience," and the adjective "empirical" are not univocal terms that can be transferred from one system to another without a change of meaning. And for this reason, when our naturalist takes the no-nonsense position that "knowledge is knowledge," as he does somewhere in the essay under examination, he is indulging in an act of oversimplification.[26] Knowledge is indeed knowledge, but what *is* knowledge? I am ashamed to have to say it, because it is something that any undergraduate who has taken a course in the history of philosophy ought to know; but I am forced to say it in view of the no-nonsense attitude of our philosopher. What knowledge is, is still an open question which Western philosophy has not succeeded in resolving in spite of the tremendous effort that has been put into the attempt to do so. Experience does not come labeled as empirical, nor does it come self-certified as such. What we call "experience" depends on assumptions often hidden beyond scrutiny, which define it and which in turn it supports. We are here caught in a kind of circular analysis we would do well to admit and accept, for it can be avoided only by abandoning our system and falling back on incoherence.

With these observations about the form of our philosopher's argument out of the way, we turn to the substantive problem that arises because of the introduction of the concept of emergence. In order to examine it, I have to call the reader's attention to the first of the two tenets that our philosopher considers central to naturalism. He states it as follows: "The first [thesis] is the existential and causal primacy of organized matter in the executive order of nature." [27]

Our problem arises because we can interpret emergence in one of two ways. Either the term "emergence" points to a place where the causal link is not known, but is assumed to exist, or to a place where it is not known because it does not exist. If we assert "the existential and causal primacy of organized matter," we must take the first interpretation of emergence. If we take the second, we are left with some sort of creation out of nothing. In a paper published over fifteen years ago Paul Henle made clear that "emergence" must be interpreted as pointing to our ignorance of causal links that have not yet been discovered.[28] If Paul Henle is not right, why are scientists and philosophers concerned with the questions whether biochemists can synthesize life in their laboratories and why are evolutionists putting forth speculative doctrines about the condition on earth that made the appearance of life possible? They are—like students of man such as Messrs. Coon and Carter—concerned with the missing links. To seek for these links relentlessly and everywhere, even where religious or other interests put up no-trespassing signs, has, after a long struggle, come to be recognized as legitimate in the civilized world— is, indeed, one of the marks by which we distinguish today a civilized society from one that is not. But to assert that we *know* that they exist before we find them is to attempt to pass off a "hunch" for a fact for which we have no evidence.

Such a conviction is no part of science; it is pure speculation. Until we find the causal links, particularly at the critical places at which they are now missing, the affirmation of the existential and causal primacy of matter is a philosophical conviction on all fours with other philosophical convictions. Or are we here confronted with privileged a priori knowledge or a scientific revelation? If we are, we should be informed that we are, for I, and I am certain many others, do not want to infringe on anyone's privileges. Until, however, the privilege is validated or the causal links are supplied, I think we have a right to say that what we have here is a bit of speculation—and a hope, the hope that the links will be found.

There are other problems generated by the improper introduction of the scientific temper into the studies of man, but although they are more or less intimately connected with the faith of the naturalist, I cannot take them up here.

On one point, before closing, I beg leave to dwell emphatically: In suggesting that Mr. Carter either argues in a circle or begs the question, I have no desire to foist on him the views of the philosopher whom I have criticized. But if his argument is not based on some formulation of the naturalistic tenet—which is to say, if he does not accept some form or other of the premise I expressed as "whatever happens happens by natural means"—what premise allows him to make the deduction from biological to human evolution? Or does he mean to deny the differences between man and his "fellow" animals that give rise to the problem? The latter cannot be his intention, and the evidence that it is not is the rhetorical effort, to which I have already referred, made by Mr. Carter to persuade the reader that in spite of the differences or alleged differences there is evolutionary continuity between man and the other animals. If these differences are accepted, Mr. Carter must make the deduction by some sort of implicit premise, for his argument is clearly enthymemic.

Or is Mr. Carter arguing as a man of faith and not as a man of science? This I can understand and accept. What is more, if the matter is thus put, I have a "hunch" that Mr. Carter is right. That is probably how man came about, although we do not know, at the critical places, how it happened. Having been born in the twentieth century, I find it impossible to entertain any other notion of how man came about. But "hunches," by whomever held and however widely held, do not constitute scientific knowledge, although some of them may be the starting point of such knowledge. And the Spirit of the Age—any age, even the greatest of all ages, the age of Belsen and Hiroshima, of genocide and of the commissar—is not always the Spirit of Truth. Had Messrs. Coon and Carter wanted to remain scrupulously within the domain of science, they would have asserted something like this: For the fact of man's biological evolution there is evidence as good as any we have in science. As to the factors, we must be prepared to modify our hypotheses with the progress of biology and other relevant sciences. But how an animal became a human being, a symbolic, culture-rearing animal, what factors led to this change and when, this is a question that scientists can answer only in the most speculative and, as yet at least, nonempirical of ways—in the way which Mr. Coon has answered it. Mr. Coon's answer could be improved considerably. It could be less fanciful, more diffident, and considerably more sophisticated. But, as yet, something like Mr.

Coon's story is all we can give in answer to the question how an unknown animal became man. Had the answer been couched in these terms, Mr. Coon could not have written his long and lively book; he would have written a much smaller one, and a more sober one. But he would not have been open to criticism.

It follows from what I have said that I do not reject the naturalistic faith because I believe in man's special creation or in divine miracles. I believe in only one miracle—the miracle of the universe. As to creation of any kind—whether that of man or the world—which is to say, as to the generative processes with which the universe teems—these are too mysterious or miraculous for me to advance anything resembling a "hypothesis" about them. I am content to let Messrs. Hoyle and Gamow speculate about them. As for myself, all I can do is to respond to these processes with awe and piety. And with unappeased wonder.

That this is not acknowledged frankly, that conscientious scientists do not see that their argument is enthymemic and the implicit premise is a philosophic assumption and not an empirically demonstrated proposition, is a fact that it is most important to notice, because only by noticing it do we grasp the true nature of the conviction that these men possess. *It is a faith.* And for this reason, when the studies of man claim to be scientific, they are merely scientistic.

NOTES

1. In the writing of this paper I have not had history in mind, for I take it that history is still fortunately free from scientistic contagion. But in so far as the assertion is made that history is a science, in the sense of the word here employed, what I say about the scientistic studies of man applies to history.
2. Gobbledygook is not to be identified indiscriminately with the technical language of a discipline, in which terms that are relatively precise are introduced by scholars to save laborious periphrasis and mental effort. For a deliberate attempt to introduce gobbledygook into a discipline, see E. W. Count *et al.* "Do We Need More Becoming Words?" *American Anthropologist,* Vol. LV, No. 3 (1953) pp. 395 ff.
3. A valuable contribution towards defining the relation of psychology to the human being is made by Paul Lafitte, *The Person in Psychology, Reality or Abstraction* (London, 1957).

4. I have been asked for "proof" of this statement. By the request, I take it, what is intended is "empirical evidence" obtained as follows: Take at least twenty freshmen (women will do, if men are not available, and upper classmen even; *in extremis,* professors, if their services can be enlisted) and divide them into two groups, one for control. Destroy the self-respect of one of the groups and observe results. The statement is taken as a "hypothesis" which, if "confirmed," becomes a "law." Will the law apply to Hindoos in Trinidad, B.W.I.? This calls for "field work," which first involves a "foundation grant" leading to a little junket in the Caribbean. Alas, I do not have this kind of evidence, and what compounds the felony, I do not have much faith in this way of getting it. The "proof" by which I back the statement is a number of years of observation of my fellow beings and speculation concerning the nature of the good life. This, I know, is a most disreputable admission for a scholar to make, and I make it in shame, for it puts me (allowing for obvious differences in stature) with men like Plato, Aristotle, Montaigne, Kant and Hume—yes, even Hume, for consider the nature of the evidence he offers in Section II of his *Enquiry Concerning the Principles of Morals*—and Veblen. A shameful group of men to be with, who make statements of an empirical nature without having taken twenty freshmen, etc.

5. Ruth L. Monroe, *Schools of Psychoanalytic Thought, an Exposition, Critique, and Attempt at Integration* (New York, 1955).

6. Radcliffe-Brown's statement is quoted by A. C. Haddon, *History of Anthropology* (London, 1934), p. 123.

7. Ralph Linton, *The Study of Man, an Introduction* (New York, 1946), p. vii.

8. Fr. Bernardino de Sahagún, *Historia general de las cosas de Nueva España,* (Mexico, D. F., 1938), I, xiv-xvi. The writer of the "Nota Preliminar" to the *Historia general,* Wigberto Jimenez Moreno, concludes his discussion of Sahagún's method in the following manner: "Sahagún followed, without knowing, the most rigorous and demanding method of the anthropological sciences." And he refers to two other writers that have studied Sahagún from this point of view. I once heard the distinguished philosopher, the late Joaquin Xirau, make the same point about Sahagún.

9. Redfield's article was published in *The Chicago Review,* Vol. VIII, No. 3 (1954), pp. 35-43. I shall refer to it below in another connection. I want to use this opportunity to express my deep sense of grief: as I was revising these notes his death occurred. American anthropology suffers irreparable loss.

   As I was engaged in the revision of this paper a review came to my attention that ought to be read by those interested in the subject of scientism and the studies of man. Entitled "The Proper Study of Mankind," it appeared in *The* (London) *Times Literary Supplement,* No. 2 946, 57th year (August 15, 1958), pp. 453-454. *See also* Abraham Maslow, *Personality and Motivation* (New York, 1954) and a paper to be published in the *Journal of Genetic Psychology* entitled "The Cognition of

Being in the Peak-Experiences." His recent papers all indicate that the subject matter in which he is interested, which is of great importance, cannot be handled within the restrictions of scientism.

10. Thus, one of the contributors to this volume, Professor von Bertalanffy, seems to hold (I say "seems," because I am not certain that I have understood him) that teleology is no longer a problem among biologists.

11. Philosophers of science will consider this account of what scientists do superficial and inaccurate. But a more accurate account of the matter would take us too far afield. The essential point I want to make is that the student of man, for complex reasons, cannot handle value data as the scientist handles merely factual, value-free data.

12. Redfield, *op. cit.,* p. 40.

13. S. F. Nadel, *The Foundations of Anthropology* (Glencoe, Ill., 1951—but the Preface is dated November, 1949). A. Irving Hallowell, "Personality Structure and the Evolution of Man," *American Anthropologist,* Vol. LII, No. 2 (April-June, 1950), pp. 159 ff. Since failure of communication at this point would lead to a total misunderstanding of my point, let me emphasize that I am not speaking here about the cluster of problems brilliantly elucidated by Redfield in *The Primitive World and Its Transformations* (Ithaca, New York, 1953). Redfield starts with beings that are already human. I am referring to the critical period during which the transition took place between a prehuman animal and the culture-rearing, symbol-using animal, the full human beings we now are.

14. Carleton S. Coon, *The Story of Man* (New York, 1954), pp. 11-12. If Hürzeler's Oreopithecus is accepted, Mr. Coon's ape took to the grass in vain, for he was too late to found a dynasty. And, what is more amusing to the student of philosophy, Bishop Wilberforce's query to Huxley had a point in spite of His Grace's prejudice and ignorance. But our problem is not changed by little Oreopithecus.

15. *Op. cit.,* p. 18.

16. *Op. cit.,* p. 28, p. 32.

17. *Op. cit.,* pp. 96 ff.

18. *Op. cit.,* pp. 45, 47, 61, 65.

19. *Op. cit.,* p. 101.

20. *Op. cit.,* p. 105.

21. *Loc. cit.* I may be giving the reader the impression of being a carping, implacable, and even picayune critic. So be it. But these are important questions, and one cannot stand by and watch them settled in such a cavalier manner by a man who speaks in the name of science. On Mr. Coon's conception of religion and of art, they are both means of restoring equilibrium. It would seem that the difference between one mode of experience and the other requires careful discrimination, in which the anthropologist would be as seriously interested as the student of philosophy. But note that I am not complaining that Mr. Coon failed to elucidate the distinction between religion and art; that is not within his professional competence. The complaint is that he did not indicate in passing that this difference constitutes a difficult problem. Is it not desirable that the scientist who writes for the general public should point

out the difficulties that perplex us when we try to grasp the nature of man and his experience?

22. G. S. Carter, "The Theory of Evolution and the Evolution of Man," in *Anthropology Today, an Encyclopedic Inventory,* prepared under the chairmanship of Λ. L. Kroeber (Chicago, 1953), p. 327 A.

23. *Op. cit.,* 339 B.

24. Ernest Nagel, "Naturalism Reconsidered," *Proceedings and Addresses of the American Philosophical Association,* 1954-55, p. 10. However, I am not quite sure exactly what attitude Mr. Nagel does take towards "emergence," and the reason for my difficulty is that earlier in the same page he says that "naturalism views the emergence and the continuance of human society as dependent on physical and physiological conditions . . ."

25. *Op. cit.,* p. 14 and p. 12 respectively.

26. *Op. cit.,* p. 14.

27. *Op. cit.,* p. 8.

28. Paul Henle, "The Status of Emergence," *The Journal of Philosophy,* Vol. XXXIX, No. 18 (August 27, 1942), pp. 486 ff.

4

Concealed Rhetoric in Scientistic Sociology

Richard M. Weaver

This inquiry concerns some problems posed by the use of rhetoric in the dissemination of a professedly scientific knowledge of man. It assumes that rhetoric in its right character is one of the useful arts and that knowledge about the nature and behavior of man can be gained and should be propagated as widely as possible. The question of what things should precede and enter into that dissemination, however, continues to raise real perplexities. Many of us who read the literature of social science as laymen are conscious of being admitted at a door which bears the watchword "scientific objectivity" and of emerging at another door which looks out upon a variety of projects for changing, renovating, or revolutionizing society. In consequence, we feel the need of a more explicit account of how the student of society passes from facts to values or statements of policy.

I would reject at the outset any assumption that the man who studies social phenomena either could or should be incapable of indignation and admiration. Such a person, were it possible for him to exist, would have a very limited function, and it is hard to see how he could be a wise counselor about the matters with which he deals. It seems probable that no one would ever devote himself to the study of society unless he had some notion of an "ought," or of the way he would like to see things go. The real focus of this study is on the point at which social science and rhetoric meet and on the question whether this meeting, in the case of what will here be labelled "scientistic" sociology, has resulted in deception rather than in open and legitimate argument. To begin the inquiry, it will be necessary to say a few things about the nature of rhetoric.

1. *Rhetorical and Scientific Discourse*

Rhetoric is anciently and properly defined as the art of persuasion. We may deduce from this that it is essentially concerned with producing movement, which may take the form of a change of attitude or the adoption of a course of action, or both. This art, whether it presents itself in linguistic or in other forms (and I would suggest that a bank or other business corporation which provides itself with a tall and imposing-looking building is demonstrating that there is even a rhetoric of matter or of scene), meets the person to whom it is addressed and takes him where the rhetor wishes him to go, even if that "going" is nothing more than an intensification of feeling about something. This means that rhetoric, consciously employed, is never innocent of intention, but always has as its object the exerting of some kind of compulsion.

Defining rhetoric thus as the art of persuasion does not, however, divorce it entirely from scientific knowledge. My view is that the complete rhetorician is the man of knowledge who has learned, in addition to his knowledge, certain arts of appeal which have to do with the inspiring of feeling. Indeed, the scientist and the rhetorician both begin with an eye on the nature of things. A rhetoric without a basis in science is inconceivable, because people are moved to action by how they "read" the world or the phenomena of existence, and science is the means of representing these in their existential bearings. People respond according to whether they believe that certain things exist with fixed natures, or whether they accept as true certain lines of cause-and-effect relationship, or whether they accept as true certain other relationships, such as the analogical. One might, speaking as a scientist, define man as an animal, or one might assert that government spending is a cause of inflation, or one might assert that war and murder are similar kinds of things. But one could also make these statements as a rhetorician. How, then, can one distinguish between the two kinds of statements?

The difference is that science is a partial universe of discourse, which is concerned only with facts and the relationships among them. Rhetoric is concerned with a wider realm, since it must include both the scientific occurrence and the axiological ordering of these facts. For the rhetorician the tendency of the statement is the primary thing, because it indicates his position or point of view in his universe of discourse. Rhetorical presentation always carries perspective. The scientific inquirer, on the other hand, is merely noting things as they exist in empirical conjunction. He is not passing judgment on them because his presentment, as long as it remains scientific, is not supposed to be anything more than classificatory. The statement of a scientist that "man is an animal" is intended only to locate man in a biological group as a result of empirical finding; but the rhetorician's statement of the same thing is not the same in effect. For him the term "animal" is not a mere positive designation, but a term loaded with tendency from the wider context in which he is using it. He is endeavoring to get a response by identifying man with a class of beings toward which a certain attitude is predictable. He has taken the term out of the positive vocabulary and made it dialectical, a distinction I shall take up presently.

It may now be suggested that if the sociologists whom I am here calling "scientistic" had been true scientists, they would have asked at the beginning: What is the real classification of the subject of our study? And having answered this, they would have asked next: What is the mode of inquiry most appropriate to that study? I am assuming that the answers to their questions would have told them that their subject matter is largely subjective, that much of it is not susceptible of objective or quantitative measurement, and that all or nearly all their determinations would be inextricably bound up with considerations of value. This would have advised them that however scientific they might try to be in certain of their procedures—as in the analysis of existing facts— the point would be reached where they would have to transcend these and group their facts in categories of significance and value.

But what some of the more influential of them did was to decide that the phenomena which they were engaged in studying were the same as those which the physical scientists were studying with such impressive results, and that the same methods and much of the same terminology would be appropriate to the prosecution of that study.

2. *The Original Rhetorical Maneuver*

My thesis is that in making this decision they were acting not as scientists, but as rhetoricians, because they were trying to capitalize on a prestige and share in an approbation, in disregard of the nature of the subject they were supposed to be dealing with. Sociology took this turn at a time when the prestige of physical science was very great, possibly greater than it is even today, since certain limitations had not then been encountered or fully considered. Physical science was beginning to change the face of the earth, and it was adding greatly to the wealth-producing machinery of mankind. It was very human for a group engaged in developing a body of knowledge to wish to hitch its wagon to that star. F. A. Hayek, in *The Counter-Revolution of Science,* has related the case as follows

Their [the physical scientists'] success was such that they came to exert an extraordinary fascination on those working in other fields, who rapidly began to imitate their teaching and vocabulary. . . . These [subjects] became increasingly concerned to vindicate their equal status by showing that their methods were the same as those of their more brilliantly successful sisters rather than by adapting their methods more and more to their own particular problems.[1]

Accordingly, the founders of scientistic sociology did not so much arrive independently at a definition of sociology (in doing which they would have been scientists) as seek identification, for external reasons, with another field of study. In proceeding thus, they were not trying to state the nature of their subject; they were trying to get a value imputed to it. That this was their original rhetorical maneuver can be shown in the following way.

Rhetoric can be visualized as altogether a process of making this kind of identification. The process is simply that of merging something we would like to see taken as true with something that is believed to be true, of merging something we would like to get accepted with something that is accepted. Such an operation can be seen in the most rudimentary of all rhetorical devices, which is sometimes termed "name-calling." To something that we wish to see accepted, we apply a name carrying prestige; to something that we wish to see rejected, we apply a name that is distasteful. Rhetoric thus works through eulogistic and dyslogistic vocabularies. It is the thing-to-be-identified-with that provides the impulse, whether favorable or unfavorable. The honest and discriminating rhetorician chooses these things with regard to reason and a defensible scheme of values; the dishonest or unthinking one may seize upon any terms which seem to possess impulse, just to make use of their tractive power.

If the foregoing analysis is correct, the scientistic sociologists applied a prestige-carrying name to their study. They were not classifying in the true sense; they were instigating an attitude. In brief, "social science" is itself a rhetorical expression, not an analytical one. The controversy over their methods and recommendations which goes on today continues to reflect that fact.

3. Positive and Dialectical Terms

Having thus assumed the role of scientists, they were under a necessity of maintaining that role. And this called for further "identifications." Perhaps the most mischievous of these has been the collapsing of the distinction between positive and dialectical terms. Since this distinction is of the first importance to those who would deal with these matters critically, I shall try to make clear what is meant by it.

Practically everyone grants that not all of the terms in our vocabulary refer to the same kind of thing. The difference between those which refer to positive entities and those which refer to dialectical ones is of decisive significance for the investigator. "Positive" terms stand for observable objects capable of physical identification and measurement. They are terms whose referents are things existing objectively in the world, whose presence supposedly everyone can be brought to acknowledge. "Rock," "tree," and "house" are examples. Positive terms thus make up a "physicalist" vocabulary, inasmuch as they represent the objects of sensory perception (even when these have to be noted by dials and meters). Properly speaking, there cannot be an argument about a positive term; there can be only a dispute, which is subject to settlement by actual observation or measurement.

"Dialectical" terms come from a different source, because they take their meaning from the world of idea and action. They are words for essences and principles, and their meaning is reached not through sensory perception, but through the logical processes of definition, inclusion, exclusion, and implication. Since their meaning depends on a concatenation of ideas, what they signify cannot be divorced from the ideological position of the user as revealed by the general context of his discourse. A scientist, as we have noted, locates things in their empirical conjunction, but the user of dialectic must locate the meaning of his entities in the logical relationships of his system, and hence his discovery of them cannot be an empirical discovery. For this reason we say that the meaning of "justice" or "goodness" or "fair play" is not "found," but rather "arrived at." It is implied by the world of idea and attitude with which the user started. A dialectical term does not stand for "motion," as the positive term out of science might do, but for "action," which cannot be freed from the idea of purpose and value.

The scientistic sociologist has tried to maintain his scientific stance by endeavoring to give the impression that all the terms he uses are positive and hence can be used with the same "objectivity" and preciseness as those of the physical scientist. I say he has endeavored to give the impression, because even an impression that this can be done is difficult to induce for any length of time, as I believe the following examples will show.

Let us take for illustration an expression fairly common in sociological parlance today: "the underprivileged," and ask ourselves how one determines its meaning. We see at once that it is impossible to reach the meaning of "the underprivileged" without reference to the opposed term, "the privileged." Evidently one has first to form a concept of "the privileged," and this will be in reference to whatever possessions and opportunities are thought of as conferring privilege. The one term is arrived at through logical privation of the other, and neither is conceivable without some original idea frankly carrying evaluation. "Privilege" suggests, of course, something that people desire, and hence "the privileged" are those in whose direction we wish to move; and "the underprivileged" constitute the class we wish to escape from. But where is the Geiger counter with which we could go out into society and locate one of the underprivileged? We would have to use some definition of privilege, arising out of an original inclination toward this or that ideal.

Or let us take the more general expression, "social problem." How is one to become aware of the supposedly objective fact or facts denoted by this expression? According to one sociologist, a social problem is "any situation which attracts the attention of a considerable number of competent observers within a society and appeals to them as calling for readjustment or remedy by social, i.e., collective, action of some kind or other." [2] At least three items in this definition warn us that a social problem is not something that just anybody could identify, like an elephant in a parade, but something that must be determined by a dialectical operation. First of all, the observer must be competent, which I take to mean trained not just in seeing objective things, but in knowing when ideas or values are threatened by their opposites. This perception appeals to him for an attitude to be followed by an action, and moreover this action must be of the putatively most beneficial kind, "social" or "collective."

The point I wish to make here is that the scientistic sociologist is from the very beginning caught up in a plot, as it were, of

attitude and action, and that he cannot divorce the meaning of
the incidents from the structure of the plot. The plot is based on
a position which takes facts out of empirical conjunction and
places them in logical or dialectical constructions.

He is therefore not dealing in positive words that have a single
fixed meaning when he uses terms that depend on a context for
their signification. Another way of expressing this is to say that
the terms in his vocabulary are polar, in that their meaning
changes according to what they are matched with. And since the
sociologist has the opportunity to match them with almost anything, he is not dealing with scientific invariables when he talks
about "the underprivileged" or "a social problem." He is being
an ethical philosopher from the beginning, with the responsibility
which that implies.

The conclusion comes down to this: Things which are discriminated empirically cannot thereafter by the same operation be
discriminated dialectically. If one wishes to arrive at a dialectical
discrimination, one has to start from a position which makes that
possible.

4. *Other Forms of "Identification"*

This ignoring of the nature of dialectical inquiry is the most
serious perversion committed by the scientistic sociologists in seeking to maintain their identification, but there are other, perhaps
more superficial, procedures, whose general end is the same kind
of simulation. One of the more noticeable is what might be called
pedantic analysis. The scientistic sociologist wishes people to feel
that he is just as empirical and thoroughgoing as the natural
scientist and that his conclusions are based just as relentlessly on
observed data. The desire to present this kind of façade accounts,
one may suspect, for the many examples and the extensive use of
statistical tables found in the works of some of them. It has
been said of certain novelists that they create settings having such
a wealth of realistic detail that the reader assumes that the plot
which is to follow will be equally realistic, when this may be far
from the case. What happens is that the novelist disarms the

reader with the realism of his setting in order that he may "get away with murder" in his plot. The persuasiveness of the scene is thus counted on to spill over into the action of the story. In like manner, when a treatise on social science is filled with this kind of data, the realism of the latter can influence our acceptance of the thesis, which may, on scrutiny, rest on very dubious constructs, such as definitions of units.

Along with this there is sometimes a great display of scientific preciseness in formulations. But my reading suggests that some of these writers are often very precise about matters which are not very important and rather imprecise about matters which are. Most likely this is an offsetting process. If there are subjects one cannot afford to be precise about because they are too little understood or because one's views of them are too contrary to traditional beliefs about society, one may be able to maintain an appearance of scientific correctness by taking great pains in the expressing of matters of little consequence. These will afford scope for a display of scholarly punctiliousness and of one's command of the scientific terminology.

At the opposite extreme, but intended for the same effect, is the practice of being excessively tentative in the statement of conclusions and generalizations. The natural scientists have won an enviable reputation for modesty in this respect: they seldom allow their desire for results to carry them beyond a statement of what is known or seriously probable. This often calls for a great deal of qualification, so that cautious qualification has become the hallmark of the scientific method. It is my impression, however, that a good many modern sociologists do their qualifying, not for the purpose of protecting the truth, but of protecting themselves. There is a kind of qualification which is mere hedging. I offer as an example a sentence from an article entitled "Some Neglected Aspects of the Problem of Poverty." The author begins his definition thus: "It would seem that it is nothing more nor less than a comparative social condition depending on a relative control over economic goods, the standard of comparison being a group possessing a maximum of such control, called the rich or wealthy." [3] There appear at the very beginning of this sentence two important qualifiers: (1) the verb is thrown into a conditional mode by the use of the auxiliary "would," and (2) the verb is not the categorical "is," but the tentative "seem," with its suggestion that one may be dealing only with appearances. This is followed by "nothing more nor less," which is a purely rhetorical flourish, evidently intended to make us feel that the author is going to be definite, whereas he has just advised us that he is not. What looks like carefulness is mere evasiveness; this writer does not want to assume the risk of saying what poverty is. Instances of such unwillingness to make a firm declaratory statement are so numerous that they almost constitute the style of a type of social science writing. With the unwary reader, unfortunately, this style may encourage confidence, whereas it should lead to challenge.[4]

5. *Appeals to Authority*

In addition to a language simulating that of science, the scientistic sociologists make use of an external means of persuasion in the form of an appeal to authority. A common practice with some of these writers when they are dealing with a subject that is controversial or involved with value judgments is to cite an impressive array of authorities. There is nothing improper in itself, of course, about the invoking of authority. But when we look at the method of certain of these authors, we are likely to find that the authorities are other social scientists who happen to share the particular view which is being presented. What looks like an inductive survey of opinions may in fact be a selection of *ex parte* pronouncements. Still, such marshalling of authorities, often accompanied by a quotation from each to heighten the sense of reality or conviction, can easily give the impression that all authority is behind the view being advanced. Thus many textbooks on social problems bristle with the names of persons whose claims to authority may be quite unknown to the reader, but whose solemn citation may be depended on to exert a persuasive force.[5] One suspects that it is the appearance rather than the real pertinence of the authority which is desired.

Along with this there is another, and a more subtle, kind of appeal to authority which takes the form of a patter of modern shibboleths. These may be taken from everyday language, but they will be words and expressions associated with leaders of opinion, with current intellectual fashions, with big projects, and with things in general which are supposed to have a great future. Professor A. H. Hobbs, in his *Social Problems and Scientism,* lists among others: *modern, rational, liberal, professional, intergovernmental, objectivity, research, disciplines, workshop, interrelations, human resources,* and *human development.*[6] I would suggest that this language represents an appeal to the authority of the "modern mind." These are expressions carrying a certain melioristic bias, which one will have difficulty in resisting without putting oneself in the camp of reaction or obscurantism. The repeated use of them has the effect of setting up a kind of incantation, so that to sound in dissonance with them is virtually to brand oneself as antisocial. The reader is left with the alternative of accepting them and of going along on assumptions he does not approve of, or of rejecting them, which would entail continuous argument and would involve taking a position almost impossible to explain to a "modern."

6. *Sociology as Deliberative Oratory*

The use of appeals based on authority brings up again the role of the sociologist as advocate.

At the beginning of his treatise on *Rhetoric* Aristotle divides the art into three kinds: deliberative, forensic, and epideictic. Epideictic rhetoric is devoted to celebrating (as in the panegyric); forensic rhetoric is concerned with the justice or injustice of things which have already happened; and deliberative oratory is concerned with the future, since the speaker is urging his audience to do, or to refrain from doing, something or other. "The end of the deliberative speaker is the expedient or the harmful; for he who exhorts recommends a course of action as better, and he who dissuades advises against it as worse; all other considerations, such as justice and injustice, honor and disgrace, are included as accessory in relation to this." [7] By the terms of this definition a considerable part of sociological writing must be classified as deliberative oratory, and the practitioners of it as rhetoricians. When one sets up to advise concerning alternative social courses, one does exactly what the ancient orator in the Areopagus or the forum was doing, however much the abstractness of one's language may tend to conceal that fact. As Kenneth Burke has pointed out:

. . . when you begin talking about the optimum rate of speed at which cultural change should take place or the optimum proportion between tribal and individualistic motives which should prevail under a given set of economic conditions, you are talking about something very important indeed; but you will find yourself deep in matters of rhetoric, for nothing is more rhetorical in nature than a deliberation as to what is too much or too little, too early or too late. . . ." [8]

A good many current texts on sociology are replete with this kind of deliberation. Martin Neumeyer, in his *Social Problems and the Changing Society,* while discussing numerous opinions on the topics with which he deals, often steps into the role of judge and advocate. Thus we read:

Homicides, suicides, illegitimate births, deaths due to venereal disease and the like seem to be more prevalent where there is low integration in cities. The more adequately a city provides for the health and welfare of its citizens, the greater the chance of preventing or controlling deviations. Well integrated cities are likely to have a better chance of survival and growth than poorly integrated urban areas.[9]

It might be contended that this passage is merely descriptive of certain laws of social phenomena. Still, the presence of such phrases as "more adequately," "health and welfare of its citizens," and "a better chance of survival and growth" show plainly that the passage is written from a standpoint of social meliorism.

The same kind of thing is done by George Lundberg, in his *Foundations of Sociology,* when he becomes a pleader on the subject of language itself. He argues that we ought to give up those terms created by the original myth- and metaphor-making disposition of the human mind in favor of a different "symbolic equipment." That he is entirely willing to utilize traditional rhetoric in making his point may be seen from the following passage:

Untold nervous energy, time, and natural resources are wasted in warfare upon or protection against entirely imaginary monsters conjured up by words. Widespread mental disorders result from constantly finding the world different from the word-maps upon which we rely for guidance and adjustment. Social problems cannot be solved as long as they are stated in terms as primitive and unrealistic as those which attributed disease to demons and witches.[10]

A feature of another kind indicating that a good many sociologists are engaged in more or less concealed deliberative oratory is the presence in their work of a large amount of enthymematic reasoning. Reasoning in this form is a rhetorical kind of convincing, and the enthymeme is actually described by Aristotle as the "rhetorical syllogism." [11] In the textbooks of logic it is defined as a syllogism with one of the propositions withheld. In the argument

All who are patriots should be willing to sacrifice for their country. You should be willing to sacrifice for your country.

the minor premise, "You are a patriot," is missing. It has been omitted because the maker of the argument has assumed that it is granted by the hearer and will be supplied by him to complete the argument.

This type of argument is rightly described as rhetorical because the rhetorician always gets his leverage by starting with things that are accepted. By combining these with things he wants to get accepted ("identification" again) he moves on to the conclusion which is his object. In other words, because the rhetorician can assume certain things—because he does not have to demonstrate every proposition in his argument—he can work from statements which are essentially appeals. He studies beforehand the disposition of his auditors and takes note of those beliefs which will afford him firm ground—those general convictions about which one does not have to be deliberative. Hence the enthymeme is rhetorical, as distinguished from the syllogism, because it capitalizes on something already in the mind of the hearer. The speaker tacitly assumes one position, and from this he can move on to the next.

A number of contemporary sociologists, as I read them, use the enthymeme for the purpose of getting accepted a proposition which could be challenged on one ground or another. They make an assumption regarding the nature or goals of society and treat this as if it were universally granted and therefore not in need of explicit assertion. I refer again to Neumeyer's *Social Problems and the Changing Society*. This work seems to rest its case on an enthymeme which, if expanded to a complete syllogism, would go as follows:

If society is democratic and dynamic, these prescriptions are valid.
Society is democratic and dynamic.
Therefore these prescriptions are valid.

What the author does in effect is to withhold his minor premise apparently on the ground that no man of sense and information will question it. Therefore he does not take seriously those who would ask "Is society really democratic and dynamic?" or "In what ways is society democratic and dynamic?" (What is to take care of societies which are aristocratic and traditional, or do they have no social problems?) Having thus assumed the premise he needs in order to get his conclusion, he can proceed to describe the techniques which would be proper in a democratic and dynamic society, as if they were the only ones to be taken into account.

There is nothing illicit about enthymematic arguments; they are to be encountered frequently wherever argumentation occurs. My point is that something significant is implied by their presence here. Even if we are clear about why the sociologist must argue, why is he employing a form of argument recognized as "rhetorical"?

This takes us back to the original question regarding his province and specifically to the relationship of what he does to the world of value. A good many current writers in the field seem rather evasive on the subject of values: they admit that the problem of value has to be faced; but then they merely circle about it and leave specific values to shift for themselves. Occasionally one takes a more definite stand, as when Francis E. Merrill declares that the values of a social scientist are the values given him by virtue of his membership in a democratic and progressive society.[12] Even so respected a thinker as Max Weber seems less than satisfactory on the two roles of the social scientist. His position is that

the distinction between the purely logically deducible and empirical factual assertions, on the one hand, and practical, ethical, or philosophical judgments, on the other hand, is correct, but that nevertheless . . . both problems belong within the area of instruction.[13]

Obviously the problem is how to encompass both of them. What Weber does is to lay down a rule for academic objectivity. The teacher must set

as his unconditional duty, in every single case, even to the point where it involves the danger of making his lectures less lively or less attractive, to make relentlessly clear to his audience, and especially to himself, which of his statements are statements of logically deduced or empirically related facts and which are statements of practical evaluations.[14]

My question would be how the sociologist can in good conscience leave the first to embark upon the second without having something in the nature of a philosophy of society. His dilemma is that he is perforce a dialectician, but he is without a dialectical basis. He must use dialectical terms, but he has no framework which will provide a consistent extra-empirical reference for them, though we may feel sometimes that we see one trying to force itself through, as in the concept of society's essence as something "democratic and progressive." It seems to me that the dilemma could be faced with more candor and realism. No practical man will deny that the student of society can make use of many of the findings of positive science. Things must be recognized in their brute empirical existence; we are constantly running into things of which we were unaware until they proclaimed their objectivity by impinging upon our senses. And there are some things which must be counted. A pure subjective idealism is a luxury which a few thinkers can afford, but it is not a prudential system. I for one can hardly believe that science is purely ancillary in the sense of finding evidence for what we already believe or wish to believe. The world is too independent a datum for that.

On the other hand, a large part of the subject matter of the student of society does consist of the subjective element in human beings. This has to be recognized as a causative agent. History shows many opinions, highly erroneous or fantastic, which have been active influences on human behavior. This factor has to be studied, but it cannot be simplistically quantified. Here at least there must be room for speculative inquiry.

Finally, the student of society should realize that he is a man writing as a man. He cannot free himself entirely from perspective. His view of things can have a definite bearing on what is regarded as a fact or on how factual units can be employed. To argue that the social scientist should adopt no perspective on matters is perhaps in itself to adopt a perspective, but a far less fruitful one than those in which, with proper regard for objective facts, a viewpoint is frankly espoused.

In view of these considerations, why does not social science call itself "social philosophy"? This would widen its universe of discourse, freeing it from the positivistic limitations of science and associating its followers with the love of wisdom. At the same time it would enable them to practice the art of noble rhetoric where it is called for, without unconscious deception and without a feeling that they are compromising their profession.

NOTES

1. F. A. Hayek, *The Counter-Revolution of Science* (Glencoe: The Free Press, 1952), pp. 13-14.
2. Clarence M. Case, *Outlines of Introductory Sociology* (New York, 1924), p. 627.

3. Merton K. Cameron, "Some Neglected Aspects of the Problem of Poverty," *Social Forces,* VII (September, 1928), 73.

4. T. H. Huxley has such admirable words of advice on this subject that I cannot refrain from including them here: "Be clear though you may be convicted of error. If you are clearly wrong, you may run up against a fact some time and get set right. If you shuffle with your subject and study to use language which will give you a loophole of escape either way, there is no hope for you." Quoted in Aldous Huxley, *The Olive Tree* (New York, 1937), p. 63.

5. For examples see F. Stuart Chapin, *Cultural Change* (New York, 1928), p. 203; and Martin H. Neumeyer, *Social Problems and the Changing Society* (New York, 1953), p. 48.

6. A. H. Hobbs, *Social Problems and Scientism* (Harrisburg: The Stackpole Company, 1953), pp. 51-52.

7. *Rhetoric,* 1358b.

8. Kenneth Burke, *A Rhetoric of Motives* (New York, 1950), p. 45.

9. Neumeyer, *op. cit.,* p. 107.

10. George A. Lundberg, *Foundations of Sociology* (New York, 1939), p. 47.

11. *Rhetoric,* 1356b. Strictly speaking, in the Aristotelian enthymeme all the propositions are present, but one of them, instead of resting on proof, rests upon "signs" or "probabilities." See George Hayward Joyce, S. J., *Principles of Logic* (London, 1916), pp. 253-255.

12. Francis E. Merrill, H. Warren Dunham, Arnold M. Rose, and Paul W. Tappan, *Social Problems* (New York, 1950), pp. 83-84.

13. Max Weber, *The Methodology of the Social Sciences,* tr. Edward A. Shils and Henry A. Finch (Glencoe: The Free Press, 1949), p. 1.

14. *Ibid.,* p. 2.

5

Fiduciary Responsibility and the Improbability Principle

JAMES W. WIGGINS

The behavioral sciences, in so far as they attempt to be sciences, share with other sciences several articles of faith. Among these are the use of relevant concepts, prediction based on probabilities, a commitment to objectivity, avoidance of value positions, a search for all the evidence, and a public methodology which allows fellow scientists to test conclusions through replication. The scientist, *qua* scientist, is committed to the presentation of the results of his studies regardless of his personal approval or disapproval of his findings. "He is neutral in the sense that he will accept without personal reservation what his evidence has revealed." [1] He is, by definition, opposed to personal or other censorship which seeks to control or direct his search for such aspects of truth as his methods allow him to apprehend.

The social scientist, then, like other scientists, has a kind of fiduciary responsibility [2] both to his fellows and to the larger society which supports him and his search. There can be little doubt that, in the long run, his fiduciary responsibility must be accepted and expressed with all care, if that society is to continue to give him its confidence and support.

The purpose of this paper is to call attention to the apparent reversal of a number of the canons of social science in consequence of the value commitments of the scientist, which threatens potential or actual loss of confidence by social scientists in their own work. But more importantly, this reversal threatens loss of public confidence that fiduciary responsibility is being honored.

1. *The Value Commitments*

The discovery of value commitments which interfere with expressions of science requires neither unusual insight nor extensive examination of the literature. Particularistic espousals are stated directly and clearly in the public pronouncements of some officers of national professional organizations and in some committees authorized to represent officially the organized membership of the behavioral science fields involved. Basic agreement on value positions and on programs of related actions are stated directly or are clearly implied in papers presented to professional meetings, sometimes published later, and in journals as reviewers address a congenial audience. These values and goals of action seem to be assumed to be so pervasive, so standardized, so monolithic, that reviewers approach the point of saying, "Of course, we all oppose (or support) this sort of thing." [3]

But nowhere are the commitments of supposed "value-free" behavioral scientists better expressed than in the platforms of some of the affiliates of national professional societies. The affiliates typically form an independent organization, dedicated to one or several programs of action, and establish a journal. The next step is for the group to petition for legitimacy, that is, for affiliation with the general—and relatively respected—national organization of their profession. This affiliation, if established, both legitimizes the "action" or value-oriented group and adds to its actions the apparent backing of the larger organization.

An analogous procedure would involve the organization of Catholic sociologists who are members of the American Sociological Association into a Society for the Propagation of the Faith. The members of the new society would then petition for affiliation with the American Sociological Association—and, as members of the latter body, vote for affiliation. Thus would the Jewish, Unitarian, and Baptist (as well as atheist) sociologists come apparently to support the propagation of the Catholic faith. It is not suggested that this effort will ever be made, and certainly not that this particular effort would ever be successful if made.

But similar efforts have been made and have been successful. The Society for the Study of Social Problems is an affiliate of the American Sociological Association. Its recurrent value statements may be derived from analysis of the various issues of *Social Problems,* the publication of this special-interest group. In the words of the respected Ernest W. Burgess:

It is fitting at this time to restate the objectives of our Society and to define the role that is envisioned for this new Journal.

First, the organization of the Society is a recognition of the growing importance of research on social problems. There is the continuing challenge presented by the crucial situations confronting American society to *the development of policies and programs of action.* Certainly the knowledge gained from social science research is basic to *wise formulation of policy and to the choice of effective programs of dealing with these situations.*[4] (Italics added.)

Professor Otto Klineberg, in the lead article of the first issue of *Social Problems,* and on pages immediately following Burgess' statement (above) expressed himself as follows:

. . . Those of us who concern ourselves with social issues or social problems, in the hope that we can contribute something to the improvement of human relations, are not infrequently looked upon with suspicion, as if we were somehow proving unfaithful to our scientific Hippocratic Oath.

The fact remains that such a concern is growing rapidly. . . .[5]

Later in the same issue, Donald V. McGranahan writes:

I think we can all agree that not much is really known about the human implications of technological change in countries that are called economically "underdeveloped." We cannot readily generalize from studies in Western culture, because the conditions are so different in the economically underdeveloped areas.[6]

But on the preceding page, Byron L. Fox had pointed out that "Accordingly, it *is* logical to apply well-established sociological principles, concepts and schemes of analysis at the world level." [7] (Italics added.)

McGranahan, however, continues:

At times social scientists who are liberal and forward-looking citizens of their own countries give an impression of conservatism[!] when they look at underdeveloped areas and stress only the dangers and evils of development. . . .[8]

One point that has impressed me recently while reading E. H. Carr's *The New Society* is the possibility that certain conditions which have been considered socially undesirable consequences of development in the West may, in fact, have played a functional role in the process of development. . . . the situation in which unemployed men in England were allowed to go hungry in the early part of the 19th century was the result of the demand created by the industrial revolution "to drive a hitherto predominantly rural working class into urban workshops and factories." . . . Two possible methods of getting labor into the new industries were considered during the period—starvation and forced labor . . . and the policy of starving labor into factories was followed.[9]

Although it must be admitted that McGranahan does not advocate either starvation or slavery, he does conclude by saying, ". . . let me repeat my plea that in viewing the human implications of technological change we do not become so fascinated by the bad as to forget the good, and so protective of the present cultures of underdeveloped areas as to wish to preserve these cultures against the very idea of progress which we embrace for ourselves." [10]

Such missionary zeal for remaking underdeveloped countries,

whatever the cost, is comparable to the remarks of Nels Anderson about the development of the underdeveloped U.S.S.R.

> . . . in most Communist countries systematic efforts have been made to change the ways of life and work of rural people. The farmer must be separated from his traditions. Thus efforts have been made, apparently with much resistance, but still with a measure of success, to force farmers into various types of modernized collective groups. Whatever the merit of these urban-conceived schemes, their objective is to hasten a process which might in the long run take place anyway . . ." [11]

This is an interestingly euphemistic way of describing the liquidation of peasants and suggests that something like genocide might well be supported if development, as conceived by some social scientists, is thus facilitated.

For some years the Society for the Study of Social Problems was closely associated with the Society for the Psychological Study of Social Issues and in fact held joint meetings with the sister group. On the instance of the latter group, this association has been ended, although it is not clear to the writer whether one or the other of these groups became too scientific or whether there was a difference about platform planks.[12] In any case, the Society for the Psychological Study of Social Issues continues its affiliation with the American Psychological Association, while it (the former) continues publication of its *Journal of Social Issues.* The imprint of the American Psychological Association on the frontispiece is a kind of *imprimatur* which has apparent value for the espousals of the Journal.

A third case in point is the Society for Applied Anthropology, with its house organ, *Human Organization.* It should be noted that this action group has *not* become an affiliate of the American Anthropological Association. Its goals are relevant, however, to the present interest. "Its primary object is 'the promotion of scientific investigation of the principles controlling the relations of human beings to one another and the encouragement of the wide application of these principles to practical problems.' " [13] And in another connection, clarifying the Code of Ethics of the Society for Applied Anthropology, the reader is informed:

It has been emphasized in discussions that the applied anthropologist may properly work for a partisan group within a society (e.g., the National Association of Manufacturers, the Congress of Industrial Organizations, the Anti-Saloon League, the Planned Parenthood League, the National Catholic Rural Life Conference, the National Conference of Christians and Jews, etc.) recognizing that such groups are a significant and important part of our social life and that improvements in the functioning and understanding of any one such group can be valuable to the whole society . . .[14]

It appears, therefore, that—discounting minor differences and interdisciplinary rivalry—one might accept the inaugural statement of Burgess on *Social Problems,* that ". . . It will join with such kindred publications as the *Journal of Social Issues* and *Human Organization* in promoting interdisciplinary exchange of ideas and cooperation in interdisciplinary research. In short, it will enable the Society for the Study of Social Problems to share its interests with a broader public and to accomplish its several missions more effectively." [15]

In summary, it is rather obvious that substantial value positions are explicitly stated as basic to the efforts of at least the identified groups of professional behavioral scientists. The determination to remake people, societies, and, in fact, the whole world shows clearly in the foregoing, regardless of costs, in some cases at least, and regardless of the resistance of part or the whole of the populations whose ways of life are displeasing to the scientists. This aim can be understood perhaps in connection with another value, held equally dear—the equalitarian orientation.[15a] The effort to show that everybody is, or is about to be, completely equal must hold an element of uncertainty. If this is the fact, or is about to be the fact, of human existence, it becomes clearly illogical and unnecessary to make it the goal of a social movement. (The social scientists are, of course, exempt from equality, since they are in charge.)

In the pursuit of the goal of new creation, the capitalist economic system must be inevitably suspect, since it distributes rewards *as if* some people were unequal. It has also become increasingly clear that the system of Communism also cannot be trusted, since it also rewards (not to say punishes) people *as if* they were unequal.[16] Almost inevitably, but certainly factually, the usurpation of the function of creator produces a consistenly negative attitude toward organized religion, which has for millennia offered its own conception of a Creator.[17]

2. *The Rejection of Concepts*

Concepts in social science gain and retain their place primarily through their varied functions in distinguishing, invoking, and predicting properties extracted from reality which are relevant to the particular science concerned.[18] Discarding concepts which have significant predictive and discriminating value because of emotional pain is hardly congruent with the public avowals of science. The following discussion will present the possibility that the equalitarian position is so strong that important concepts have withered if they stood in the way.

The chief identified inequality under active consideration by social scientists at present in the United States is the inequality of so-called minority groups. The term itself suggests persecution and is primarily open to argument, since the people so identified include such majorities as Catholics in Boston, Jews in parts of New York City, and Negroes in southern Mississippi. And technically, they are not groups, but categories.

However that may be, within the minority category, the inequalities between the Caucasian and Negroid races attract most attention and continuing efforts to reduce inequality. As a social movement, this has much to commend it. As science, it is scientism. This effort has led its exponents to seek the abolition of a significant concept from the language of social and physical science.

The concept of race is significant for psychology if it is useful, ultimately, in predicting the emergence of properties (behavior) in which the psychologist is interested. It is a valid concept for sociology if through its use significant social or sociological phenomena may be clarified, identified, or predicted. The same can be said for other sciences, such as biology, anatomy, or physical anthropology.[18]

This is not to say that the specific *word* is crucial. The concept may be identified as "tepic," or NMC^2, or by any others of an almost limitless range of symbols. The point under consideration is the nature of the concept, not the symbol.

A. L. Kroeber, perhaps the "dean" of living anthropologists, has written, "A race is a valid biological concept. It is a group united by heredity: a breed or genetic strain or subspecies . . . Physical anthropology, being concerned with man's organic features, is properly and necessarily concerned with the human races." [19] This statement is supported by anatomists, who can cite hundreds of structural differences between physical types classified by the concept of race, by physicians who accept patients from more than one race, and by a variety of researchers in other fields.

A fairly early effort to discredit the concept was that of anthropologist Ashley Montagu, in the publication of *Man's Most Dangerous Myth: The Fallacy of Race.*[19a] A more recent example is the somewhat testy correction by biologist Bentley Glass of a quotation in *Saturday Review* ascribed to Glass, and stating that differences in intelligence between races of men do exist. Glass had said *"may* exist, but we have no way of knowing." Professor Glass does not even believe in intelligence tests, apparently, but he certainly does not believe in race.[20]

One of the most direct admissions of the impact of values on concepts, and even on the concealment of findings causing emotional anguish, came out of extended discussions of the "Statement of Human Rights," [21] published by the American Anthropological Association during the immediate post-World War II period. For present purposes it is well to begin with a communication from anthropologist John W. Bennett, in reply to previous comments by Julian Steward and H. G. Barnett. Barnett and Steward, said Bennett, were incomplete and unrealistic.

The arguments of Julian Steward and H. G. Barnett in their interesting critiques of the Statement on Human Rights, published under the sponsorship of the Executive Board of this Association, may be summarized as follows: (1) Science cannot, through the medium of scientific method, demonstrate the validity or "rightness" of any particular point of view toward what is "good" for society and personality. (2) An attempt to do so perforce involves the scientist in contradictions and pushes him into the peculiar position of elevating his empirical knowledge to the level of values. (3) Therefore, science, on the one hand, and value-making, policy-making, and moral-making, on the other, are incompatible, and the individual must choose which of these he intends to pursue. (4) They conclude that (a) professionals as a group had best avoid the field of social pronouncement and value-supporting and adhere to science (Steward) ; and (b) the support of social movements and causes is all right and even advisable, but let us do so honestly with a frank declaration of our position, abandoning the attempt to justify our stand scientifically (Barnett) .[22]

Having thus discarded a reasoned statement of the method, function, and goals of science, Bennett stated what he considered the anthropologist's position and warned that science must stand aside while the position is defended.

. . . In the quarter-century of our discussion of racism a similar contradictory argument has been used: on the one hand, we have said that there are no differences between human groups; on the other, we have specified the scientific possibilities of difference and *have discovered some*. Scientifically we know that differences between human varieties can and do exist; ideologically it serves our purpose to deny them. We have had our cake and eaten it too, but few anthropologists would deplore our participation in the racist issue. We apparently took the course in that particular issue of not daring to admit the existence of differences, since we felt that a categorical denial had more social value than a half-admission of difference.[23] (Italics added.)

But it is in his footnote that he drops the seventh veil:

Some of us say that the differences, while present, are unimportant. We say this, however, with a sinking feeling, since it always throws us open to the sneer: "See, first you said all races were equal, and now you say they aren't. Make up your mind." In the whole racist struggle we have done much more than merely say, "Your facts are wrong," but have always insisted that the use of the myths for purposes of repression and discrimination were also wrong. *Barnett's position would really tend to imply that we must withdraw from antiracist propagandizing.*[24] (Italics added.)

These quotations were originally published more than a decade ago and may consequently be considered out of date. The recent presidential address of E. Adamson Hoebel, of the American Anthropological Association, in December, 1957, promised a continuing dedication to science and antagonism to propagandizing:

. . . Professional anthropology achieves its basic strength through its freedom from major concern with immediately practical problems. Freedom from dominance by public policy and social reform interests lends to anthropology, as Riesman has observed, a greater degree of objectivity and scientific imaginativeness than obtains in political science and sociology. . . .[25]

The day after the delivery of his address, however, Dr. Hoebel was quoted in *The New York Times* as having said, "The question of where they [children] should go to school is a burning issue, but the anthropologists are joined together on the side of integration."[26]

It is not difficult at this point to understand why the anthropologist who wishes to study race and to publish his findings feels oppressed. Dr. Carleton S. Coon, University of Pennsylvania, outstanding physical anthropologist, said in 1951: "This tendency has been carried so far that it is difficult to have a truly scientific, objective book on race published or reviewed"; and in 1954, "Basing their ideas on the concept of the brotherhood of man, certain writers, who are mostly social anthropologists, consider it immoral to study race, and produce book after book exposing it as a 'myth.' Their argument is that because the study of race once gave ammunition to racial fascists who misused it, we should pretend that races do not exist." [27]

But let us look in on the deliberations of the American Association of Physical Anthropologists. These are the men who are dedicated to the study of the structure of man as an index to human behavior. Anthropologist John Gillin, having publicly challenged statements by Dr. W. Critz George, of the University of North Carolina's Medical School faculty, to the effect that there are significant differences between the races, appealed to the physical anthropologists to support his position. What was the action of the physical anthropologists?

Amidst qualifications that this scientific *(sic)* society could not pass on any political matter (Coon and Thieme), that Gillin's quoted newspaper statement was not quite accurate since there have not been "hundreds of investigations" bearing on racial superiority (Spuhler), that it (the report) could be adopted unchanged (Tappen), that the statement was unclear as it stood (Howell) and ineffective (Gavan), two general feelings emerged: *that the society should back a man in a difficult position asking for the society's support* (Cobb, Coon, Howells, Howell, Gruber, Thieme, Aginsky, etc.) and that we might stress the lack of anthropological data which might justify racial discrimination (Washburn, Greulich, Spuhler, Kraus, etc.). Brozek pointed out that this hydra-headed subject of discussion raised (1) the question of what we can do to help John Gillin [Note: This is a *scientific* question?], (2) racial and ethnic discrimination as a social phenomenon, and (3) the need for a scientific statement with proper definitions on the subject of biological superiority versus inferiority.[28] (Italics added.)

After further consideration of what could be done to help John Gillin in his argument with Dr. George, the society voted "overwhelmingly" that "They support Dr. John Gillin in his recent position in this respect." [29]

3. *The Improbability Principle*

Physical anthropologists do not concentrate on the study of behavior, but rather attend to structure. Sociologists and psychologists study behavior and have a number of interests in common. Both fields of study, when they are most scientific, depend on statistical methods expressing probabilities. The concept of statistical significance describes a degree of association between an independent variable (cause) and a dependent variable (effect) greater than can be explained by chance. Such a statement oversimplifies and is especially unsatisfactory in the inferential use of cause and effect.

Nevertheless, it seems reasonable to expect that, if specified classes of phenomena are associated with other specified phenomena more frequently than would be explained by chance, this finding would be useful in prediction. Thus, the concept of race and certain other phenomena are more frequently associated than chance would allow.

In this area the sociologist and the psychologist are not without data. Otto Klineberg's often cited *Race Differences* is used as a basic source. An exhaustive study for the period, and a careful one, it is ordinarily mentioned in support of the statement that Northern Negroes made higher scores on World War I Army Alpha tests than did Southern Whites. Seldom is the fact mentioned that Northern Whites consistently surpassed Northern Negroes.[30]

A more recent study of the many published comparisons of intelligence by racial categories, *The Testing of Negro Intelligence*, by psychologist Audrey M. Shuey, has been met so far by silence from the reviewers in professional journals. One reviewer did give it attention, under the title, "Cat on the Hot Tin Roof," which suggests the unfavorable verdict. (An almost automatic party line of silence or sneer comparable to the one in this country does not yet seem to exist in Great Britain. Thus, Professor Shuey's book is praised as a "painstaking and valuable contribution to the literature of social and racial differences" by W. D. Wall of the National Foundation for Educational Research in England and Wales in his review of the book in the *Sociological Review* [December, 1959], published by the University College of North Staffordshire.)

It is possible to follow the propagandizing scientist one step further. It is not only difficult for him to examine and report findings suggesting significant correlations between race and other variables, but he may also completely reverse his methodology and embrace the principle of improbability. The logic of improbability is illustrated by this reasoning. Far from accepting the statement of the anthropologists that race is not a significant discriminating concept, the improbability scientist calls attention to his occasional finding that an exceptional member of the "minority" race performs better than the average of the "privileged" race. He then seeks to convince us that the "minority" is superior by citing the improbable finding of a negligible number of cases. When the data all point overwhelmingly in an undesired direction, they may be explained away through the application of special criteria ordinarily ignored in the evaluation of scientific research.

Sociologist George Lundberg recently commented insightfully on this "state of affairs."

There are doubtless many reasons for this state of affairs. I should like to call special attention to only one of them because, although it reveals a laudable human quality, it is inimical to objective analysis. I refer to the sympathy of social scientists, as well as most other people, for certain currently disadvantaged minorities. One shrinks from too rigorous or objective examination of people whose misfortunes one recognizes and deplores. As one of my friends (the editor of a leading journal of opinion) put it on reading the analysis which follows below: *"Regardless of the logic and the facts, we must lean over backwards* in the special cases before us because a more realistic view would merely be seized upon by the prejudiced as vindication of their hostility. Any aid or comfort to this group is in the direction of Hitlerism, convent-burning, etc. That danger transcends all other considerations." This attitude is certainly understandable, and one cannot help but admire it as a finely motivated position. Yet I believe that in the long run it only injures the cause it seeks to advance. In objective *scientific analysis* there can be *no* "leaning over" *backwards or forwards,* of the type contemplated. Any leaning toward or away from conclusions *scientifically warranted* in order to conform to desired ulterior ends, however laudable under existing mores, is recognized by all scientists as a negation of science.[31]

That there are some publicly identified social scientists who do not let the problem interfere with their espousals is shown in the exchange some years ago between Gustav Ichheiser and the late Louis Wirth. Ichheiser rather innocently pointed out that "It is a universal human fact that people tend to consider different those who look different. . . . minorities are likely to interpret as a plot what is only a natural majority reaction to personal differences." [32]

Wirth wrote that these statements could not possibly be correct because there were people who had been socialized to ignore differences in skin color and hair form. Furthermore, he added that "White people who even share more intimate experiences with Negroes [than dancing] are not necessarily deceiving themselves in thinking there is no significant difference between them." [33]

Wirth said that the ability to discern differences and to relate oneself to people in terms of these recognized differences was prejudice. "I . . . consider anyone prejudiced who . . . approaches a new experience with a preconceived judgment and assigns that experience to a preformed category." [34] Prejudice clearly is not, by this definition, a valid concept, since the typical relationship of man to man is based on such classification, not to mention the relationship of man to maid.

Wirth's scientific language was gracefully expressed when he vented his spleen (*scientifically?*) on Ichheiser, thus:

As far as I know, no one with any sense in the field of race relations [i.e., no scientist] seeks to deny differences in physical characteristics [This excludes the physical anthropologists cited above, because they have no sense] or even in cultural characteristics. They do, however, object to the chauvinistic [scientific epithet?] racialist suggestion that the two *invariably* [Italics added. Very high positive correlation which absolutely nobody suggests] go together.

Ichheiser concluded by a resort to analogy:

We treat dogs and cats as two different animals, not because of a cultural definition, but because cats and dogs look different, and if social scientists (as presidents of a council on dog-cat relations) would start to convince the common man that dogs and cats are alike, and "only" look different, the sole result of such an action would be that the common man would start to laugh about social scientists. Even dogs and cats themselves would not accept this redefinition.[35]

The present writer has no interest, for the purposes of this presentation, in the question of racial differences. Certainly he has no interest in restricting opportunity arbitrarily beyond the absolute minimum required for social order in any society. But he is publicly identified as a sociologist, and, being so identified, he is alarmed at the cited tendencies to ignore the rigorous requirements of the scientific quest for knowledge because of value commitments. It is amazing that the threat to the profession is not more widely recognized and that there is so little effort to allay the "sinking feeling" to which Bennett referred above.

It would be unfair to conclude the paper on a note of complete pessimism about the behavioral scientists, in spite of the value positions, the rejection of concepts, and the acceptance of the improbability principle. The "minorities" which attract most attention are the loudest, and it is hoped that the "scientists" who have been considered here are themselves a minority.

Fortunately there is a model available. Dr. C. P. Oberndorf, in his presidential address to the American Psychopathological Association in 1954, described the necessity of overcoming personal preferences in the light of scientific "truth."

Terms such as option, discrimination, preference, selectivity, and segregation are generally in disfavor in the social scheme and philosophy of a democracy such as we live in. So, at the outset, I wish to make unequivocally clear my agreement with this philosophy and opposition to legalized segregation in the social scheme. . . .

The need for a second hospital for the insane in New Mexico is great. . . . However it is likely that should a new hospital be designated exclusively for Spanish and Indians, or Anglos and Indians, staffed correspondingly, incensed protestations against such segregation might arise from each of the three groups concerned—and this in the face of the obvious benefits, from the psychiatric angle, which such separations might yield. . . .

Certain groups to which we belong, being biologically determined, never change. They are: sex, (2) age, and (3) color groupings. The question of separating the first group (sex) in hospitalization is never questioned and rarely is the second, namely, the undesirability of mixing children with adults, and more recently, of ever growing numbers of old-age psychotics with the average adult age group.

. . . Some years ago the question came up in the Committee for Mental Hygiene Among Negroes of the impossibility for Negroes to avail themselves of treatment in the best private mental hospitals in the New York area. An ever-increasing number of Negroes, mostly from the fields of amusement, literature, and sports, can afford such accommodation. Therefore, in line with the contention of this presentation, I suggested the establishment of an endowed mental hospital for Negroes with private quarters, similar to the one (Hillside Hospital) I had proposed in 1922 for Jews, which would cater to the latter's linguistic and ritual needs. It was based solely upon the opinion that it is simpler to achieve a restitution to health when the patient's confidence is gained and this is more readily attainable in a setting in general sympathy and empathy with his previous experience. However, a Negro member of this committee, a journalist, quietly replied, "Doctor, others see a different solution of the problem"— distinctly indicating the exertion of pressure to force a change in the position of established white institutions, completely misunderstanding the psychiatric basis of my proposal.

It would seem, then, that an institution such as the Veterans Hospital at Tuskegee, where an all-Negro staff of psychiatrists and nurses administers treatment to an all-Negro patient population, serves this particular group more efficiently than would be possible with a white staff.[36]

Dr. Oberndorf thus states his value position, but clearly and logically moves it aside when his professional and scientific decisions must be made. He, it appears, is willing to "accept the consequences of scientific discovery, even when it makes him emotionally uncomfortable."

I can find no conclusion for this paper that compares with an excerpt from an article by Morton Cronin, who, strangely for present purposes, is a professor of English. After pointing out that the intellectual (under which concept we may subsume the social scientist) always enjoys a larger measure of freedom than the average citizen, he continues:

Now it may be that a given population as a whole should be freer than it is to express opinions. But no matter how free it becomes in this respect, its intellectuals—if it has any—must be freer. This may be undemocratic, as the scientist's *(sic)* special right or the judge's may be, but without these special rights we can have no scientists, judges, or intellectuals.

I must now recite the killjoy lesson that exceptional privileges usually entail exceptional obligations. The intellectual's most important obligation consists in maintaining a greater degree of independence, integrity, and candor in his relations with the world than can be reasonably expected of most men. His primary duty is to tell the whole truth as he sees it, in detail as well as in general. *His primary duty is not to make that truth prevail.* In fact, if he slips too deeply into the tactical maneuvers of social action, especially those which require close organizational ties, he will, like a judge who wades in politics, evoke the suspicion that he can no longer be trusted with his special prerogative. And this suspicion will be justified by the common experience of mankind. For when an individual becomes profoundly involved in a program of political action, he usually cannot be counted on to make a fair assessment of opposing programs. Such involvement on the part of an intellectual will be enough to establish the presumption that he has stopped being an intellectual and can now with propriety be treated as factionalists treat one another.[37]

NOTES

1. Arnold W. Green, *Sociology* (New York: McGraw-Hill Book Company, 1960), 3rd ed., p. 7.
2. Talcott Parsons, "Some Problems Confronting Sociology as a Profession," *American Sociological Review,* Vol. XXIV, No. 4 (August, 1959), pp. 547-559.
3. Curiously, and perhaps unfortunately, most of these values and goals of action seem to have one basic source: resentment. Professor George Simpson of Brooklyn College in his book *Sociologist Abroad* (The Hague: Martinus Nijhoff, 1959) writes with charming candor: "Anyone who hopes to wind up as a good sociologist must, I think, start originally with some hurt, some feeling of resentment against the society existent, which leads him to find out what is wrong with that society. Wishing to relieve his own dissatisfaction, he seeks to universalize his hurt and is thus led on to discover why human beings have to suffer. And he will remain a good sociologist only so long as the hurt or resentment continues to exercise some influence on his professional behavior." (p. 168.)
4. "The Aims of the Society for the Study of Social Problems, "*Social Problems,* Vol. I (1953), pp. 2-3.
5. "Prospects and Problems in Ethnic Relations," *Social Problems,* Vol. I (1953), p. 4.

6. "Some Remarks on the Human Implications of Technological Change in Underdeveloped Areas," *Social Problems*, Vol. I (1953), p. 13.
7. "The Cold War and American Domestic Problems," *Social Problems*, Vol. I (1953), p. 12.
8. *Op. cit.*, p. 14.
9. *Op. cit.*, pp. 13, 14.
10. *Op. cit.*, p. 14.
11. Nels Anderson, *The Urban Community: A World Perspective* (New York, 1959), pp. 101, 475.
12. It is not impossible that this development is related to the extension of state laws for licensing professional psychologists in recent years. There is some inference here that sociologists and anthropologists are no longer legitimately concerned with the social issues staked out by psychologists. See discussions in *American Sociological Review*, Vol. XXIV, Nos. 3, 4 (1959).
13. *Human Organization*, Vol. IX, No. 1 (Spring, 1950), p. 1.
14. *Ibid.*, Vol. X, No. 2 (Summer, 1951), p. 32.
15. Burgess, *op. cit.*, p. 3.
15a. For those who reject this value, the label "authoritarian personality" has been developed and documented at length, and with multiple tabulations.
16. See Milovan Djilas, *The New Class* (New York, 1957).
17. Auguste Comte, it will be remembered, established a new "organized" religion. But a cursory glance into introductory textbooks in sociology will confirm this point. While there are a few exceptions, the very popular *Sociology*, by Wm. F. Ogburn and Meyer Nimkoff, in its various editions has divided events into two categories: fact (i.e., science) and fantasy (religion). It is not suggested that science should espouse organized religion, but neither should science attack it—as science. See also, in this connection, C. P. Oberndorf, "Selectivity and Option for Psychiatry," *American Journal of Psychiatry*, April 1954, p. 754.
18. Professor Wolfram Eberhard, sociologist and anthropologist at the University of California in Berkeley, pointed to the mental block produced by egalitarian commitments in much of American social science, when he examined why the ethnologist Richard Thurnwald has had so little impact in the United States: "Thurnwald started out from the point from which many theories started, the obvious connections between the economic system of a society and its societal structure. But keeping away from the one-sidedness of economic determinism, he tried by careful field-work or by painstaking study of the reported data to uncover the exact type of economic-social interrelations. . . . This led him to his theory of 'superstratification' as a factor of decisive importance. . . . Resistance against this theory in the United States seems to stem basically from a feeling that to accept as 'normal' a hierarchical order of people in all higher organized societies would go against a belief in democracy." ("In Memoriam Richard Thurnwald," *Revista do museu Paulista*, Sao Paulo, Vol. IX, 1955, pp. 297 f.)
19. A. L. Kroeber, *Anthropology* (New York: Harcourt, Brace and Company, 1948), p. 124.

19a. New York, 1943.
20. *Saturday Review,* Nov. 16, p. 58.
21. *American Anthropologist,* N. S., Vol. **XLIX** (1947), pp. 539-543.
22. *Ibid.,* Vol. LI (1949), p. 329.
23. *Ibid.,* p. 331.
24. *Ibid.,* pp. 334, 335.
25. *American Anthropologist,* N. S., Vol. LX (1958), p. 635.
26. December 30, 1957.
27. *Atlantic Monthly,* Vol. CXCVIII (Nov., 1956), p. 31.
28. *American Journal of Physical Anthropology,* N. S., Vol. XIV (1956), pp. 366-7.
29. *Loc. cit.* Gillin's statement included the remark that "Science has shown that all living human beings are members of a single zoological species, Homo sapiens." The concept of species is a useful, although arbitrary, taxonomic device. But scientism consists in part of dramatically invoking scientific jargon to overawe the layman. It is probable that both Professor Gillin and laymen recognize differences among members of single species and really consider some of them important.
30. New York, 1935.
31. "Some Neglected Aspects of the Minorities Problem," *Modern Age,* Vol. II (Summer, 1958), pp. 287-288. It would be interesting to know the reaction of an editor of a professional journal if offered the manuscript of this balanced and realistic treatment.
32. "Factors in Race Relations," *American Journal of Sociology,* Vol. LIV, No. 4 (January, 1949), p. 395.
33. *Op. cit.,* p. 400.
34. *Loc. cit.*
35. *Op. cit.,* p. 401.
36. "Selectivity and Option for Psychiatry," *American Journal of Psychiatry,* April, 1954, pp. 754-758.
37. "The American Intellectual," AAUP *Bulletin,* Vol. XLIV, No. 2 (June, 1958), pp. 409-410.

6

Knowledge: Unused and Misused

HELMUT SCHOECK

I

Probably there is no way of knowing what it pays most to know first. Laymen and many of our students, even after they have gained some familiarity with a chosen discipline, rarely realize the elements of chance and willful or unconscious bias in every field of science and scholarship which are inescapably linked to the fact that we have to conduct our work in a time series of now and later.

There is not only the possibility that a wrong choice of priority will exhaust time, funds, scarce experimental materials (for instance, the minute quantity of a new element or compound isolated for the first time) or the scholar's creative haul. A wrong choice of priority in research can also lead to effective blocking, for an indefinite time, of those research paths which would have yielded the desired or the most important result. This problem is essentially the same for all human efforts to widen knowledge. When "science," i.e., an individual scholar or team of scholars, selects the less productive avenue of investigation, the results can be disastrous. The phenomenon of fatigue in metals can remain a marginal research problem until one day airplanes of a new type start plunging to earth mysteriously.[1]

Evidently man can do little to avert such calamities. If he knew always in advance which approach would yield most, he would

119

have to possess, in many cases, so much knowledge already that the particular research problem might not be a problem at all.

Not long ago a physicist, comparing natural and historical studies, emphasized the importance of seeing, or seeking, relevant lacunae in the realm of specific experience chosen by a given scholarly discipline.[2] The social sciences, i.e., the systematic efforts to study man in social action, might well profit from a similar emphasis.

Sometimes a proved lacuna—the nearly total absence of a trait, value complex, or expectation—in a society or culture will be more indicative of its potentialities than a dozen surveys proving the presence of certain values, attitudes, or habits. Of course, as teachers of all disciplines well know, few tasks are as hard as teaching the students how to watch out for significant lacunae, for meaningfully empty slots in a multidimensional realm of hypothetically possible referents.

Obviously, like every other researcher and scholar, the person who "derives satisfaction" from studying man as a social being makes subjective decisions when he chooses hypotheses, approaches, units, classes, places, and many other possible or necessary limitations on what he actually will and can examine. We can survey the failures in a given society, and, curiously, social scientists show a preference for them; or we can, as Carle C. Zimmerman of Harvard has done, focus on a unit such as the "successful American high school family." [2a]

More important, however, than a mere shift of attention might be a systematic search for indicative lacunae in social reality. Of course, here the research situation is not comparable to the work of the natural scientist. In society we miss such seemingly simple situations as a substance turning out to be sterile when it should show growth of germs. There are very few, if any, "either-or," "all-or-nothing" propositions. Even a proof of what we take to be, say, genuine altruism will not rule out the presence of intense potential hatred and egotism, though some social scientists seem to proceed on that assumption. Nor can we count on exact complementariness or correspondence between polar entities or referents which we use in the social sciences. (For that reason, I am suspicious of polar typologies, e.g., *Gemeinschaft-Gesellschaft* dichotomies. They lure us into fallacious, and yet perhaps sometimes self-fulfilling, prophecies of decline and decay.) [3]

For instance, is it not a testimony to the blindness of social scientists and critics that they ignore such a significant social lacuna in America as the paid blood donor? In 1956, of all blood donated in the United States, only two percent came from people who received payment for it. Even in Germany, during the height of "social solidarity" under Hitler's war propaganda, the paid donor was the rule. In 1959 in West Germany one of the smaller political parties could urge its members to donate blood for pay to earn money for the party treasury. The bloodmobile, collecting blood on a voluntary and unpaid basis, left a group of Soviet medical officials, visiting New York in September, 1956, speechless. In the Soviet Union one would not dream of collecting blood on a noncommercial basis. Has anyone ever bothered to use this "social fact" for correcting the caricature of American society that the world has received, and still gets, from official social science? [4]

II

There are quite a number of foci of research and general scholarly concern that, in my judgment, omit crucial aspects. For instance, I am not encouraged or comforted by *all* attacks that are currently carried on in the name of a crusade against scientism.

In current trends of criticism, a number of my friends in the world of scholarship engage in a particular vein which troubles me. It is their organized hostility toward various forms of advertising.

This hostility is in reality an old prejudice among some intellectuals. They would be amazed to know how much of their criticism stems from men such as Fourier, who merely dreamed of things to come in the field of "hidden persuasion."

In America, I could name Joseph Wood Krutch and W. H. Whyte, Jr., among the more congenial authors, and John Galbraith, Vance Packard, and Leopold Kohr, among the less congenial, as critics whose worst fear of "scientism" is focused on its use in the economic market.

It is perhaps quite interesting to observe how criticisms of advertising—which have been commonplace in America and England during the past two decades—are now being reformulated in some West German philosophical quarters as ideas which no one since Fourier and Karl Marx knew how to express.

The gist of these criticisms can be given in a few words. Man—they say—is caught in a vicious circle. He is the slave of a system which must use any and all methods of hidden persuasion to sell him things under false pretenses, things which he does not need and which are often worth much less than claimed. Man loses his humanity (*"Selbstentfremdung des Menschen"* according to Marx) because of his fixation on acquiring things for consumption, a fixation imposed upon him by others.

Sometimes the critics assert that this advertising apparatus of mass persuasion is especially dangerous because it lends itself to misuse by seekers after political tyranny.

This last assertion is not intrinsically related to the other criticisms of advertising. But even this assertion does not stand up. For after all, hidden mass persuasion could also be used by persons wanting to get rid of an obnoxious government. See, for example, the subtle slights on the planned economy in Great Britain by a little Mr. Sugar whose image, I believe, appeared on all sugar products.

As long as there is some freedom of communications—of the press, of advertising, of broadcasting—the same methods can be used by all antagonists. As long as we believe that one party or group may have a better case than another, there is no reason why the case for a free society should not be advanced for some voters by methods that do not require intellectual virtuosity for comprehension.

Politics could be separated from the methods of hidden persuasion only if our modern mass democracies could bring themselves to reintroduce a highly unpopular limitation: a restricted suffrage.

So long as we adhere to the theory that all human beings ought to take part in the political process, even those who are eighteen or twenty-one years of age, and regardless of signs of sane judgment, no politician will ever be able to refrain from using methods of hidden persuasion. And so long as we believe that some politicians will protect the interests of a free society better than other politicians (even though most of these may not protect it fully to our own liking), it is hardly good judgment to argue for the abolition of such methods of persuasion. As we have come to see in our times, the political party which we think represents the lesser evil will abide by the ban on hidden persuasion, whereas the political party which we most fear will not abide by the ban.

I should like to examine the case against advertising, against "hidden persuasion," put forward on grounds of human dignity and freedom of choice.

To clear the decks, let me first dispose of the false notion that the use of hidden persuasion, of "all-out" advertising, is more or less restricted to a capitalist economy. The facts are to the contrary. If the state industries in the Soviet Union happen to misjudge consumer wants and needs, and turn out too many ill-constructed, poorly working TV sets at a time when people prefer Hi-Fi sets, we now have evidence that the Minister of Economics will use hidden persuasion to make Russians buy poor TV sets instead of good gramophones. (See *Foreign Affairs,* July, 1960, p. 629.)

As far as the question of free and wise choice is concerned, I fail to see any special problem or villainy in the consumer goods industries when they are compared with other fields of activity. So long as we want men to be free to marry the wrong girl at the wrong time, we can hardly advocate a curb on the advertising of baby carriages and washing machines. No misjudgment in the purchase of *durable* goods can be as much a threat to happiness as misjudgment in selecting a mate. Women are much more permanent than motor cars, as many alimony-payers no doubt are well aware!

The other argument against our present economic system (often made by people who wish it well in general) is this: We are deprived of some intrinsic human values when we are conditioned to take a fleeting attitude toward our material possessions. We know that we shall buy another car, household appliance, suit, etc., before long. Leopold Kohr goes so far in his book, *The Breakdown of Nations,* published in 1958, as to attribute supreme happiness to men of former centuries who could wear a cloth for life.[5]

Speculation on what makes human beings happy probably is not a proper subject for scholars. Least of all, however, do I like it from those (J. Galbraith, Leopold Kohr, and others) who once attacked our capitalistic society when it was allegedly rigged for scarcity.

I submit that interpersonal relations in a society of abundance can be much better than in a society having to make do with a few things for a lifetime. It is in precisely the latter that relations are such that human beings are slaves to things.

Some of us may remember years and decades of extreme scarcity. Replacement of lost or damaged things was virtually impossible. And most people behaved accordingly. A child who made cracks in an appliance or furniture, who broke windows, a stranger who accidentally made a cigarette-burn in another person's jacket, a maid or husband who dropped a china plate, all these became the subjects of strained and often extremely tense human relationships. We were slaves to things because we knew they had to last indefinitely.

In comparing human behavior under conditions of scarcity and abundance, it is interesting to read Hilde Thurnwald's published survey of family relations in Berlin after World War II. I recall from her observations the case of a well-bred, intelligent father who carried his CARE packages home and secretly devoured the contents in the basement. Is he a more encouraging figure of a man than the typical upper-middle-class American father of today who, with his family, indulges in a perhaps overstylized barbecue ritual in a backyard with dozens of what the antiadvertising intellectuals call "unnecessary frills and gadgets"?[6]

Relations between motorists involved in an accident, parents and children, supervisors and employees, and countless other relations of daily life become much more tolerable, much less of a strain, much less fraught with anxiety when all those who take part are aware that no thing has to last for ever.

I contend that the industry which is geared to make last year's car obsolete is far from being the materialistic threat to a good society which it is almost invariably pictured as being by the anti-advertising propagandists. If we just want it to be so, and if we refuse to let the hidden persuaders of the Galbraith variety spoil our attitude toward reality, it ought to be much easier to become less materialistic and less attached to any given thing today than it was in times when most men were "stuck" for life with all the things they had to use.

I believe it would not take unusual labor to find in psychiatric literature a number of cases showing mental disorder precisely on the basis of a pathological attachment to a thing which the owner believed to be irreplaceable. I have observed, in otherwise perfectly sane families, ugly scenes between normal people at the very moment when one member of the family thoughtlessly used a thing or commodity which the specific owner deemed (often irrationally) unique or extremely difficult to replace or refill.

I am equally sceptical of the Pavlov conditioning theory when it is used to promise social harmony between incompatible groups provided they "can be made to get used to each other."

Man's sphere of free choice and privacy has shrunk in recent decades, partly because of the transfer of experimental findings from the level of animals to that of human beings. Social reformers, while professing concern for the unique dignity of man when asking for individualistic legislation, often show a remarkably cynical and brutal concept of man when they use facts of experimental conditioning of rodents to dispel the warnings of those who think that Sumner's *mores* will outlast many generations of reformers to come.

Several observers noted the perfectionism of the reformer as a cause of the shrinkage of personal freedom in our time. In a particular yet important case, this perfectionism resembles the quest of natural scientists for pure systems, compounds, elements, and the like. It expresses a wish to see the absolute maximum of

a given process. Physicists try hard to produce the lowest temperature theoretically possible. Similarly, reformers insist on a satura-
tion point of contact between disparate groups. They detest any
sign of what might be called rough spots between members of the
human race. They promise a future without tensions—a term
characteristically adopted from mechanics. This desire results in
an anomaly—altruism by decree. The administration of this Uto-
pia proceeds by means of informal social controls, of "group dynamics," and of legislated or discretionary governmental power.

In all cases this administration is based essentially on a transfer
of certain discoveries made about animals, and about human
beings under very specific conditions, to human social action at
large. It is based on the theory that if only we can bring together
in long enough contact the members of some groups that have not
previously shown great sympathy for one another, they will eventually acquire altruistic and sympathetic attitudes toward one another.

In the musical play *The King and I*, this is the theme which
Oscar Hammerstein put into the lyrics of the song "Getting to
Know You" as a remedy for the social and political ills of our
times. When Edward R. Murrow asked Mr. Hammerstein over the
air why he supports so many "liberal" causes, Mr. Hammerstein
cited that theme song and suggested that if we knew all about one
another, as the English school teacher knew about her Siamese
pupils, the age of bliss would be near.

When we review hundreds of supposedly scientific articles about
"intergroup relations," they appear to add little beyond what is
implied in Mr. Hammerstein's song. The concept of "mixed neigh-
borhoods" in city planning—a source of considerable waste and
disappointment—assumes, as does the scholastically nondiscrimi-
nating comprehensive high school, that permanent brotherhood
will emerge between people of different outlook and achievements
if we can keep them in physical proximity long enough for human
nature to evaporate.

When the proponents of such schemes are pressed for reasonable
proof of a sound basis for their optimism, they usually cite some
"psychological facts of learning" derived from experiments with

rats. However, the moment we ignore these experiments and consider the meagre responsiveness of human beings to various forms of knowledge and propaganda in nonlaboratory situations, we find little basis for such optimism.

I have probably been exposed to thousands of the most intriguing advertisements and broadcast commercials for various tobacco products. None has succeeded in turning me into a smoker. On the other hand, the rather overwhelming and threatening scientific correlations between smoking and serious ailments have registered remarkably little persuasion with medical men, who go on smoking as usual.

It may be one of the most arrogant errors of social science to claim and enlist legislative support for the hypothesis that men could become predominantly altruistic creatures without strong hostilities toward anyone if only they could be properly conditioned.

It is still fashionable to belittle or ignore the existence of human nature and to disregard its stubborn and mischievous potentialities. On the other hand, the same people who ignore human nature are only too eager to assume there is a world-wide identity of human nature when they dream of a world free from conflict and with equal standards of living. Obviously, either one or the other of these views must be given up.

It would call for much longer treatment than is possible in this essay to try to analyze the fluctuations in the concept of human nature set forth by influential public figures and commentators in recommending mutually exclusive remedies for social and political problems, depending on where the sore spot happens to be located.

Domestically we are asked to expect wonders from coerced conditioning, from shows of force by wise men who, by contrast, are convinced that a show of force and strength is entirely lost on peoples of the Middle and Far East. And if there is an ethnocentric tendency to suicidal resentments in human being (and I have observed it in many forms), then it would seem at least as unrealistic to expect lasting peace to be created by paratroopers in Arkansas as in Algeria.[7]

While studying animals, our students of human behavior have

completely failed to reckon with the phenomenon of cumulative resentment in human beings of a kind that is a negligible drive in animals.

Of course, I am aware of the possibility that some authors make merely political and expedient use of these inconsistencies when judging social problems. But I think, nevertheless, that indulgence in such hypocrisies is made easy for them by the failure of the contemporary anthropological disciplines to commit themselves to a firm concept of human nature.

III

The term "scientism" refers only to the fallacious use of the methods of certain natural sciences when we ought to study man as a unique being with emotional, mental, and social potentialities above those of known animals.

Obviously, a critique of scientism does not imply wholesale condemnation of the adoption of the methods of natural science. Indeed, some of the worst culprits of scientism have merely introduced the wrong tools and procedures of the natural sciences into the social and moral sciences. They have ignored a number of powerful intellectual and observational instruments of the biological sciences which we could well have used in the study of man in his social context. I am thinking here of criteria of form, of congruity v. incongruity, considerations of symmetry—in short, of morphological approaches to reality.[8] Sociologists, for instance, are most reluctant to recognize persistent styles of social life, for fear of being undemocratic. And yet it is the integrating reality and indefinite life-span of such diverse styles of human life which permit almost unlimited peaceful coexistence of capsular group life.

Much of the damage which has been done to fairly well-functioning systems of existing societies, in the name of social science, might have been avoided if sociologists and social psychologists were held, by the profession, to that minimum observation of natural morphological criteria which we expect the anatomist to respect. One of my academic teachers, the zoologist Karl von

Frisch, in his course in comparative anatomy, called the human pelvis the worst possible solution nature could have found for the birth-act. But I have yet to hear a doctor urging compulsory pubic symphysectomy for all females of our species.

On the contrary, the natural childbirth fad, with its emphasis on "constructive pain," gained favor exactly among our "progressive" social scientists, such as Margaret Mead, who would, in social life, gladly turn society upside down in order to eliminate (largely imaginary) *social* pains of some members of society.[9]

I reject the organismic concept of society, especially when used in rhetoric for recommending public policy. No group of individuals becomes more accessible to theoretical comprehension if understood as an organism. No "diseased" part of society *necessarily* impairs any other, although, of course, some pathological condition in society might spread because of contiguity. Why should we expect much good to come from telling members of a society that they owe each other a great deal because they are all part of an organism? If this is urged, we usually end up with a system in which we constrain one another rather than release the individual creativity. Moreover, should we not justly resent the bureaucrat who wants to plan *our* welfare because he defines himself as head and us as limbs of the "good society"?

Some of the foregoing may seem redundant. After all, who has taken the organismic theory of society seriously in recent years? But when we examine the speeches of contemporary politicians, presidents, and prime ministers, it is quite easy to show that their grandiose flights of thought and rhetorical promises often implicitly rest on an organismic concept of society.[10]

It is especially disheartening to see some intellectuals insist that it is about time for them to take charge of the "organism society," because life has become too complex for the common man.[11]

Much of the current attack on the political and economic system we live in (and some "really advanced" critics are "farsighted" enough to include in their condemnation East and West in order to be still right if and when the Soviet Union can satisfy all consumer wants) stems from a peculiar kind of scientism. It is partly historicism, partly a kind of philosophic trespassing. Perhaps it grows in part from the organismic theory of civilization. Plato, Rousseau, Fourier, Marx, and others are cited with their models of man and community in order to declare our present society doomed.

But is it fair, either to the present structure of our economy and to today's people or to the originators of social ideas and philosophies in centuries past, to force them together in an analysis of current social reality? In doing this we perpetrate a historical incongruity. It is unfair to Plato when we use his concept of a true polis to measure our sorry state of politics. At the same time we are unfair to our fellow citizens when we measure *their* actions and attitudes against the what-might-have-been in the time of Plato had he succeeded in saving the old Greek polis.

We have no way of knowing what Plato would have thought, felt, and advised had he had even a faint glimpse of societies (or nations) with 50, 170, 200, or 650 million citizens. Nor can we estimate the stature of any contemporary man by supposing his arrival in a Greek polis of 500 B.C.

Of course, there are specific existential—ethical, philosophical —situations where a man must seek his place in a field of conflicting values. These situations can be essentially the same in ancient as well as modern times. But this is different from attempts to apply what we know of the ancient polis as a real ideal-type to the study of contemporary society. I am wary of the theme of the "lost community." This is a crypto-quantitative comparison which tries to match wholly incongruous societies for the purpose of learning something about the quality of human relations.

When we examine publications in the field of theoretical and applied social science, two trends seem to run parallel: There is the preference for reducing the study of man in his social interaction to the measurement of the percentage of incidence of clumsily extracted attitudes and hypothetical responses to hypothetical situations. The other trend is the habit of crediting the arbitrarily delineated collective with all those faculties and potentials which are no longer attributed to individual members of society. A good example of this tendency to throw individuals to the mercy of "wise society" can be found in the proceedings and final resolution of the American Assembly in 1953, called together to discuss "social security in modern times." [12] But any actuarial examination of social security schemes in advanced democracies shows that these collectives have less wisdom and long-range foresight in planning the welfare of society than has the average head of a family for his dependents.

One reason for this, of course, is that the head of a family can be sure of love and support even if he has to make, in the interest of long-range goals, economic decisions which frustrate the immediate preferences of some members of the family. The governments of democracies usually believe that they cannot afford such sanity. It is "politically impossible."

Possibly, as Richard LaPiere shows in his book, *The Freudian Ethic* (1959), the same sentiments and pseudo ethics that have rendered impotent whatever wisdom may be available to some men in government now tend to corrupt at least certain families in America. Parents read that they ought to run the family by public opinion polls among brats. If this should become a dominant feature of our families, it is likely that more and more of them will become incompetent. In so far as this stems from the same source as the cancer in government—a vulgar misunderstanding of democracy and equality—I see little reason for optimism when the more powerful of two incompetents, a certain type of modern government, tells a certain type of modern family that it needs the central government to protect it from its own folly. A collusion of two fools will hardly lead to a sane public policy.

In some circles of contemporary sociology it is fashionable to view society and its subdivisions as "systems." Often, however, it seems to me, not enough care is taken in regard to important ontological distinctions. For instance, Karl von Frisch, in his studies of the bees, conceives of their state as a highly articulate system; but we hardly assume the bees to know themselves as constituent members of a system. In other words, there are at least two different possibilities when we speak of a social system. The researcher and theorist, in order to make puzzling phenomena comprehensible, may try to sort out specific units from a range or cluster of phenomena and call their interdependency, their functioning, a system. This does not require conscious behavior on the part of those units, or of a majority of them, as members (and in terms) of a system. The "system," its functional value, may have come about by natural selection. We might think here also, for instance, of the nervous *system* or certain ecological systems made up of different plants and lower organisms.

And even when we speak of "American society," for the most part we have a system before us that functions in all its complexity on a level of mutual consciousness and recognition not very much higher than the systems mentioned above. Except for a few intellectuals perhaps, most Americans, whose daily activities over centuries helped to create a complex and highly productive socioeconomic system, did not, and do not now, go about their business all the time thinking of their social system.

By contrast, there are social systems that are *systems* precisely because of a theory of a specific system that preceded them in time. They remain functioning systems only as long as most of their members remain intensely conscious of the theory that has welded them into a system. Any complex group of human beings performing a highly specialized service, whether it be Lloyd's of London, an opera company, or the general staff of an army, might be mentioned as illustrations. Yet again, there is a difference between the social system of Lloyd's, a modern opera house, and the German General Staff. Unlike the former, which grew gradually by trial and error, the German General Staff was an articulate and functioning social system mostly by virtue of all its members' constant and intense dedication to the theory which had put the system into existence.

If these different meanings of the term "social system" are confused, naive yet ambitious legislators and policy-makers often may come to expect from "society" a continuous performance on a level of cohesion and dedication which we could expect only in the best circumstances from a system of the type illustrated by the General Staff.

IV

As several papers in this book argue, without conscious commitment to value judgments we can hardly hope to gain a concept of the true, i.e., least coercive and least fragile, relationship between man and his society. I should like to show that even our "highly scientific" natural sciences cannot do without such value judgments. (Michael Polanyi, in his *Personal Knowledge: Towards a Post-Critical Philosophy*, published both in Britain and the United States in 1958, presents the same argument in detail.)

Let us examine the work of the chemist. He serves one of the oldest true natural sciences. His knowledge caused some of the most spectacular transformations of our internal and external environments. Chemistry, among other deeds, helped medical art become, in part, scientific. Laymen and social scientists accept chemistry as a true representative of the exact and nonsubjective natural sciences where measurement rules and the subjectivity of human sensory experience has been replaced by apparatuses recording in figures and decimals.

Especially, the public may believe, chemistry without exception is an exact science with demonstrable nonevaluative proof when the judgment and findings of a chemist are introduced in court and a man can be convicted on such evidence. This is a fairy tale.

Recently I refreshed my memory of my own studies in that field in a long talk with a young doctor of chemistry who works in a state laboratory controlling foods and beverages. Quite a number of his analyses, on the basis of which a manufacturer or innkeeper may be sentenced to jail, depend on the simple fact that chemist and judge agree on a single sensory perception which most people would call a culture-bound value judgment. A stench is a loathsome stench in certain cultures only. Yet, I was told, it may suffice for conviction even if a sample of suspect fat eludes all other methods of quantitative and qualitative analysis. However, even though chemist and judge agree on a stench as the criterion of unfitness for human consumption, the same intrinsic *sensory* experience might make the same sample of food a delicacy in another culture.

The most recent reference books in the field of food chemistry abound in value judgments when stating criteria for finding butter or meat unfit for human consumption. Delicate and highly subjective syndromes of color, odor, and texture, of just plain "looks," guide the chemist when he has to pass his scientific, expert judgment on butter. Often it is not a question of poisonousness at all, but simply a question of aesthetics.[13]

Psychologists of language know that the olfactory sense of humans permits distinctions for which no general verbal referents exist. When chemists communicate about a certain analytical fact, they rely on reasonable identity of subjective experiences which are completely absent for some members of the human race.[14]

When the chemist applies his science and expertness to the judgment of food samples in criminal cases, for instance, he is permitted the use of words such as "loathsome," "sickening," "repulsive," and judge and jury are likely to agree. But if a sociologist should be caught by his profession calling polygamy, communism, or the system of the Soviet Union "loathsome," he is immediately attacked as "unscientific" or "unscholarly." (The censure is less likely to follow should he label capitalism or profit-seeking a loathsome business!) And yet the weight the chemist's expertness gathers in court is due to the fact that what he refuses to eat a layman also refuses to consume. This is not made invalid by the fact that we can always find some people who would love, or could be "brainwashed" to consume, that particular sample of food.

Therefore, what is so "unscientific" about a political scientist or economist who calls a planned or an egalitarian economy a "loathsome" affair? Surely he can find plenty of common folk who would know what he means as precisely as does the public which agrees with the food chemist.

A man whose sense of color is impaired could hardly work as chemist or physician. Only recently have methods and apparatuses become available which substitute for the human faculty of recognizing a change in color.

And yet studies of individual variations show that human beings vary considerably in their faculty of identifying specific stimuli for the senses. What the chemist or physician relies upon is average, a reasonable, and sometimes probably culture-bound ability of ordinary people to find identical verbal referents or memory images ("smells like . . .").

However, it is very doubtful whether today's political science or sociology would permit me to size up the future actions of a Castro or Nasser on the basis of comparing my impression of his performance in a television interview with my memory images of a Hitler. I may do this, perhaps, as an essayist or journalist, but not as an observer who claims scholarly or scientific authenticity.

And yet I believe I can show that the essential complexity of the syndromes perceived is not greater in the last case than in the case of a chemist or medical pathologist who testifies about his findings in court. Is it not strange that an audience of ordinary people, when shown successively a movie of Hitler and one of Nasser or Fidel Castro, each addressing a crowd, would instantly, without even understanding German, Arabic, or Spanish, recognize some intrinsically common features; whereas, I am afraid, a professional group of political scientists might squeamishly refuse to commit themselves to any cognition from which inferences for policy decisions could be drawn?

It seems we know much more about men and their likely actions and potentials than the behavioral and "policy sciences" permit us to know and say officially. We may lack "scientific" methods, especially quantitative ones—as does the analytical chemist—for assessing and recording the rottenness of a form of leadership, but there is no reason why we could not reaffirm the freedom of qualitative judgment when studying, let us say, a labor union monopoly or junta.

What we students of man and his organization need more than new fancy methods and methodologies is a general recognition that sometimes our judgments may be as old-fashioned as those of a modern food chemist. We must recapture the scholarly legitimacy of ordinary observation when deciding between better and worse, between more or less functional, more or less apt to cause friction. This could bridge the gap between a lost discipline—moral philosophy—and comparative political science, sociology, and economics.

In saying this, I do not ignore the element of human freedom and its role in our specific subject matter, human action. True, there is the (remote) possibility that a labor union hierarchy, after being called rotten to the core, might pick itself up and become a bevy of altruistic stewards of power. Obviously, rancid butter will never respond to the verdict of a chemist.

We touch here a most vexing problem. It has been discussed under such titles as "private versus public prediction" or "self-fulfilling and self-defeating prophecies." Robert K. Merton, K. R. Popper, and others have dealt with it. Value judgments as well as seemingly neutral bodies of data in the social sciences have consequences within their subject matter, men and groups of men.

Again we have to guard against an overstatement of this fact. It is not an exclusive faculty of human beings. Lower forms of life also may evade—as if rational—the application of human intellectual concepts. Certain stocks of germs are known to outwit the antibiotics researcher by selectively outbreeding his luck with resistant strains. In other words, it may be as difficult for man to freeze advantageously his relationship to his nonhuman environment as it is toward his fellow men. We seem as capable of overreaching our supply of natural resources (experimenting in the name of material progress) as we are capable of overextending our resources of altruism, good will, and patience (experimenting in the name of social progress). A biologist enthralled by the beauty of a theory can destroy an ecological equilibrium in nature as surely as can a sociologist or economist in society.

Almost every time a finding or a hypothesis is made public by a student of human action, it leads to an artifact. In this regard there is little difference in effectiveness (dangerousness) between the various methods. A bluntly evaluative term can cause as violent a response as the dry publication of a set of telling figures. Consequently, limiting ourselves to quantitative behavioral science, seemingly free from value judgments, will not prevent the occurrence of unexpected or unwanted reactions in the groups and societies we are studying.

As social scientists, as students of social interaction, we are inescapably responsible for a stream of artifacts unless we remain forever silent about what we believe we know. We cannot prevent the intrusion of novel facts and data-providing processes into the field of study as a result of our work. We share this problem with the natural scientists, but sometimes we suffer more from its consequences.

What troubles me, however, is the failure of so many social scientists to concern themselves with their artifacts as systematically and conscientiously as the microscopic anatomists did when they wondered whether their dyes had caught structures in nerve cells or merely made cracks in a formerly unstructured whole. Too many social scientists seem unequipped to tell cracks from structures, especially when they produce the former.

The pathologist or the haematologist, in reaching a crucial differential diagnosis, may rely on criteria of form, color, texture, contiguity, and configuration which defy verbal, let alone quantitative, objectification. The same is true of the engineer, the architect, the physicist, and the mathematician.[15] These scientists and scholars may declare a certain solution to a problem less elegant, less desirable, than another without being obliged to offer any other reasons save their cultivated sense of form and coherence. But woe to the sociologist, economist, or political scientist who can cite no statistical figments to buttress his preference for one type of organization over another. Is it really so significant whether or not a socialist economy *could* solve the problem of allocation and distribution in some fashion as long as enough sane men agree that the market mechanism is a more elegant and aesthetically pleasing method for these tasks? Do we need quantifying policy sciences to find (or doubt) that political succession by election or hereditary monarchy is more elegant and aesthetically pleasant than one by murder?

Ironically, natural scientists possess the privilege of falling back

on intrinsic human experiences as ultimate and axiomatic proof—
and reason for preferences—whereas the students of man are no
longer allowed to argue on the basis of their introspective knowledge of what fits man best.

V

It shows the present-day delusions of behavioral scientists that
they scoff at methods and criteria of cognition which still belong
to the standard arsenal of chemistry.

Sub rosa, of course, we know that all we have for telling a difference in our social environment are our traditional terms of reference, no matter how far out of line they are with the "progress"
of social science. For instance, what is the test for the degree of
deterioration of a city section?

The New York Times can hardly be accused of unfairness to
nonwhite racial minorities. Yet, in a long and learned survey of
the disturbing decline of "urban quality" in the city blocks surrounding Columbia University, the writer for the *Times,* with
apologies, admitted that the only genuine criterion for the worsen-
ing of an urban area is the influx of Negroes and Puerto Ricans.
He wrote: This is an unpopular criterion, but it is the best yardstick of urban decline.

And the University of Chicago, desperately trying to get rid of
slums around its campus, helped build a belt of luxury apartment
houses with rents assuring a white neighborhood, a sin against the
times for which this bastion of racial egalitarianism was attacked
in the press.[16]

In brief, no matter how social scientists may measure "progress"
in "social" or "democratic" attitudes, when it comes to city planning as a means of saving cultural centers from going under in a
sea of slums, "liberals" and conservatives often employ the same
traditional criteria for what is good and what is worse.

I have tried to show the scholarly legitimacy of subjective (depending on impressions of a sensory and cultural quality) value
judgments in the study of social man.

But it is not enough if, for instance, I can show the scholarly respectability and epistemological legitimacy of a statement such as "communism smells." Harold J. Laski, in his last book, criticized Sir Winston Churchill who, by rallying the Atlantic community of nations, committed a crime against history when he saved central and western Europe from Moscow, thus, as Laski put it, perpetuating the bad odor of decaying capitalistic society.[17] Whose sense of smell shall prevail? I think egalitarianism smells. Many others say every sign of social stratification emits an odor of rotten social fabrics.

Of course, there are some tests, inductive at best, which should support one kind of value judgment against another. For instance, we could examine the net migration of man. Many more people constantly flee from state socialism to the West than from the "decaying West" into "flourishing empires" of the East. The egalitarian *kibbutzim* in Israel are losing members as did all such utopias that ever existed.[18] But this test would not help us in all cases of social and political analysis.

Hitler Germany, for instance, succeeded in luring back into the "community" many ethnic Germans from abroad, even Austrians from Italy. I recall an Austrian-Italian waitress in a hotel by the Mediterranean in Nervi near Genoa in 1949. She spoke to us about fellow Austrian-Italians, including her brother, who followed Hitler's call to "return" north ten years earlier. She was still wondering what had made them run: "All of a sudden," she said, "the blue sea was no longer blue. Why?"

Is it that some personalities can best win a sense of importance, temporarily perhaps, by following the charism of the collective, while others, for their sense of well-being, need personal freedom, even at the cost of temporary hardship and disappointment, to such a degree that they move away from planned, paternalistic or collectivistic systems whenever they can?

Perhaps it is so difficult to develop a social science congruent with human nature because we are always faced with "mixed societies," made up of both types of people, thus never allowing even an approximate congruousness of theory and actual behavior, save for short periods and specific instances.

Thus, at any rate, even if Red China, for example, somehow

could induce many of the overseas Chinese to flock back to the mainland, instead of the present exodus of her nationals, her fellow-traveling friends in the West could not use that fact as a criterion of her goodness unless they retroactively granted the same to Hitler's Third Reich.[19]

NOTES

1. The problem of priority in research obviously can become crucial in medical science. Errors in choice of strategy may be fatal. See, for instance, the controversy over "Probability, Logic and Medical Diagnosis" (a paper by R. S. Ledley and L. B. Lusted) in *Science,* CXXX, July 1, 1959, and October 9, 1959.
2. Henry Margenau, "Physical versus Historical Reality," *Philosophy of Science,* XIX (July, 1952), 203.
2a. Carle C. Zimmerman and Lucius F. Cervantes, *Successful American Families* (New York: Pageant Press, 1960).
3. For the concept of self-fulfilling prediction, see Robert K. Merton, *Social Theory and Social Structure* (Glencoe: The Free Press, revised edition, 1957), chap. XI, "The Self-Fulfilling Prophecy." For a very sane critique of the *Gemeinschaft-Gesellschaft* dichotomy, see Richard T. LaPiere, *A Theory of Social Control* (New York: McGraw-Hill Book Company, 1954), chap. I.
4. Kathleen McLaughlin, "U. S. Blood-Giving Baffles Russians," *New York Times,* September 13, 1956. See also *New York Times,* April 27, 1958, p. 15, on blood donors.
5. *See also* Leopold Kohr, "Toward a New Measurement of Living Standards," *American Journal of Economics and Sociology,* XV (October, 1955), 93-102.
6. According to a poll in October, 1959, the vast majority of Americans, and, interestingly enough, especially the upper-middle class, approve of advertising. Could it be that our professional intellectuals, as in so many other areas of life, worry themselves to pieces about a problem which is of little concern to those on whose behalf they worry?
7. Compare, for instance, the *New York Times* of August 3, p. 10 E, and August 17, p. 5 E, 1958, for the entirely different moral verdict on the use of force, as well as the estimate of its success, when it comes to dealing with Nasser versus dealing with a state of the United States.
8. For a meaningful use of the concept of asymmetry in sociology, see, for instance, Richard L. Meier, "Explorations in the Realm of Organization Theory," *Behavioral Science,* IV (July, 1959), 242.
9. See Margaret Mead's attack on the book *Don't Be Afraid of Your Child* by Hilde Bruch, *American Journal of Orthopsychiatry,* XXIV, 426-428, and the defense of Bruch's book by William S. Langford, *ibid.,* 838 ff.
10. For typical illustrations, see text of President Eisenhower's address at

Abilene, *New York Times,* October 14, 1959, or text of American Assembly Report, *New York Times,* October 19, 1959. See also *American Assembly on Economic Security,* Columbia University, 1954, p. 7, n. 16.

11. The canard that modern society and modern "life" have become too complex and too "big" for individuals and local agencies to handle is being heard over and over again. Arthur Larson, for instance, said: ". . . you ask yourself if any private-enterprise firm, any insurance company or combination of insurance companies, any state government or local government could administer Social Security. Of course, it couldn't. Social Security covers hundreds of millions of people [really that many?] going all over the earth." ("A Mike Wallace Interview with Arthur Larson," The Fund for the Republic, 1958, p. 10). Professor Larson, formerly a Special Assistant to President Eisenhower, forgets to explain only one thing: Why should it be necessary at all for a *single* agency to cover all those "hundreds of millions of people going all over the earth"? Why not let a multitude of local and smaller agencies and insurance companies administer the voluntarily chosen insurance schemes of individual families?

The rhetoric of "complexity" is also found in a Senate bill to "establish a permanent Advisory Commission on Intergovernmental Relations," S. 2026, *Congressional Record,* May 21, 1959, p. 7851: "Because the complexity of modern life intensifies the need in a federal form of government. . . ."

The lack of empirical basis, the emptiness of the complexity-argument is brought out by D. R. Price-Williams in his review of *Mental Health Aspects of the Peaceful Uses of Atomic Energy* in *Population Studies,* July, 1959, p. 126.

12. See reference 10 above, last item.

13. Much of the following information I received from Dr. Heinz Grimm, chemist and pharmacologist at the Austrian federal institute for pure foods in Vienna. For this method of applied chemistry *see* Kurt G. Wagner, "Zur Theorie der Bewertungsschemata für Lebensmittel," *Deutsche Lebensmittel-Rundschau,* XLV (June, 1949), 145-149. Wagner stresses "that the exaggerated preference for numerically measurable facts" [scientism too!] among chemists led to the relative neglect of the organoleptic method with its somewhat subjective statements, although it is still in many instances the only useful method. Wagner also complains—and here the chemist sounds almost like a nonscientistic sociologist—that some of his fellow chemists should have devoted as much time and mental effort to the systematization of the *sensory* methodology as they wasted on playing with apparatuses (p. 145), especially in view of the fact that the chemistry of nutrients cannot do without judgments of smell and taste. Wagner knows that only people with special gifts of these senses ought to work as nutritional chemists and fears errors from the less gifted.

More recently, Professor D. J. Tilgner gave a brilliant defense and survey of the sensory analysis of nutrients. His bibliography includes a number of items in English. ("Der gegenwärtige Stand der quantitativen und qualitativen sensorischen Analyse der Qualität von Lebensmitteln," *Deutsche Lebensmittel-Rundschau,* LIV [May, 1958], 99-108). I should like to cite some of them here: H. S. Groninger, Tapperl and Knapp, "Some Chemical and Organoleptic Changes in Gamma-irradiated Meats," *Food Res.,* XXI (1956), 555-564. D. Sheppard, "The Importance of Psychophysical Errors," *J. Dairy Res.,* XIX (1952), 348-355. E. L. Pippin, A. A. Campbell and Streeter, "Flavour Studies," *J. Agric. and Food Chemistry,* II (1954), 354-367. M. M. Boggs and H. L. Hanson, "Analysis of Foods by Sensory Difference Tests," *Adv. Food Research,* II (1949), 219-258. H. L. Hanson *et al.,* "Sensory Test Methods," *Food Techn.,* IX (1955), 50-59. D. R. Peryam, "Hedonic Scale Method of Measuring Food Preferences," *Food Engng.,* XXIV (1952), 7. E. C. Crocker, "The Nature of Odor," *Techn. Associat. of the Pulp and Paper Industry,* XXXV (1952), 9.

Tilgner emphasizes the differences in talent and gifts in sensory competence among chemists, especially the varying gift of feeling *(Gefühlsbegabung)* which is important when it comes to deciding qualities and degrees of appetizingness or loathsomeness. And yet, Tilgner joins the Australian chemist, D. W. Crover, ("Progress in Food Analysis." *Food Manuf.,* XXV, 1949) in saying that the present status of the sensory (organoleptic) method permits results so precise that this method belongs to the chemical-analytical methodology. Microchanges in protein molecules, for instance, which elude ordinary chemical analyses, can be discovered quickly and definitely by the sensory method (p. 100). Incidentally, at this point, the method of the food chemist and the medical haematologist become similar epistemologically.

Thus, in practice, the natural sciences are far from being reduced to the study of the measurable. Curiously enough, E. C. Harwood ("On 'Measurement as Scientific Method in Economics,'" *American Journal of Economics and Sociology,* XVII [October, 1957], 101) challenges Leland B. Yeager's claim that there are social scientists narrow enough to restrict science to measurement. At any rate, I can name one: the sociologist Franz Adler, who wants to restrict to pure measurement even so delicate a field as the sociology of knowledge. The original view that *science is measurement,* of course, was given by Galileo, who wrote: "My program is to measure what can be measured and to make measurable what cannot be measured yet." (Galilei, *Opere,* ed. by Alberi, IV, 171). But it is very doubtful whether Galileo ever would have thought of "making measurable" those phenomena which our scientistic students of man insist on measuring.

14. Biochemical individuality and the sense of smell is one of the problems intriguing Roger J. Williams. See his books *Free and Unequal* (Austin: University of Texas Press, 1953), p. 32, and *Biochemical Individuality* (New York: John Wiley & Sons, 1956), p. 180.

15. The issues of qualitative versus quantitative judgment and the element of subjectivity in the field of haematology are discussed, in a vein supporting my argument, by St. Sandkühler, "Über Dokumentation von Knochenmarkbefunden," *Röntgen- und Labor-Praxis,* X, 278-280. Or,

take another area of medical diagnosis, the perception of macroscopic syndromes, e.g., the first diagnosis of coronary occlusion as reported in R. H. Major, *Classic Descriptions of Disease* (2nd ed.; Springfield: Charles C. Thomas, 1939), pp. 464 ff. Similar problems of subjectively differentiating diagnosis face the archeologist: "Modern archeology has reached a point where many possible patterns and hypotheses can be suggested, each of which seems to propose cultural 'facts' that are not necessarily mutually exclusive and that do not necessarily contradict each other but which *in the same body of materials* reflect various aspects of a many-sided reality. . . . In the case of cultural pattern or configuration, however, the 'reality' of proposed fact is less apparent because the particular interests of the investigator, and perhaps the historical development of the science, intrude more strongly into the result." (Joseph R. Caldwell, "The New American Archeology," *Science,* CXXIX [February 6, 1959], 305.)

For the problem of elegance in research and theory, see, for instance, John D. Tsilikis, "Simplicity and Elegance in Theoretical Physics," *American Scientist,* XLVII (Spring, 1959), 87-96.

16. "Renewal Project Divides Chicago," *New York Times,* September 28, 1958, and Sol Tax, "Residential Integration: A Chicago Case," *Human Organization,* XVIII (Spring, 1959).

17. H. J. Laski, *The Dilemma of Our Times* (London, 1952), pp. 46 f.

18. Seth S. King, *New York Times,* February 20, 1958; *see also* Amitai Etzioni, "The Functional Differentiation of Elites in the Kibbutz," *American Journal of Sociology,* LXIV (March, 1959), 476-487.

19. Ironically, and pertinent to this point, Walter Lippmann, in the early spring of 1960, used migration figures from West Germany to East Germany cited by the Communists as evidence that all could not be so bad in East Germany as to warrant a strong stand on the part of the West in regard to the Berlin question. And yet, a few weeks later a flood of refugees, unprecedented in recent years, began to reach West Berlin and has not yet subsided at the time of this writing.

7

Scientism in the Writing
of History

Pieter Geyl

When I was invited to take part in the Symposium on Scientism and the Study of Man, I happened to be preparing the valedictory oration I was to deliver on the occasion of my retirement as Professor of Modern History in the University of Utrecht. The organizers were good enough to allow me to use that paper as my contribution to the symposium but, although it gave rise to an animated, and to me enlightening, discussion, I had felt all along that it was not really very closely related to the central theme of the symposium.

What I spoke about to my audience in the Aula of Utrecht University on May 31, 1958, was "The Vitality of Western Civilization." I used an occasion which was bound to attract attention to speak my mind on a matter that had for a long time irritated me and that I consider to be a danger to our Western community, viz., the irresponsible depreciation of our civilization, the wallowing in visions of decay, the belief that a new world was beginning, or had begun, in which we should take our tune, if not from the Russians, then from the Asiatics or the Africans.

That oration of mine [1] should not be interpreted as a hymn of praise to the times we live in; it was not meant as such. Nor did I want to extol Western civilization as the salt of the earth or to decree a permanent inferiority for races which are obviously coming into their own. I only wanted to affirm, as strongly and persuasively as I could, that no matter what was happening to the rest of the world, we still have a duty to ourselves, above all to believe in ourselves, to believe that we still have a contribution to make, and that the only way in which we can do this is by remaining faithful to our own traditions. All this seemed to me, and it still seems to me, of such overriding importance, not only because of the awakening of the Asian and of the African peoples, but especially because there is Russia, or there is Russian-Chinese communism, threatening us directly and ready to make use of all our weaknesses.

We *are* suffering from weaknesses. Generally speaking, these do not, in my view, spring from factual conditions; they belong to the realm of the spirit. They result from a mood, or a combination of moods. In analyzing these I indicated a variety of sources. One is the disgruntlement of the once dominating class at the irresistible emancipation and growth in material well-being of the working classes. Another is the concern of the religious-minded at what seems like an equally irresistible development of dechristianization. Then there is the anger, the feeling of frustration, of an ex-colonial power suddenly thrown out of a position of which it had been proud, not only on account of the wealth and influence that went with it, but on account of the task we had fulfilled, with conviction, and not without benefit for the peoples under our rule. Anger and a feeling of frustration are not all. Along with them there goes a more complicated psychological reaction of an opposite tendency, a feeling of guilt, a feeling of having transgressed against these peoples and of having to make up to them now.

I need hardly say that, while my oration was intended for a Dutch public, all these various factors have their parallels in other, more important, European countries.

In expounding the state of mind that I have just adumbrated, and in trying to counter the fallacies to which it gives rise, I spoke as a historian. Or perhaps I should say that, while speaking from a conviction that is rooted in the whole of my outlook on life, or in my personality, I felt my views supported by what I consider to be true history; in any case, I thought it particularly incumbent upon me to expose the false history so often adduced by the pessimists.

The pessimists? This word, too, stands in need of qualification. Pessimism often enough takes on the appearance of optimism and adopts the tone of cheerfulness and hope. Our civilization is, so we are told (by Marx, for instance, and his followers), in the last stage of decay, but what will come after its final dissolution will be of a higher quality and worth all the upsets and the sufferings that we have still to face. Not that this disguise of optimism is required to tempt everyone. There is in human nature an inclination which responds to visions of ruin and decay. Against them the divine promise of eternal bliss can shine with greater radiance. Take Augustinus; take Bilderdijk, the great Dutch counterrevolutionary poet. But even Spengler's unadulterated pessimism found a receptive public.

Now all these prophets of woe and of repentance, and the joyful announcers of a new and blissful dispensation as well, like to appeal to history. History in their hands is made to conform to the system which they need for their gloomy or hopeful visions.

It is, I suppose, an ingrained habit of the human mind—and, indeed, it is a noble ambition—to try to construct a vision of history in which chaos, or apparent chaos, is reduced to order. The historical process is made to conform to a line, a rhythm, a regularity—a movement, in other words, which obeys definable and intelligible laws and whose continuation can, therefore, be predicated by the observer beyond the moment of his own life.

So I expressed myself, ten years ago, when setting out on a discussion of the works of Sorokin and of Toynbee. "A noble ambition." But also: "The historical process is *made* to conform." In other words: Violence is done to the historical process. Some years later, when I was invited to deliver the Terry Lectures at Yale University, I chose the use and abuse of history for my subject.[2] In dealing with it, I naturally devoted a good deal of attention to the problem of scientism, that is, the undue application of the terminology and of the methods of science to the study of man, and I had indeed faced it before, as the passage quoted from my essay of 1949 makes clear. Yet I must confess that until I received the invitation to this symposium, I had not, as a matter of fact, ever dealt with the problem exclusively, let alone exhaustively.

Now, instructive and at times revealing as I have found the four days' discussion to which it has been my privilege to listen and in which I took part, I am still inclined to view scientism primarily as one method out of several in the service of an attitude of mind—of a mood, be it of a compelling desire to recast the world in conformity with an ideal, or merely of dissatisfaction, of despair. And perhaps it is enough to point to the more general human trait to which I alluded in the passage quoted, a trait stronger in some men than in others, of being liable to be fascinated by a system, any system. This tendency, if examined more closely, will generally prove to be connected with the habit of thinking in absolutes, which may be characteristic of a minority of men only, but which can develop great dynamic power and carry away simple-minded multitudes; or with the craving for certainty which all of us can observe in ourselves, although here again some are less able to bear uncertainty than are others.

Now the historian, as I have insisted time and again (and I never imagined that I was saying anything new or original), moves in a sphere of uncertainty. We keep on trying to get into touch with the realities of past life; the inexhaustible attraction of history is in that it does help us to achieve this miracle; yet at the same time its revelations will always be incomplete; there always remains something mysterious and unfathomable.

As I wrote in the first page of my essay on Ranke,[3]

History is infinite. It is unfixable. We are trying all the time to reduce past reality to terms of certainty, but all we can do is to render our own impression of it. No book can reproduce more than a part of that reality, even within the confines of its particular subject; and each book contains something else, which gets mixed up with historical truth in an almost untraceable manner, which does not necessarily turn it into falsehood, but which nevertheless transforms it into something different from the simple truth—I mean the opinion, or the sentiment, or the philosophy of life, of the narrator; or in other words, the personality of the historian.

No certainty, no finality. "History," so I put it in my *Napoleon For and Against*,⁴ "is an argument without end." The discussion is not fruitless, far from it. But every conclusion reached, helpful and satisfying as it may be, and seemingly well established, will lead to further questioning, which will reveal in it weak spots or unsuspected implications, and at any rate the debate will continue.

The ambitious systems, the philosophies of history as they used to be called, in which the whole of mankind's historic life was surveyed and the stages of development categorically indexed, do not really belong to this debate. They were derived by their authors from other sources than the patient and devoted contemplation of the past, sources which promised certainty. St. Augustine was inspired by the revelations and the prophecies of Holy Writ. In the eighteenth century the French philosophers deified Reason, but in their visions the past was fashioned so as to appear the predestined preparation of their earthly "heavenly city." ⁵ Hegel was in a way no more than a secularized St. Augustine. *His* conception of history, too, is of a *purposeful* development, its motive force, instead of the God of the Christians, being the Absolute, realizing itself. Hegel's influence was profound, and he taught generations of historians—especially, but by no means solely, in Germany—to present historical events as the inevitable and predetermined working out of ideas or currents governing the epochs. And then, in the nineteenth century, this conception of history, which had at first, in spite of its rationalist appearance, thrived on the support of the spirit of romanticism, entered into a very different, but perhaps even more powerful, alliance with science.

This was largely the doing of Comte. I shall here insert a few comments from *Use and Abuse of History*: ⁶

Comte, the father of positivism, had his own system of historical development, in so many stages, a system founded more exclusively than that of Hegel on science. The scientific method applied to history —this is his great contribution. "History," he wrote, with the confidence characteristic of so many philosophers, "has now been for the first time systematically considered as a whole and has been found, like other phenomena, subject to invariable laws."

The great task before the historian, he thought, must henceforth be to discover those laws. Given the ever-increasing prestige of science as the nineteenth century saw it advance from one great victory to another, historians must be tempted to tackle the job. To talk the language of science, to pride themselves on having applied its methods, became a habit with historians. The concepts of Darwin, for instance, intended for biology, were eagerly annexed for history. Marxism sailed merrily along on this same current. A pure positivist of Comte's school, Buckle, wrote the ambitious *History of Civilization in England,* which purported to show the laws by which the progress of civilization toward ever more complete enlightenment is governed. Buckle is now forgotten, but there was Taine, one of the most brilliant minds among historical writers in the second half of the century. In Taine's system, the influence of Comte predominates although fused with that of Hegel.

He solemnly declared history to be dominated by the three factors of race, surroundings, and moment, a formula which has a fine scientific ring about it, but which can be handled in almost any case with the most widely different results. In successive prefaces he asserted that man is an animal of a superior kind which produces philosophies more or less as silkworms make cocoons; that vice and virtue are products in the same way that vitriol or sugar are; that he regarded his subject, the transformation of French civilization in the course of the eighteenth century, with the eyes of a natural scientist observing the metamorphosis of an insect; while he presented his volume on the Reign of Terror as a treatise on "moral zoology." Renaissance, classicism, Alexandrine or Christian epoch—"there is here, as everywhere, nothing but a problem of mechanics." "What matters is," he wrote in a private letter twenty years after that statement, "a scientific opinion. My impressions don't count. What I want is to collaborate in a system of research which will in fifty years' time permit honest men to have something better than sentimental or egoistic impressions about the public affairs of their own day."

The fifty years have long passed (the letter was written in 1885), but although the mass of well-established facts relating to innumerable aspects of the past has constantly grown, and although the severest methods of sifting and testing, comparing and combining have been and are still being applied—although, in short, we historians have done and are still doing our best—few of us will nowadays maintain that the day is near when sentiment or egoism can be eliminated from the interpretation or presentation of the past.

The provocative crudity with which Taine expressed himself in these prefaces, and the glaring contradiction presented by the highly sensitive and personal quality, even violent partisanship, of the books they introduced to the public alienated many of his contemporaries. There was particularly Sainte-Beuve, who in the heyday of philosophic or systematized or symbolic history was in the habit of making comments of astringent and wholesome skepticism, to the effect that the individuality of the actor and the uniqueness of the event in history should not be forgotten, that the observer should humbly remember his human quality and not pretend to be in control of the fortuitous and the unforeseeable.

Today, at any rate, most of us know that it is not so simple. Large regions of history have no doubt proved suitable for methods of research which may be called scientific. The collaboration of historical scholars can yield valuable results. Yet, notwithstanding, or rather by very reason of, our half-century more of experience, we know that history will not so readily give up her secret at the bidding of the magic word "science." We have grown somewhat wary of this scientific terminology applied to history. The view of history as an organic development has proved extraordinarily fertile; it is still helpful, but it should not be thought that the word "organism" in its biological sense can represent a historical reality. It is no more than a metaphor; it is a token used for a working method. In Taine's own day, however, the spirit animating professions of faith such as the ones quoted exercised an influence not often leading to unconditional acceptance, but so extensive as to set a mark on the period, and this for the whole of the Western world. And, as a matter of fact, that spirit has by no means been cast out, nor has the mark been effaced.

"The spirit has not been cast out." It reigns supreme in the Communist world. At the International Historical Congress, held in Rome in 1955, there appeared a number of Russian historians, and several of them read papers. Their leader, Sidorov, was proud to affirm that "the materialistic conception of history has triumphed completely in our country and has the unanimous adherence of historians both of the younger and of the older generation." [7] I shall not enter into the question *how* unanimity has been achieved in a field that, in my opinion, ought to be dedicated to discussion. But what, in fact, we saw before us in Rome was an array of well-drilled historians all speaking of "we Soviet historians," "the school to which I belong, of historical materialism," and going on to treat us to an extraordinary display of "certainty." "The materialistic tradition has completely realized its possibilities in Marxism," Sidorov told us, "and it enabled Lenin to offer new explanations of all great events in Russian history and in modern world history." No less! And this new history is "scientific." "By adopting the materialistic conception of history," so Madame Pankratova tells us, "and only thus, can the laws of historical development be rightly understood and can we learn to apply them towards the solution of contemporary problems." Similarly Nikonov: "History has become a systematized science"; and he goes on to tell us how, by the light of "modern, progressive historical science," [8] Soviet historiography has succeeded in unravelling the mystery, by which bourgeois, or reactionary, historians still allow themselves to be baffled, of the causation of wars.

Nikonov then proceeds to explain to us the origins of World War II. The critical reader will soon be struck by the incredible bias of the account here presented, and he will notice that the real intention of the essay is to excuse the Russian rulers' action in concluding the pact with Hitler in August, 1939, and to lay the guilt for the outbreak of the war on the shoulders of the "reactionary" politicians of the West. The pretentious introduction and the talk about science and the laws of history are the merest make-believe. I have no doubt, however, but that the writer himself took this verbiage quite seriously. It helped him to convince himself of the impeccable accuracy of his garbled presentation of the episode. The magic word "science" made him feel virtuous; it confirmed him in his "certainty."

This is why scientism is practised so frequently, and this is why it is so dangerous.

It is practised, and it has always been practised, by conservatives as well as by progressives. To deduce from our "fallible understanding of a largely imaginary past or a wholly imaginary future" . . . . "some fixed pattern" in reality dictated by "absolute categories and ideals," is (I am paraphrasing Isaiah Berlin in his recent inaugural oration) "an attitude found in equal measure on the right and left wings in our days." [9] Comte's immediate progeny consisted largely of left-wingers, but I mentioned Taine, who, in the name of science, denounced the French Revolution. And I have before this called attention to the absolutist attitude of mind as well as to the deceptive appeal to science in writers like Sorokin and Toynbee, neither of whom can be regarded as left-wingers.

The system in which Sorokin ranges the civilizations rests on the distinction between ideational and sensate characteristics. In order to carry through and support that distinction, he shows tables for which, as I wrote in my essay "Prophets of Doom," [10]

the numbers of casualties in wars over twenty-five centuries have been estimated and compared; and so have the numbers of books or of paintings showing a prevalent percentage either of sensate or of ideational characteristics in any given period.

I must say that these immensely elaborate tables strike me as entirely unconvincing. To me it seems an illusion to think that so complicated, so many-sided, so protean and elusive a thing as a civilization can be reduced to the bare and simple language of rows and figures. The idea that by such a device the subjective factor in the final judgment can be eliminated is the worst illusion of all. The criteria by which the classifications are to be made cannot really reduce the humblest assistant to a machine (for much work is often left to assistants as if it were something mechanical or impersonal). When it comes to comparative statistics ranging over the whole history of the human race, does not Sorokin forget how scanty are the data for some periods, how unmanageably abundant for others? Is it possible, in using the statistical method, to guard against the difficulty presented by the fact that what survives from the remote past are mostly the thoughts and works of art of an élite, while in our view of our own age the activities and idiosyncrasies of the multitude take an infinitely larger, but perhaps a disproportionate, place? A balance has to be struck between these and many other aspects of history, that is to say, between the records of human activities in so many countries and in many ages, that are so scrappy, or again so full, so dissimilar, and mutually impossible to equate. The question imposes itself: Can anybody, in attempting this, claim that he is guided by the sure methods of science? Can he embrace with his mind the whole of that immense chaos and derive from it a conclusion which would be evident to every other human intellect, as would a proposition in Euclid?

I doubt it, or rather—I deny it.

Statistics are not often used by historians, as is done by Professor Sorokin, to support large theories about the world's future (a very dark one, in his view). But statistics are much in vogue with writers of social history nowadays, who believe that with their aid they can get away from the controversial problems raised by ideological differences and achieve objectivity. Now I am not arguing against statistics, nor am I, in a more general sense, contending that the methods of science can never be of any use in the study of man. What I am tilting at is the *undue* application of such methods, which is what I understand is meant by scientism. Statistics can be useful to the historian. To think, however, that by their means one can avoid ideological issues and make a short cut to objectivity seems to me a dangerous illusion. History can in that way only be devitalized. The historian should be very careful not to be imposed upon by the scientific appearance of an array of figures and of elaborate calculations based upon them, as if the reality of the past must now let itself be captured without fail. A striking instance of the deceptiveness of statistics in history was discussed by Professor Hexter in an essay on the great Tawney-Trevor Roper controversy about the gentry which appeared in last year's *Encounter*.

Toynbee, in his *Study of History*, does not deal in statistics so much, but occasionally he prints, to illustrate his argument, tables which are similarly intended to set upon it the mark of scientific precision and order. "It looks beautifully 'simple,'" was my comment on one such table in Volume IX.[11] "I shall say no more than that I have rarely seen a more arbitrary juggling with the facts of history."

Toynbee, the prophet of a world one in the love of God, provides a classic example of systematic scientism. This is what I had said about him a few years earlier: [12]

The worst of Toynbee's great attempt is that he has presented it under the patronage of a scientific terminology. A patently aprioristically-conceived, Augustinian-Spenglerian scheme of the history of mankind he wants to pass off as the product of the empirical method, built up out of what he calls facts, without troubling to analyze their precise nature or test their reliability for the purposes of system construction. When, in a radio debate with him in January, 1948, I remarked upon the bewildering multiplicity as well as baffling intangibility of historical data, he asked: "Is history really too hard a nut for science to crack?" and added: "The human intellect, sighs Geyl, 'is not sufficiently comprehensive.' " Of course I had not sighed; why should I sigh about what I regard as one of the fundamental truths of life? But Toynbee's rejoinder was: "We can't afford such defeatism; it is unworthy of the greatness of man's mind." In short, he belongs to those who obstinately blind themselves to the limitations of our comprehension of history.

In all my various essays devoted to *A Study of History* I have attempted to show the insufficiency, or the complete irrelevance, of Toynbee's pretended scientific arguments, formulations, and conclusions. Here, for instance, is a passage in which I derided his portentous use of the word "laws." In arguing that civilizations thrive on challenges, he admits that sometimes challenges are so severe as to be deadly. The growth of civilization, therefore, is best served by the "Golden Mean." Or, "in scientific terminology," what is needed is "a mean between a deficiency of severity and an excess of it." Now follows my comment: [13]

So here we have a "law," scientifically established, or at least scientifically formulated. But what next? When we try to apply it, we shall first of all discover that in every given historical situation it refers to only one element, out of many, one which, when we are concerned with historical presentation, cannot be abstracted from the others. Moreover, is it not essential to define what is too much and what too little, to stipulate where the golden mean lies? As to that, the "law" has nothing to say. That has to be defined anew each time by observation.

But indeed, these "laws" of Toynbee's, which in some cases he has had to formulate in so distressingly vague a manner, rest on very insecure foundations. They are, if we will take the author's word for it, the result of an investigation carefully proceeding from fact to fact. But what are facts in history?

I contend (so I wrote some years ago) [14] that his conception of what a historical fact really is, of what a historical fact is worth, of what can be done with it, is open to very grave objections.

Toynbee, with his immense learning, has a multitude of historical illustrations at his fingers' ends at every turn of his argument, and he discourses with never-failing brilliance and never-failing confidence on careers and personalities of statesmen or thinkers, on tendencies, movements of thought, social conditions, wars, customs of all countries and of all ages. Now the critical reader will feel that each single one of his cases might give rise to discussion. Each could be represented in a slightly or markedly different way so as no longer to substantiate his argument. They are not facts; they are subjective presentations of facts; they are combinations or interpretations of facts. As the foundations of an imposing superstructure of theory, they prove extraordinarily shifting and shaky, and this in spite of the dexterity and assurance with which Toynbee handles them.

Now let me say explicitly that I am far from wanting to confine history within the narrow bounds of the factual account. In another essay I wrote: [15]

I don't mean that the historian (as he is sometimes advised) should "stick to the facts": The facts are there to be used. Combinations, presentations, theories, are indispensable if we want to understand. But the historian should proceed cautiously in using the facts for these purposes. It goes without saying that he should try to ascertain the facts as exactly as possible; but the important thing is that he should remain conscious, even then, of the element of arbitrariness, of subjectivity, that necessarily enters into all combinations of facts, if only because one has to begin by selecting them; while next, one has to order them according to an idea which must, in part at least, be conceived in one's own mind.

The restrictions, the self-restraint, here indicated, are irksome to those who want to attain certainty or manage to persuade themselves that they have attained it. To me this acknowledgment of limitations seems imposed upon us by the nature of life itself. And let me add that I try to avoid being dogmatic here as well. I know that there will always remain a residuum of uncertainty. There will always remain matter for discussion. But at the same time, "this discussion does lead to a gradual, even though forever partial, conquest of reality." [16] When, in the exchange of thought at Sea Island, Professor Vivas suggested that in the sciences of man you cannot distinguish between *the true* and *the pseudo* as you can in physical science, I was not prepared to follow him.

I do not, of course (so, more or less, ran my reply), dispute that history does not yield absolute and unquestionable results. There are, and there will always be, contending schools, not one of which can claim to represent history to the exclusion of the others. But they can, all of them, be united by a respect for the true method. And by the true method I simply mean what was described by Professor Werkmeister as "the scholarly punctiliousness in dealing with facts, the desire to provide rational explanations on sound, logical, or, simply, honest, argumentation." In contradistinction to this, history, that is, a view or an interpretation of the past, can be so dominated by fanaticism, by an emotion, by the craving for a system, by the desire to make it a preface to the future, or rather to the picture of the future of which the historian's mind is full, by detestation, also, of the world and of the direction in which it seems to be moving—that all these safeguards of the true method are thrown to the winds. The past, of course, cannot protest. The unscrupulous historian can fashion it after his fancy. And the myths which are created in this way can have practical effects of the most disturbing or pernicious nature. But the application of unsound methods can be detected, and I regard it as one of the historical scholar's obligations towards the community that he should do what he can to expose such "abuse of history."

I have, in my time, waged a good many fights against what I

considered to be pseudo history. I was moved, I hope, by a genuine regard for true history, but also, undoubtedly (and I do not think that I have any cause to apologize), by a wish to counter the evil influences which I observed that the false presentations of history were having in the present, by detestation of the particular prejudices or passions which I detected behind them. First, I attacked the misconception of Netherlands history by which it was intended to erect a barrier between the Dutch and the Flemings.[17] Then it was national-socialist historiography that drew my fire.[18] Since the last war it has been particularly the gloomy prognostications about Western civilization and the blithe universalist visions, the tendency of which I regard as no less perniciously defeatist. In all these cases I discerned that the effect was obtained by distortions, omissions, fantasies, which did not stand the test of criticism in accordance with the true historical method. Scientism, not always, but frequently, supplied some of the defective links which were needed to make the argument hang together on paper.

History is one of the great conserving forces of our civilization; and it also provides guidance, indispensable if never categoric, in our laborious and adventurous progress towards the unknown future. But in order to fulfill its function, history should stick to its own laws.

NOTES

1. "De Vitaliteit van de Westerse Beschaving" (1958), English translation, "The Vitality of Western Civilization," *Delta* (Amsterdam: 1959, quarterly). The essay will be included in a volume entitled *Excursions and Encounters in History* to be published by Meridian Books, New York, in 1960.
2. Pieter Geyl, *Use and Abuse of History* (New Haven: Yale University Press, 1955).
3. See *From Ranke to Toynbee,* Smith College Historical Series (1952); or *Debates with Historians* (1955), (paperback edition, 1958).
4. Pieter Geyl, *Napoleon For and Against* (Cape, London, and Yale University Press, 1949), p. 16.
5. See Carl Becker, *The Heavenly City of the Eighteenth Century Philosophers* (1932).
6. *Loc. cit.,* pp. 45-49.
7. *Relazioni* (of the Historical Congress at Rome), VI, 391. English version in *Editions de l'Académie des Sciences de l'URSS* (1955), p. 209.

8. See *Editions de l'Académie des Sciences de l'URSS* (1955), p. 53.
9. Isaiah Berlin, *Two Concepts of Liberty* (Oxford, 1958), p. 56.
10. Pieter Geyl, "Prophets of Doom," *Virginia Quarterly* (1950); see *Debates with Historians*, p. 134.
11. Pieter Geyl, "Toynbee the Prophet," *Journal of the History of Ideas* (New York, 1955); see *Debates with Historians*, p. 175.
12. Pieter Geyl, *Use and Abuse of History* (New Haven: Yale University Press, 1955).
13. Pieter Geyl, "Toynbee's Systeem der Beschavingen," *Verslag van het historisch Genootschap* (1950); English version in *Journal of the History of Ideas* (1949); see *Debates with Historians*, pp. 101-102.
14. Pieter Geyl, "Prophets of Doom"; see *Debates with Historians*, p. 140.
15. *Ibid.*
16. Pieter Geyl, *Use and Abuse of History* (New Haven: Yale University Press, 1955).
17. See the "National State and the Writers of Netherland History," *Debates with Historians*, pp. 179-197.
18. See, for instance, essays on German works edited respectively by H. Klosz and R. P. Oszwald, also on Steding and on Rauschning, published in various Dutch reviews 1938, 1939, and before May, 1940, and republished in *Historicus in de Tijd* (1954).

8

The Mantle of Science

Murray N. Rothbard

In our proper condemnation of scientism in the study of man, we should not make the mistake of dismissing *science* as well. For if we do so, we credit scientism too highly and accept at face value its claim to be the one and only scientific method. If scientism is, as we believe it to be, an improper method, then it cannot be truly scientific. Science, after all, means *scientia,* correct knowledge; it is older and wiser than the positivist-pragmatist attempt to monopolize the term.

Scientism is the profoundly unscientific attempt to transfer uncritically the methodology of the physical sciences to the study of human action. Both fields of inquiry must, it is true, be studied by the use of reason—the mind's identification of reality. But then it becomes crucially important, in reason, not to neglect the critical attribute of human action: that, alone in nature, human beings possess a rational consciousness. Stones, molecules, planets cannot *choose* their courses; their behavior is strictly and mechanically determined for them. Only human beings possess free will and consciousness: for they are conscious, and they can, and indeed must, choose their course of action.[1] To ignore this primordial fact about the nature of man—to ignore his volition, his free will—is to misconstrue the facts of reality and therefore to be profoundly and radically unscientific.

Man's necessity to choose means that, at any given time, he is

159

acting to bring about some *end* in the immediate or distant future, i.e., that he has purposes. The steps that he takes to achieve his ends are his *means*. Man is born with no innate knowledge of what ends to choose or how to use which means to attain them. Having no inborn knowledge of how to survive and prosper, he must learn what ends and means to adopt, and he is liable to make errors along the way. But only his reasoning mind can show him his goals and how to attain them.

We have already begun to build the first blocks of the many-storied edifice of the true sciences of man—and they are all grounded on the fact of man's volition.[2] On the formal fact that man uses means to attain ends we ground the science of *praxeology,* or economics; *psychology* is the study of how and why man chooses the contents of his ends; *technology* tells what concrete means will lead to various ends; and *ethics* employs all the data of the various sciences to guide man toward the ends he should seek to attain, and therefore, by imputation, toward his proper means. None of these disciplines can make any sense whatever on scientistic premises. If men are like stones, if they are not purposive beings and do not strive for ends, then there is no economics, no psychology, no ethics, no technology, no science of man whatever.

1. The Problem of Free Will

Before proceeding further, we must pause to consider the validity of free will, for it is curious that the determinist dogma has so often been accepted as the uniquely scientific position. And while many philosophers have demonstrated the existence of free will, the concept has all too rarely been applied to the "social sciences."

In the first place, each human being knows universally from introspection that he chooses. The positivists and behaviorists may scoff at introspection all they wish, but it remains true that the introspective knowledge of a conscious man that he is conscious and acts is a fact of reality. What, indeed, do the determinists have to offer to set against introspective fact? Only a poor and misleading analogy from the physical sciences. It is true that all mindless matter is determined and purposeless. But it is highly inappropriate, and moreover question-begging, simply and uncritically to apply the model of physics to man.

Why, indeed, should we accept determinism in nature? The reason we say that things are determined is that every existing thing must have a *specific* existence. Having a *specific* existence, it must have certain definite, definable, delimitable attributes, i.e., every thing must have a specific *nature*. Every being, then, can act or behave only in accordance with its nature, and any two beings can interact only in accord with their respective natures. Therefore, the actions of every being are caused by, determined by, its nature.[3]

But while most things have no consciousness and therefore pursue no goals, it is an essential attribute of *man's* nature that he has consciousness, and therefore that his actions are self-determined by the choices his mind makes.

At very best, the application of determinism to man is just an agenda for the future. After several centuries of arrogant proclamations, no determinist has come up with anything like a theory determining all of men's actions. Surely the burden of proof must rest on the one advancing a theory, particularly when the theory contradicts man's primary impressions. Surely we can, at the very least, tell the determinists to keep quiet until they can offer their determinations—including, of course, their advance determinations of each of our reactions to their determining theory. But there is far more that can be said. For determinism, as applied to man, is a self-contradictory thesis, since the man who employs it relies implicitly on the existence of free will. If we are determined in the ideas we accept, then X, the determinist, is determined to believe in determinism, while Y, the believer in free will, is also determined to believe in his own doctrine. Since man's mind is, according to determinism, not free to think and come to conclusions about reality, it is absurd for X to try to convince Y or anyone else of the truth of determinism. In short, the determinist must rely, for the spread of his ideas, on the nondetermined, free-will choices of others, on their free will to adopt or reject ideas.[4] In the same way, the various brands of determinists—behaviorists, positivists, Marxists, etc.—implicitly claim special exemption for themselves from their own determined systems.[5] But if a man cannot affirm a proposition without employing its negation, he is not only caught in an inextricable self-contradiction; *he is conceding to the negation the status of an axiom.*[6]

A corollary self-contradiction: the determinists profess to be able, some day, to determine what man's choices and actions will be. But, on their own grounds, their own knowledge of this determining theory is itself determined. How then can they aspire to know *all*, if the extent of their *own* knowledge is itself determined, and therefore arbitrarily delimited? In fact, if our ideas are determined, then we have no way of freely revising our judgments and of learning truth—whether the truth of determinism or of anything else.[7]

Thus, the determinist, to advocate his doctrine, must place himself and his theory outside the allegedly universally determined realm, i.e., he must employ free will. This reliance of determinism on its negation is an instance of a wider truth: that it is self-contradictory to use reason in any attempt to deny the validity of reason as a means of attaining knowledge. Such self-contradiction is implicit in such currently fashionable sentiments as "reason shows us that reason is weak," or "the more we know, the more we know how little we know." [8]

Some may object that man is not really free because he must obey natural laws. To say that man is not free because he is not able to do anything he may possibly desire, however, confuses freedom and power.[9] It is clearly absurd to employ as a definition of "freedom" the power of an entity to perform an impossible action, to violate its nature.[10]

Determinists often imply that a man's ideas are necessarily determined by the ideas of others, of "society." Yet A and B can hear the same idea propounded; A can adopt it as valid while B will not. Each man, therefore, has the free choice of adopting or not adopting an idea or value. It is true that many men may uncritically adopt the ideas of others; yet this process cannot regress infinitely. At some point in time, the idea originated, i.e., the idea was *not* taken from others, but was arrived at by some mind independently and creatively. This is logically necessary for any given idea. "Society," therefore, cannot dictate ideas. If someone grows up in a world where people generally believe that "all redheads are demons," he is free, as he grows up, to rethink the problem and arrive at a different conclusion. If this were not true, ideas, once adopted, could never have been changed.

We conclude, therefore, that true science decrees determinism for physical nature and free will for man, and for the same reason: that every thing must act in accordance with its specific nature. And since men are free to adopt ideas and to act upon them, it is never events or stimuli external to the mind that *cause* its ideas; rather the mind freely adopts ideas about external events. A savage, an infant, and a civilized man will each react in entirely different ways to the sight of the same stimulus—be it a fountain pen, an alarm clock, or a machine gun, for each mind has different ideas about the object's meaning and qualities.[11] Let us therefore never again say that the Great Depression of the 1930's *caused* men to adopt socialism or interventionism (or that poverty *causes* people to adopt Communism). The depression existed, and men were moved to think about this striking event; but that they adopted socialism or its equivalent as the way out was not determined by the event; they might just as well have chosen laissez faire or Buddhism or any other attempted solution. The deciding factor was the *idea* that people chose to adopt.

What *led* the people to adopt particular ideas? Here the historian may enumerate and weigh various factors, but he must always stop short at the ultimate freedom of the will. Thus, in any given matter, a person may freely decide either to think about a problem independently or to accept uncritically the ideas offered by others. Certainly, the bulk of the people, especially in abstract matters, choose to follow the ideas offered by the intellectuals. At the time of the Great Depression, there were a host of intellectuals offering the nostrum of statism or socialism as a cure for the depression, while very few suggested laissez faire or absolute monarchy.

The realization that ideas, freely adopted, determine social institutions, and not vice versa, illuminates many critical areas of the study of man. Rousseau and his host of modern followers, who hold that man is good, but corrupted by his institutions, must finally wither under the query: And who but *men* created these institutions? The tendency of many modern intellectuals to worship the primitive (also the childlike—especially the child "progressively" educated—the "natural" life of the noble savage of the South Seas, etc.) has perhaps the same roots. We are also told repeatedly that differences between largely isolated tribes and ethnic groups are "culturally determined": tribe X being intelligent or peaceful because of its X-culture; tribe Y, dull or warlike because of Y-culture. If we fully realize that the men of each tribe created its own culture (unless we are to assume its creation by some mystic *deus ex machina*), we see that this popular "explanation" is no better than explaining the sleep-inducing properties of opium by its "dormitive power." Indeed, it is worse, because it adds the error of social determinism.

It will undoubtedly be charged that this discussion of free will and determinism is "one-sided" and that it leaves out the alleged fact that all of life is multicausal and interdependent. We must not forget, however, that the very goal of science is simpler explanations of wider phenomena. In this case, we are confronted with the fact that there can logically be only one *ultimate sovereign* over a man's actions: either his own free will or some cause outside that will. There is no other alternative, there is no middle ground, and therefore the fashionable eclecticism of modern scholarship must in this case yield to the hard realities of the Law of the Excluded Middle.

If free will has been vindicated, how can we prove the existence of consciousness itself? The answer is simple: to *prove* means to make evident something not yet evident. Yet some propositions may be already evident to the self, i.e., self-evident. A self-evident axiom, as we have indicated, will be a proposition which cannot be contradicted without employing the axiom itself in the attempt. And the existence of consciousness is not only evident to all of us through direct introspection, but is also a fundamental axiom, for the very act of doubting consciousness must itself be performed by a consciousness.[12] Thus, the behaviorist who spurns consciousness for "objective" laboratory data must rely on the consciousness of his laboratory associates to report the data to him.

The key to scientism is its denial of the existence of individual consciousness and will.[13] This takes two main forms: applying mechanical analogies from the physical sciences to individual men, and applying organismic analogies to such fictional collective wholes as "society." The latter course attributes consciousness and will, not to individuals, but to some collective organic whole of which the individual is merely a determined cell. Both methods are aspects of the rejection of individual consciousness.

2. *The False Mechanical Analogies of Scientism*

The scientistic method in the study of man is almost wholly one of building on analogies from the physical sciences. Some of the common mechanistic analogies follow.

Man as Servomechanism: Just as Bertrand Russell, one of the leaders of scientism, reverses reality by attributing determinism to men, and free will to physical particles, so it has recently become the fashion to say that modern machines "think," while man is merely a complex form of machine, or "servomechanism." [14] What is overlooked here is that machines, no matter how complex, are simply devices made by man to serve man's purposes and goals; their actions are preset by their creators, and the machines can never act in any other way or suddenly adopt new goals and act upon them. They cannot do so, finally, because the machines are not alive and are therefore certainly not conscious. If men are machines, on the other hand, then the determinists, in addition to meeting the above critique, must answer the question: Who created *men* and for what purpose?—a rather embarrassing question for materialists to answer.[15]

Social Engineering: This term implies that men are no different from stones or other physical objects, and therefore that they should be blueprinted and reshaped in the same way as objects by "social" engineers. When Rex Tugwell wrote in his famous poem during the flush days of the New Deal:

> I have gathered my tools and my charts,
> My plans are finished and practical.
> I shall roll up my sleeves—make America over,

one wonders whether his admiring readers thought themselves to be among the directing engineers or among the raw material that would be "made over." [16]

Model-Building: Economics, and recently political science, have been beset by a plague of "model-building." [17] People do not construct theories any more; they "build" models of the society or economy. Yet no one seems to notice the peculiar inaptness of the concept. An engineering model is an exact replica, in miniature, i.e., in exact quantitative proportion, of the relationships existing in the given structure in the real world; but the "models" of economic and political theory are simply a few equations and concepts which, at very best, could only approximate a few of the numerous relations in the economy or society.

Measurement: The Econometric Society's original motto was "Science is measurement," this ideal having been transferred intact from the natural sciences. The frantic and vain attempts to measure intensive psychic magnitudes in psychology and in economics would disappear if it were realized that the very concept of measurement implies the necessity for an objective *extensive* unit to serve as a measure. But the magnitudes in consciousness are necessarily *intensive* and therefore not capable of measurement.[18]

The Mathematical Method: Not only measurement, but the use of mathematics in general, in the social sciences and philosophy today is an illegitimate transfer from physics. In the first place, a mathematical equation implies the existence of quantities that can be equated, which in turn implies a unit of measurement for these quantities. Secondly, mathematical relations are *functional;* i.e., variables are interdependent, and identifying the causal variable depends on which is held as given and which is changed. This methodology is appropriate in physics, where entities do not themselves provide the causes for their actions, but instead are determined by discoverable quantitative laws of their nature and the nature of the interacting entities. But in human action, the free-will choice of the human consciousness is the cause, and this cause generates certain effects. The mathematical concept of interdetermining "function" is therefore inappropriate.

Indeed, the very concept of "variable" used so frequently in econometrics is illegitimate, for physics is able to arrive at laws only by discovering *constants*. The concept of "variable" only makes sense if there are some things that are *not* variable, but constant. Yet in human action, free will precludes any quantitative constants (including constant units of measurement). All attempts to discover such constants (such as the strict quantity theory of money or the Keynesian "consumption function") were inherently doomed to failure.

Finally, such staples of mathematical economics as the calculus are completely inappropriate for human action because they assume infinitely small continuity; while such concepts may legitimately describe the completely determined path of a physical particle, they are seriously misleading in describing the willed action of a human being. Such willed action can occur only in discrete, non-infinitely-small steps, steps large enough to be perceivable by a human consciousness. Hence the continuity assumptions of calculus are inappropriate for the study of man.

Other metaphors bodily and misleadingly transplanted from physics include: "equilibrium," "elasticity," "statics and dynamics," "velocity of circulation," and "friction." "Equilibrium" in physics is a state in which an entity remains; but in economics or politics there is never really such an equilibrium state existing; there is but a *tendency* in that direction. Moreover, the term "equilibrium" has emotional connotations, and so it was only a brief step to the further mischief of holding up equilibrium as not only possible, but as the ideal by which to gauge all existing institutions. But since man, by his very nature, must keep acting, he cannot be in equilibrium while he lives, and therefore the ideal, being impossible, is also inappropriate.

The concept of "friction" is used in a similar way. Some economists, for example, have assumed that men have "perfect knowledge," that the factors of production have "perfect mobility," etc., and then have airily dismissed all difficulties in applying these absurdities to the real world as simple problems of "friction," just as the physical sciences bring in friction to add to their "perfect" framework. These assumptions in fact make *omniscience* the standard or ideal, and this cannot exist by the nature of man.

3. *The False Organismic Analogies of Scientism*

The organismic analogies attribute consciousness, or other organic qualities, to "social wholes" which are really only labels for the interrelations of individuals.[19] Just as in the mechanistic metaphors, individual men are subsumed and determined, here they become mindless cells in some sort of social organism. While few people today would assert flatly that "society is an organism," most social theorists hold doctrines that imply this. Note, for example, such phrases as: "Society determines the values of its individual members"; or "The culture determines the actions of individual members"; or "The individual's actions are determined by the role he plays in the group to which he belongs," etc. Such concepts as "the public good," "the common good," "social welfare," etc., are also endemic. All these concepts rest on the implicit premise that there exists, somewhere, a living organic entity known as "society," "the group," "the public," "the community," and that that entity has values and pursues ends.

Not only are these terms held up as living entities; they are supposed to exist *more* fundamentally than mere individuals, and certainly "their" goals take precedence over individual ones. It is ironic that the self-proclaimed apostles of "science" should pursue the sheer mysticism of assuming the living reality of these concepts.[20] Such concepts as "public good," "general welfare," etc., should, therefore, be discarded as grossly unscientific, and the next time someone preaches the priority of "public good" over the individual good, we must ask: Who *is* the "public" in this case? We must remember that in the slogan justifying the public debt that rose to fame in the 1930's: "We owe it only to ourselves," it makes a big difference for every man whether he is a member of the "we" or of the "ourselves." [21]

A similar fallacy is committed, alike by friends and by foes of the market economy, when the market is called "impersonal." Thus, people often complain that the market is too "impersonal" because it does not grant to them a greater share of worldly goods. It is overlooked that the "market" is not some sort of living entity making good or bad decisions, but is simply a label for individual persons and their voluntary interactions. If A thinks that the "impersonal market" is not paying him enough, he is *really* saying that individuals B, C, and D are not willing to pay him as much as he would like to receive. The "market" is individuals acting. Similarly, if B thinks that the "market" is not paying A enough, B is perfectly free to step in and supply the difference. He is not blocked in this effort by some monster named "market."

One example of the widespread use of the organismic fallacy is in discussions of international trade. Thus, during the gold-standard era, how often did the cry go up that "England" or "France" or some other country was in mortal danger because "it" was "losing gold"? What was actually happening was that English*men* or French*men* were voluntarily shipping gold overseas and thus threatening the banks in those countries with the necessity of meeting obligations (to pay in gold) which they could not possibly fulfill. But the use of the organismic metaphor converted a grave problem of banking into a vague national crisis for which every citizen was somehow responsible.[22]

So far we have been discussing those organismic concepts which assume the existence of a fictive consciousness in some collective whole. There are also numerous examples of other misleading biological analogies in the study of man. We hear much, for example, of "young" and "old" nations, as if an American aged twenty is somehow "younger" than a Frenchman of the same age. We read of "mature economies," as if an economy must grow rapidly and then become "mature." The current fashion of an "economics of growth" presumes that every economy is somehow destined, like a living organism, to "grow" in some predetermined manner at a definite rate. (In the enthusiasm it is overlooked that too many economies "grow" backward.) That all of these analogies are attempts to negate individual will and consciousness has been pointed out by Mrs. Penrose. Referring to biological analogies as applied to business firms, she writes:

. . . where explicit biological analogies crop up in economics they are drawn exclusively from that aspect of biology which deals with the nonmotivated behavior of organisms . . . So it is with the life-cycle analogy. We have no reason whatever for thinking that the growth pattern of a biological organism is *willed* by the organism itself. On the other hand, we have every reason for thinking that the growth of a firm is willed by those who make the decisions of the firm . . . and the proof of this lies in the fact that no one can describe the development of any given firm . . . except in terms of decisions taken by individual men.[23]

4. *Axioms and Deduction*

The fundamental axiom, then, for the study of man is the existence of individual consciousness, and we have seen the numerous ways in which scientism tries to reject or avoid this axiom. Not being omniscient, a man must learn; he must ever adopt ideas and act upon them, choosing ends and the means to attain these ends. Upon this simple fundamental axiom a vast deductive edifice can be constructed. Professor von Mises has already done this for economics, which he has subsumed under the science of praxeology: this centers on the universal formal fact that all men use means for chosen ends, without investigating the processes of the concrete choices or the justification for them. Mises has shown that the entire structure of economic thought can be deduced from this axiom (with the help of a very few subsidiary axioms.)[24]

Since the fundamental and other axioms are qualitative by nature, it follows that the propositions deduced by the laws of logic from these axioms are also qualitative. The laws of human action are therefore qualitative, and in fact, it should be clear that free will precludes quantitative laws. Thus, we may set forth the absolute economic law that an increase in the supply of a good, given the demand, will lower its price; but if we attempted to prescribe with similar generality *how much* the price would fall, given a definite increase in supply, we would shatter against the free-will rock of varying valuations by different individuals.

It goes without saying that the axiomatic-deductive method has been in disrepute in recent decades, in all disciplines but mathematics and formal logic—and even here the axioms are often supposed to be a mere convention rather than necessary truth. Few discussions of the history of philosophy or scientific method fail to make the ritual attacks on old-fashioned argumentation from self-evident principles. And yet the disciples of scientism themselves implicitly assume as self-evident *not* what cannot be contradicted, but simply that the methodology of physics is the only truly scientific methodology. This methodology, briefly, is to look at facts, then frame ever more general hypotheses to account for the facts, and then to test these hypotheses by experimentally verifying other deductions made from them. But this method is appropriate only in the physical sciences, where we begin by knowing external sense data and then proceed to our task of trying to find, as closely as we can, the causal laws of behavior of the entities we perceive. We have no way of knowing these laws directly; but fortunately we may verify them by performing controlled laboratory experiments to test propositions deduced from them. In these experiments we can vary one factor, while keeping all other relevant factors constant. Yet the process of accumulating knowledge in physics is always rather tenuous; and, as has happened, as we become more and more abstract, there is greater possibility that some other explanation will be devised which fits more of the observed facts and which may then replace the older theory.

In the study of human action, on the other hand, the proper procedure is the reverse. Here we *begin* with the primary axioms; we know that men are the causal agents, that the ideas they adopt by free will govern their actions. We therefore begin by fully knowing the abstract axioms, and we may then build upon them by logical deduction, introducing a few subsidiary axioms to limit the range of the study to the concrete applications we care about. Furthermore, in human affairs, the existence of free will prevents us from conducting any controlled experiments; for people's ideas and valuations are continually subject to change, and therefore nothing can be held constant. The proper theoretical methodology in human affairs, then, is the axiomatic-deductive method. The laws deduced by this method are *more,* not less, firmly grounded than the laws of physics; for since the ultimate causes are known directly as true, their consequents are also true.

One of the reasons for the scientistic hatred of the axiomatic-deductive method is historical. Thus, Dr. E. C. Harwood, inveterate battler for the pragmatic method in economics and the social sciences, criticizes von Mises as follows:

Like the Greeks, Dr. Von Mises disparages change. "Praxeology is not concerned with the changing content of acting, but with its pure form and categorial structure." No one who appreciates the long struggle of man toward more adequate knowing would criticize Aristotle for his adoption of a similar viewpoint 2,000 years ago, but, after all, that *was* 2,000 years ago; surely economists can do better than seek light on their subject from a beacon that was extinguished by the Galilean revolution in the 17th century.[25]

Apart from the usual pragmatist antagonism to the apodictic laws of logic, this quotation embodies a typical historiographic myth. The germ of truth in the historical picture of the noble Galileo *versus* the antiscientific Church consists largely in two important errors of Aristotle: (a) he thought of physical entities as acting teleologically, and thus in a sense as being causal agents; and (b) he necessarily had no knowledge of the experimental method, which had not yet been developed, and therefore thought that the axiomatic-deductive-qualitative method was the only one appropriate to the *physical* as well as to the human sciences. When the seventeenth century enthroned quantitative laws and laboratory methods, the partially justified repudiation of Aristotle in physics was followed by the unfortunate expulsion of Aristotle and his methodology from the human sciences as well.[26] This is true apart from historical findings that the Scholastics of the Middle Ages were the forerunners, rather than the obscurantist enemies, of experimental physical science.[27]

One example of concrete law deduced from our fundamental

axiom is as follows: Since all action is determined by the choice of the actor, any particular act demonstrates a person's preference for this action. From this it follows that if A and B voluntarily agree to make an exchange (whether the exchange be material or spiritual), both parties are doing so because they expect to benefit. [28]

5. *Science and Values: Arbitrary Ethics*

Having discussed the properly scientific, as contrasted to the scientistic, approach to the study of man, we may conclude by briefly considering the age-old question of the relationship between science and values. Ever since Max Weber, the dominant position in the social sciences, at least *de jure,* has been *Wertfreiheit:* that science itself must not make value judgments, but confine itself to judgments of fact, since ultimate ends can be only sheer personal preference not subject to rational argument. The classical philosophical view that a rational (i.e., in the broad sense of the term, a "scientific") ethic is possible has been largely discarded. As a result, the critics of *Wertfreiheit,* having dismissed the possibility of rational ethics as a separate discipline, have taken to smuggling in arbitrary, *ad hoc* ethical judgments through the back door of each particular science of man. The current fashion is to preserve a façade of *Wertfreiheit,* while casually adopting value judgments, not as the scientist's own decision, but as the consensus of the values of others. Instead of choosing his own ends and valuing accordingly, the scientist supposedly maintains his neutrality by adopting the values of the bulk of society. In short, to set forth one's own values is now considered biased and "nonobjective," while to adopt uncritically the slogans of other people is the height of "objectivity." Scientific objectivity no longer means a man's pursuit of truth wherever it may lead, but abiding by a Gallup poll of other, less informed subjectivities.[29]

The attitude that value judgments are self-evidently correct because "the people" hold them permeates social science. The social scientist often claims that he is merely a technician, advising his clients—the public—how to attain their ends, whatever they may be. And he believes that he thereby can take a value position without really committing himself to any values of his own. An example from a recent public finance textbook (an area where the economic scientist must constantly confront ethical problems):

The present-day justification for the ability principle (among economists) is simply the fact that . . . it is in accord with consensus of attitudes toward equity in the distribution of real income and of tax burden. Equity questions always involve value judgments, and tax structures can be evaluated, from an equity standpoint, only in terms of their relative conformity with the consensus of thought in the particular society with respect to equity.[30]

But the scientist cannot thereby escape making value judgments of his own. A man who knowingly advises a criminal gang on the best means of safe-cracking is thereby implicitly endorsing the end: safe-cracking. He is an accessory before the fact. An economist who advises the public on the most efficient method of obtaining economic equality is endorsing the end of economic equality. The economist who advises the Federal Reserve System how most expeditiously to manage the economy is thereby endorsing the existence of the system and its aim of stabilization. A political scientist who advises a government bureau on how to reorganize its staff for greater efficiency (or less inefficiency) is thereby endorsing the existence and the success of that bureau. To be convinced of this, consider what the proper course would be for an economist who *opposes* the existence of the Federal Reserve System, or the political scientist who would like to see the liquidation of the bureau. Wouldn't he be betraying his principles if he helped what he is against to become more efficient? Wouldn't his proper course either be to refuse to advise it, or perhaps to try to promote its *in*efficiency—on the grounds of the classic remark by a great American industrialist (speaking of government corruption): "Thank God that we don't get as much goverment as we pay for"?

It should be realized that values do not become true or legitimate because many people hold them; and their popularity does not make them self-evident. Economics abounds in instances of arbitrary values smuggled into works the authors of which would never think of engaging in ethical analysis or propounding an ethical system. The virtue of equality, as we have indicated, is simply taken for granted without justification; and it is established, not by sense perception of reality or by showing that its negation is self-contradictory—the true criteria of self-evidence—but by assuming that anyone who disagrees is a knave and a rogue. Taxation is a realm where arbitrary values flourish, and we may illustrate by analyzing the most hallowed and surely the most commonsensical of all tax ethics: some of Adam Smith's famous canons of "justice" in taxation.[31] These canons have since been treated as self-evident gospel in practically every work on public finance. Take, for example, the canon that the costs of collection of any tax be kept to a minimum. Obvious enough to include in the most *wertfrei* treatise? Not at all—for we must not overlook the point of view of the *tax collectors*. They will favor high administrative costs of taxation, simply because high costs mean greater opportunities for bureaucratic employment. On what possible grounds can we call the bureaucrat "wrong" or "unjust"? Certainly no ethical system has been offered. Furthermore, if the tax itself is considered bad on other grounds, then the opponent of the tax may well favor high administrative costs on the ground that there will then be less chance for the tax to do damage by being fully collected.

Consider another seemingly obvious Smith canon, viz., that a tax be levied so that payment is convenient. But again, this is by no means self-evident. Opponents of a tax, for example, may want the tax to be made purposely inconvenient so as to induce the people to rebel against the levy. Or another: that a tax be certain and not arbitrary, so that the taxpayers know what they will have to pay. But here again, further analysis raises many problems. For some may argue that uncertainty positively benefits the taxpayers, for it makes requirements more flexible, thus allowing more room for possible bribery of the tax collector. Another popular maxim is that a tax be framed to make it difficult to evade. But again, if a tax is considered unjust, evasion might be highly beneficial, economically and morally.

The purpose of these strictures has not been to defend high

costs of tax collection, inconvenient taxes, bribery, or evasion, but to show that even the tritest bits of ethical judgments in economics are completely illegitimate. And they are illegitimate whether one believes in *Wertfreiheit* or in the possibility of a rational ethic: for such *ad hoc* ethical judgments violate the canons of either school. They are neither *wertfrei* nor are they supported by any systematic analysis.

6. *Conclusion:*
Individualism vs. Collectivism in the Study of Man

Surveying the attributes of the proper science of man as against scientism, one finds a shining, clear thread separating one from the other. The true science of man bases itself upon the *existence of individual human beings,* upon individual life and consciousness. The scientistic brethren (dominant in modern times) range themselves always against the meaningful existence of individuals: the biologists deny the existence of life, the psychologists deny consciousness, the economists deny economics, and the political theorists deny political philosophy. What they *affirm* is the existence and primacy of social wholes: "society," the "collective," the "group," the "nation." The individual, they assert, must be value-free himself, but must take his values from "society." The true science of man concentrates on the individual as of central, epistemological and ethical importance; the adherents of scientism, in contrast, lose no opportunity to denigrate the individual and submerge him in the importance of the collective. With such radically contrasting epistemologies, it is hardly sheer coincidence that the political views of the two opposing camps tend to be individualist and collectivist, respectively.

NOTES

1. Human action, therefore, does not occur apart from cause; human beings *must* choose at any given moment, although the contents of the choice are *self*-determined.
2. The sciences which deal with the functioning of man's automatic organs —physiology, anatomy, etc.—may be included in the physical sciences,

for they are not based on man's will—although even here, psychosomatic medicine traces definite causal relations stemming from man's choices.

3. *See* Andrew G. Van Melsen, *The Philosophy of Nature* (Pittsburgh: Duquesne University Press, 1953), pp. 208 ff., 235 ff.

    While free will must be upheld for man, determinism must be equally upheld for physical nature. For a critique of the recent fallacious notion, based on the Heisenberg Uncertainty Principle, that atomic or subatomic partices have "free will," see Ludwig von Mises, *Theory and History* (New Haven: Yale University Press, 1957), pp. 87-92; and Albert H. Hobbs, *Social Problems and Scientism* (Harrisburg: The Stackpole Company, 1953), pp. 220-232.

4. "Even the controversial writings of the mechanists themselves appear to be intended for readers endowed with powers of choice. In other words, the determinist who would win others to his way of thinking must write as if he himself, and his readers at least, had freedom of choice, while all the rest of mankind are mechanistically determined in thought and in conduct." Francis L. Harmon, *Principles of Psychology* (Milwaukee: The Bruce Publishing Company, 1938), p. 497, and pp. 493-499. *Also see* Joseph D. Hassett, S.J., Robert A. Mitchell, S.J., and J. Donald Monan, S.J., *The Philosophy of Human Knowing* (Westminster, Md.: The Newman Press, 1953), pp. 71-72.

5. *See* Mises, *op. cit.,* pp. 258-260; and Mises, *Human Action* (New Haven: Yale University Press, 1949), pp. 74 ff.

6. Phillips therefore calls this attribute of an axiom a "boomerang principle . . . for even though we cast it away from us, it returns to us again," and illustrates by showing that an attempt to deny the Aristotelian law of noncontradiction must end by assuming it. R. P. Phillips, *Modern Thomistic Philosophy* (Westminster, Md.: The Newman Bookshop, 1934-35), II, 36-37. *Also see* John J. Toohey, S.J., *Notes on Epistemology* (Washington, D. C.: Georgetown University, 1952), *passim,* and Murray N. Rothbard, "In Defense of 'Extreme Apriorism,'" *Southern Economic Journal,* January, 1957, p. 318.

7. In the course of a critique of determinism, Phillips wrote: "What purpose . . . could advice serve if we were unable to revise a judgment we had formed, and so act in a different way to which we at first intended?" Phillips, *op. cit.,* I, 282.

    For stress on free will as freedom to think, to employ reason, *see* Robert L. Humphrey, "Human Nature in American Thought," *Political Science Quarterly,* June, 1954, p. 269; J. F. Leibell, ed., *Readings in Ethics* (Chicago: Loyola University Press, 1926), pp. 90, 103, 109; Robert Edward Brennan, O. P., *Thomistic Psychology* (New York: The Macmillan Company, 1941), pp. 221-222; Van Melsen, *op. cit.,* pp. 235-236; and Mises, *Theory and History,* pp. 177-179.

8. "A man involves himself in a contradiction when he uses the reasoning of the intellect to prove that that reasoning cannot be relied upon." Toohey, *op. cit.,* p. 29. Also see Phillips, *op. cit.,* II, 16; and Frank Thilly, *A History of Philosophy* (New York: Henry Holt and Co., 1914), p. 586.

9. *See* F. A. Hayek, *The Road to Serfdom* (Chicago: University of Chicago Press, 1944), p. 26.

10. John G. Vance, "Freedom," quoted in Leibell, *op. cit.,* pp. 98-100. *Also see* Van Melsen, *op. cit.,* p. 236, and Michael Maher, *Psychology,* quoted in Leibell, *op. cit.,* p. 90.

11. Thus, cf. C. I. Lewis, *Mind and the World Order* (Dover Publications, 1956), pp. 49-51.

12. *See* Hassett, Mitchell, and Monan, *op. cit.,* pp. 33-35. *Also see* Phillips, *op. cit.,* I, 50-51; Toohey, *op. cit.,* pp. 5, 36, 101, 107-108; and Thilly, *op. cit.,* p. 363.

13. Professor Strausz-Hupé also makes this point in his paper in this symposium.

14. *See* Mises, *Theory and History,* p. 92.

15. "A machine is a device made by man. It is the realization of a design and it runs precisely according to the plan of its authors. What produces the product of its operation is not something within it but the purpose the constructor wanted to realize by means of its construction. It is the constructor and operator who create and produce, not the machine. To ascribe to a machine any activity is anthropomorphism and animism. The machine . . . does not move; it is put into motion by men." *Ibid.,* pp. 94-95.

16. See *ibid.,* pp. 249-250.

17. On this and many other points in this paper I am greatly indebted to Professor Ludwig von Mises and to his development of the science of praxeology. *See* Ludwig von Mises, "Comment about the Mathematical Treatment of Economic Problems," *Studium Generale,* Vol. VI, No. 2 (1953); Mises, *Human Action, passim;* and Mises, *Theory and History,* pp. 240-263. The foundations of praxeology as a method were laid by the English classical economist, Nassau Senior. Unfortunately, the positivistic John Stuart Mill's side of their methodological debate became much better known than Senior's. *See* Marian Bowley, *Nassau Senior and Classical Economics* (New York: Augustus M. Kelley, 1949), chap. I, especially pp. 64-65.

18. For a critique of recent attempts to fashion a new theory of measurement for intensive magnitudes, *see* Murray N. Rothbard, "Toward a Reconstruction of Utility and Welfare Economics," in M. Sennholz, ed., *On Freedom and Free Enterprise,* Essays in Honor of Ludwig von Mises (Princeton: Van Nostrand, 1956), pp. 241-243.

19. On the fallacy of conceptual realism (or Platonic ultra-realism) involved here, and on the necessity for methodological individualism, *see* F. A. Hayek, *The Counter-Revolution of Science* (Glencoe, Ill.: The Free Press, 1952), *passim,* and Mises, *Human Action,* pp. 41 ff., and 45 ff.

20. We may therefore say with Frank Chodorov that "society are people." Frank Chodorov, *Society Are People* (Philadelphia: Intercollegiate Society of Individualists, n.d.). For a critique of the mystique of "society," *see* Mises, *Theory and History,* pp. 250 ff.

21. See the delightful essay by Frank Chodorov, "We Lose It to Ourselves," *analysis,* June, 1950, p. 3.

22. A similar error of metaphor prevails in foreign policy matters. Thus: "When one uses the simple monosyllabic 'France' one thinks of France as a unit, an entity. When . . . we say 'France sent *her* troops to conquer Tunis'—we impute not only unity but personality to the country. The very words conceal the facts and make international relations a glamorous drama in which personalized nations are the actors, and all too easily we forget the flesh-and-blood men and women who are the true actors . . . if we had no such word as 'France' . . . then we should more accurately describe the Tunis expedition in some such way as this: 'A few of . . . thirty-eight million persons sent thirty thousand others to conquer Tunis.' This way of putting the fact immediately suggests a question, or rather a series of questions. Who were the 'few'? Why did they send the thirty thousand to Tunis? And why did these obey? Empire-building is done not by 'nations,' but by men. The problem before us is to discover the men, the active, interested minorities in each nation, who are directly interested in imperialism and then to analyze the reasons why the majorities pay the expenses and fight the wars . . ." Parker Thomas Moon, *Imperialism and World Politics* (New York: The Macmillan Company, 1930), p. 58.

23. Edith Tilton Penrose, "Biological Analogies in the Theory of the Firm," *American Economic Review,* December, 1952, p. 808.

24. In his *Human Action.* For a defense of this method, *see* Rothbard, "In Defense of 'Extreme Apriorism," *loc. cit.,* pp. 314-320; and Rothbard, "Praxeology: Reply to Mr. Schuller," *American Economic Review,* December, 1951, pp. 943-946.

25. E. C. Harwood, *Reconstruction of Economics* (Great Barrington, Mass.: American Institute for Economic Research, 1955), p. 39. On this and other examples of scientism, *see* Leland B. Yeager, "Measurement as Scientific Method in Economics," *American Journal of Economics and Sociology,* July, 1957, p. 337. *Also see* Yeager, "Reply to Col. Harwood," *ibid.,* October, 1957, pp. 104-106. As Yeager wisely concludes, "Anthropomorphism, rightly scorned in the natural sciences as prescientific metaphysics, is justified in economics because economics is about human action."

26. *See* Van Melsen, *op. cit.,* pp. 54-58, 1-16.

27. As Schumpeter declared: "The scholastic science of the Middle Ages contained all the germs of the laical science of the Renaissance." The experimental method was used notably by Friar Roger Bacon and Peter of Maricourt in the thirteenth century; the heliocentric system of astronomy originated *inside* the Church (Cusanus was a cardinal and Copernicus a canonist); and the Benedictine monks led the way in developing medieval engineering. *See* Joseph A. Schumpeter, *History of Economic Analysis* (New York: Oxford University Press, 1954), pp. 81 ff.; and Lynn White, Jr., "Dynamo and Virgin Reconsidered," *The American Scholar,* Spring, 1958, pp. 183-212.

28. For a refutation of the charge that this is a circular argument, *see* Rothbard, "Toward a Reconstruction of Utility and Welfare Economics," *loc. cit.,* p. 228.

29. "When they [the practical scientists] remember their vows of objectivity, they get other people to make their judgments for them." Anthony Standen, *Science Is a Sacred Cow* (New York: E. P. Dutton and Co., 1958), p. 165.

30. John F. Due, *Government Finance* (Homewood, Ill.: Richard D. Irwin, 1954), p. 122.

31. Adam Smith, *The Wealth of Nations* (New York: Modern Library, 1937), pp. 777-779.

9

Growth, in Biology and in Education

RALPH W. LEWIS

The purpose of this paper is to examine briefly the bodies of knowledge in biology and in education which are concerned with the phenomena generally known as "growth." The kinds of facts and the few laws and theories present in these segments of biology and education will be discussed. Attention will be given to the internal structure of the laws and theories that give organization within these bodies of knowledge and to some of the limitations of these laws and theories. Predictions made from the laws and theories will be scrutinized as a means of determining the worth of the concepts.* With the discussion on growth as a background, plus a few statements about other concepts that have been applied to the detriment of education, a set of criteria will be presented by which one can decide if concepts are worthy of being used as a basis for making decisions about human affairs.

1. *Biological Growth*

Biological growth consists basically of increase in the amount of protoplasm usually accompanied by differentiation of the protoplasm. Because of the great complexity of the problem, biol-

* I use the word "concept" loosely in this paper to mean idea, law, or theory.

ogists have conceptually and experimentally separated the two aspects of growth, increase and differentiation, even though in the growth of organisms they are not separate activities. Since there is no general theory of growth that deals with growth *in toto* by subsuming the two huge categories of facts concerning the two aspects of growth, one must examine each separately.

Even a quick look at the quantitative aspects of growth in biological writings soon leads one to the Verhulst-Pearl law of growth (19) or some modification of this law. This law says that under the right conditions an individual or a population starting anew in a favorable environment will grow through the following phases (9):

1. Lag phase: growth rate null.
2. Acceleration phase: growth rate increases.
3. Exponential phase: growth rate constant.
4. Retardation phase: growth rate decreases.
5. Stationary phase: growth rate null.
6. Decline phase: growth rate negative.

The usual method of determining quantitative growth is to measure the amount of protoplasm present at intervals of time. Measurement of the amount of protoplasm is never a direct process. Wet weight, dry weight, number of cells, linear measurement, and the like are assumed to give a figure which is directly proportional to the amount of protoplasm in the organism. When the growth measurements are plotted against time, the growth curve will be the so-called S-shaped curve and will show the phases noted above. The curve is not really S-shaped. The lag phase starts parallel to the horizontal time coordinate. During the acceleration phase the growth curve bends upward along the growth measurement coordinate until it reaches the exponential phase, which is represented by nearly a straight line sloping at an angle dependent upon growth rate. This maximum rate of growth begins to slow down as the retardation phase sets in. Gradually growth slows down until decline balances growth and the stationary phase is reached, the curve in this phase being again horizontal. Decline follows, and growth rate is negative.

This law of growth, despite its narrow limitations, has been very useful in biology. It forms the basis for the development of assay methods for vitamins and other biologically important substances; it permits comparisons of different diets; it forms the basis for recognizing and analyzing variability in populations; it is useful in exploring the problem of enzymatic adaptation; and other problems such as the exploration of factors in the environment that affect growth.

One often finds that growth fails to follow the expected S curve. Deviations in the curve suggest that unexpected factors are at work. These factors may be in the external or in the internal environment. The work of Braun (2) describes a situation in which an internal genetic factor and external nutritional factors are at work simultaneously in modifying the typical growth curve. Knowledge of the law of growth, plus much other knowledge, often makes it possible for scientists to explain apparent deviations from the law, and thus the law of growth forms the basis for advances in biological knowledge.

The growth of populations or of individuals in nature seldom follows the law of growth in detail. The smooth curves are based chiefly upon laboratory data. Varying factors in a natural environment, such as temperature, rainfall, food supply, disease, usually disturb the even growth curve that is so often found under laboratory conditions.

Inherent factors will cause pronounced deviations from the law of growth in many organisms, whether growing in nature or in the laboratory. In mammals the inherent characteristic of carrying the young internally through early stages of growth greatly affects the growth curve of each individual. The onset of activity in some endocrine glands may also affect growth to a considerable extent. Both of these effects are pronounced in human growth.

In this brief look at the law of growth we have already noted some of the applications and limitations of the concept. Even when we consider its application to quantitative growth alone, the law has stringent limitations. As a descriptive tool the law serves fairly well under carefully controlled conditions, but even here difficulties exist. A statement by Sholl (17) points out some of these difficulties when considering the growth of an animal.

To illustrate this discussion it is convenient to consider the array of points resulting from plotting the weight of an organism against its age; the principles will apply to any other measure of size while the extremely difficult problem of shape (Medawar, 1945) will not be considered. In general, this array of points will lie scattered about some line which is a picture of the general trend of growth of the animal, and our first problem is the description of this line. Such a line can give no information about fine details, but is rather like the line depicting the track of a railway on a continental map; the general direction of the railway is shown, but small variations do not appear.

There was a time when many workers thought it possible to find the formulation of such a line by a priori methods, by thinking of chemical metabolism, surface absorption, and similar notions. There have been numerous examples of this kind, and perhaps the best known is Robertson's autocatalytic theory and the resulting curve. We are now more fully aware of our inability to specify the many factors that may be responsible for growth in terms of a few parameters, let alone finding a mathematical statement about their relationships; in any case, such a relationship would be of such a complexity that it would not be expressible in terms of simple mathematical functions. Further it must be remembered that if any such function were fitted to the data, no demonstration of closeness of fit can ever prove the curve to be that one which is in any sense the unique "true" curve.

At the other methodological extreme we should be tempted to use the purely mathematical approach and use a polynomial of such a degree that the fit was adequate. This would be statistically highly satisfactory, but it would be very difficult to interpret the resulting curve and to assign a biological interpretation to the parameters involved.

Consequently, we must consider a more empirical approach, and the two criteria for choosing a curve would seem to be that it must provide a good statistical fit and also have a reasonably simple functional expression involving the number of interpretable parameters. . . . Naturally, we shall draw on our biological experience where possible and choose curves whose parameters have a biological significance.

. . . As is often the case in the application of mathematics to biology, we see that we are well advised to combine our intuitive approach with suitable mathematical methods. . . .

Because of the large number of significant variables that can affect growth, the growth law has rather limited predictive powers. For example, I have determined the growth of a fungus on a simple medium under carefully controlled conditions. I have determined growth curves when different amino acids or vitamins were included in the medium. From these data I would like to predict what will happen when I use other vitamins or amino acids singly or in combinations. But from the growth data which I have accumulated I cannot predict new situations. Of course, I can say that if growth occurs at all, its plot will be an S curve. Also, if I have controlled the amount of energy food, I can usually predict the level of the stationary phase; but that is all. As a predictive tool, the growth law has not yet proved very fertile.

Von Bertalanffy (21) has related, in many animal species, the metabolic rate of an organism to the type of growth curve produced by the organism. He says that there are three classes of animals as determined by plotting their growth curves and that the class to which an animal belongs can be predicted from a determination of the "metabolic type" of the organism. Thus, this work, "aimed at establishing connections between metabolism and growth," has greatly extended the importance of growth studies and, the author says, forms the basis for a general growth theory.

Studies on the relative quantitative growth of different parts of a single organism, called "allometric growth," have produced a law of fairly wide applicability among both animals and plants. This law can be stated simply by saying that if the logarithm of the measurement of one organ is plotted against the logarithm of the measurement of another organ of the same animal, and if this is repeated several times during growth, the points will fall on a straight line. Bonner (1) considers this law of allometric growth to be descriptive only and without the capacity to reveal hidden biological secrets.

Because the law of allometric growth compares two organs of one organism, it can be expected to be free from many fluctuations due to internal or external environmental factors; thus, in the future it may have great value when eventually it is related by new concepts to other biological laws. At present the limitations of the law are apparent in the facts it interrelates and the few predictions it permits.

The study of differentiation has produced an enormous collection of facts. These facts deal with changes that occur in organisms as they grow and mature. Most of the facts have come from observations of gross and microscopic structures as they change during the development of an adult from a zygote. The observations have revealed structures and activities that are so complex that no theory has yet been produced which is even partially adequate in providing a general explanatory system with fruitful predictive powers. Several broad and important generalizations arrived at by simple enumeration are present, but there is as yet no general theory comparable to the theory of evolution or the gene theory which are so fruitful in other areas of biology.

2. *Educational Growth*

Educational growth is a much confused concept. A goodly portion of the confusion arises from the willingness of many individuals to accept weak, tentative hypotheses as truth or as a good approximation of truth. Additional confusion arises from an extrapolation (sometimes willfully, but more often unwittingly) of a small understanding of biological growth into the area of educational growth. Some basis for analogy between the two exists, but it remains analogy, and good scientists would not use knowledge of the biological growth of babies as an argument to support an idea concerning the educational growth of children. Examples of this kind of argument are noted below under *Resistance to Displacement and Convergence* and under *Developmental Theory in Education*.

The term "growth" as used in its fullest sense in the science of education subsumes both the biological growth of human beings and all other aspects of human growth such as intellectual, artistic, personality, social, moral, emotional, and perceptual growth (3, 8, 12). Physical growth in humans is determined by the same kinds of methods that can be used on almost any higher animal. In addition to height and weight measurements, other criteria such as strength of grip, carpal development as determined from X-ray photographs, and dental development are often used for determining physical growth.

Growth of mental attributes is measured by a number of different kinds of psychological tests and by verbal descriptions. Some of the tests used and the attributes they are presumed to measure are: Kuhlmann-Binet, mental age; Gates and Stanford, reading age; Stanford, educational age; Doll, social age; Furfey and Sullivan, developmental age.

The scores on these tests and the biological measurements are not used directly in the studies considered below, but are converted to "growth ages." Norms have been established for each test and for each biological characteristic by determining the average of representative groups of children of different chronological ages for each of the biological and mental attributes. The measurement or score of the testee is compared to the set of norms, and his "growth age" is that of the norm equaled by his measurement or score. Thus, if a seven-year-old receives a score on a Kuhlmann-Binet test equal to the norm for nine-year-olds, he will be given a mental age rating of nine. If his height measurement equals the norm for eight-year-olds, his height age will be eight. Collectively mental age, height age, weight, reading age, etc., are called growth ages.

Although most of the following discussion will be concerned with growth ages for both biological and mental attributes, a word about intelligence quotient, I.Q., will explain the virtual omission of the term. An I.Q. score is the mental age, as determined above, divided by the testee's chronological age multiplied by one hundred. This kind of score does not permit a ready comparison with the age units as determined for the other attributes and so is not used for studies of "total" growth discussed below.

The most comprehensive and the most scientific studies on the growth of the "whole" child are those of Olson (12). He and his colleagues have determined growth ages of many children, usually from age five to age twelve. The growth ages for each child are determined several times during the seven-year span. The published data resulting from the tests and measurements are usually presented on graphs with the chronological age on the horizontal axis and the growth age on the vertical axis. The height ages for a child are plotted above the corresponding chronological ages, and the points are joined successively by straight lines. All the other growth ages are plotted in like manner on the same graph. Since all the attributes usually increase in time, the graph of a child's growth consists of a series of lines ascending across the graph to the right.

Olson and Hughes (15) thought "it would be of interest in testing hypotheses of children as wholes [sic!] to study the center of gravity of growth systems and the relation of separate aspects of growth to the whole." In order to do this they plotted an "organismic age" curve for each child so studied. The organismic age for any one chronological age was computed by averaging all the growth ages for that chronological age. After an organismic age was computed for each chronological age, the points were plotted and connected in sequence, thus producing the organismic age curve.

After studying many children by means of growth age curves, Olson has arrived at some conclusions and definitions, a theory of growth, and a number of applications of his views to the problems of education. In the remainder of this essay I shall describe and criticize several of these ideas. I am omitting for the sake of brevity any critical examination of the raw "facts," the bases upon which they rest, and their statistical manipulation. In the present discussion I shall assume that growth curves are a "true" representation of the attribute for which they stand.

Pattern.

A *pattern* of growth refers to the relationship of various measured characteristics within an individual at a given point in time, or to a succession of changes with time. Thus a child who at the age ten has a high mental age, a high reading age, and a somewhat lower height age, weight age, carpal age, and dental age, differs from one who has high physical ages and relatively low mental and achievement ages.

One might also speak of a given child's pattern of growth in reading as showing a period of plateau from ages six to nine with a rapid increase or spurt in the period from ages nine to twelve.[11]

A study of the patterns of growth of large numbers of children has led Olson (12, 16) to rather definite ideas about the growth of children. Some of these ideas are "unfolding design," "going togetherness," "variation," "stability of the center of gravity," "resistance to displacement," "convergence," and "deprivation."

Unfolding Design. Everyday experience supplies us with the information that, as children grow physically, some kind of "unfolding" of mental attributes occurs and that this unfolding roughly parallels physical development. No one doubts this. Nor does anyone doubt that children are as different in mental attributes as they are in physical attributes. But as a person goes from an examination of biological growth to an examination of early and late mental development of children, he will recognize the stringent limitations of "unfolding design" as a scientific concept.

Olson (12) states ". . . that a child has a design for growing, that optimum nurture fulfills this design." What does he mean by "design"? Does he mean that "design" and "optimum nurture" are singular and fixed for a developing child? In this quotation it seems that he does consider them singular and fixed, yet in his discussions of nature and nurture he seems not to take such a limited view of the potentialities of human development.

Once the data are in and the growth curves are plotted, a single, limited design for a child certainly is present on the graph. Consider, however, a child of five. Is there a single design to be followed by this child in his growth? As a biologist I cannot conceive of the design as fixed except within very wide and, at present, very indefinite limits. Several years ago I became aware that the biological concept of optimum nutrition was of little use. Innumerable combinations of nutrients produce maximum growth in weight, while some of these combinations and perhaps still others unidentified produce optimum qualitative characteristics. The same can be said for other environmental factors. Thus, at the biological level the "design" present at the start of growth has before it in time a huge number of possible designs. There is no such thing as an optimum nurture. Dozens, possibly thousands, of different combinations of environmental factors may supply the conditions for achieving a single kind of optimum or a number of different optima simultaneously. Many kinds of optima are known, and probably many are yet to be discovered. Therefore, for an individual of any species, I hesitate to speak of "optimum nurture" and of "design" for growth without a careful qualification of "optimum" and of "nurture."

Since mental growth stems from, but greatly supersedes, the complexities of biological growth, the term "design" should be discarded in talking of the growth of children, especially when presented against a background of growth curves. So presented, it may be even more readily misused than were I.Q. scores in their day (18, 20). Some term which conveys the idea of the plural potentialities of children should be coined before the textbooks of education take up such statements as the following: "Every child progresses toward a specific maximum." "Each child is apparently born with potentialities for growing according to a specific design" (8). The "design" as seen in growth graphs is *ex post facto* and should never be taken to represent what was fixed there before the design was recorded.

Going Togetherness, Variation, Center of Gravity of Growth, and Readiness. The literature at hand (6, 7, 8, 12, 13, 16) contains graphs of sets of growth age curves for a total of twenty children. Each child's record is a pattern unto himself. In one paper (16) four graphs are chosen to illustrate a "going togetherness" of all growth attributes in each child. These four graphs do illustrate this, and the author says that based upon other graphs of fifty-six boys and girls (which he does not show) ". . . one secures a most dramatic picture of the generalization that growth tends towards unified patterns."

But among the twenty growth graphs shown in the six publications, only eleven show "trends toward unified patterns"; nine do not. From these data, therefore, I find it difficult to see that the ideas of "going togetherness" and "variations" are much refined beyond the common-sense understanding of these that an experienced teacher possesses without any special study of growth.

Hughes (5) has examined variability among and within a hundred boys, ages four to twelve. Instead of plotting all growth ages for one boy on a graph, he has used a single growth age, such as height age, on the vertical axis and the chronological age on the horizontal. The curves for the one hundred boys are plotted on one graph. Ten graphs for ten biological and mental attributes are thus presented. Concerning these graphs he says: "The evidence is clear in showing that there are great differences in the distribution of measures (ordinate values) when the chronological age is held constant. In addition it should be noted that the variation of age (abscissa values) is almost equally great when the value of the measure is constant."

Some idea of the differences in distribution is secured by examining the height age and the mental age curves. At height age ten about ninety percent of the curves spread over a horizontal distance of three chronological years. At mental age ten about ninety percent of the curves spread over a horizontal distance of three and a half chronological years. The other sets of curves are quite similar in spread to the mental age curves.

Hughes' paper develops a new view of organismic growth. Instead of being satisfied with the organismic growth curve of an individual as the measure of the "center of gravity" of growth, he plots a narrow band and wider band over the organismic curve by specified mathematical techniques. The organismic curve is approximately at the center of these two bands. The inner band is about half the width of the wider band.

Concerning these graphs Hughes says:

The central dense band has been labeled the organismic area and has been presented to suggest that for management and educational purposes the child is generally "mature" within the limits of the band on an ordinate and generally "ready" to fit a level on any abscissa. Also the organismic area is shown to illustrate more clearly the fact that both maturity and readiness are distributed as necessary consequences of variation within the individual rather than narrowly fixed as the organismic age line would imply.

The peripheral lighter band has been added to the pattern to insure recognition of another fact of within variability [sic!]; namely, that for about 20 to 25 percent of growth items, maturity and readiness are, indeed, very broadly distributed.

Within some individual graphs and from graph to graph, there is in the organismic area a variation in "readiness" from one half to three chronological years and a variation in "maturity" of about the same number of growth years. For the peripheral band, that is, for about twenty percent of the growth items, readiness and maturity extend twice as far—from one to six chronological years.

Most teachers will agree that Hughes' treatment of "readiness" and "maturity" expresses these concepts in a manner much closer to reality as determined by observations of growing children. The concepts in this form appear to agree with Olson's (12) observation that "one of the striking abilities of the human organism is the power to take on new modifications throughout its lifetime." With these views of variability in mind, one wonders if possibly "readiness" in most students may not be more a matter of being ready for persistent work at studies rather than being some innate developmental factor which cannot be overcome by insistence upon reasonable standards of accomplishment.

Resistance to Displacement and Convergence. Under the heading "Resistance to Displacement" Olson (12) says:

A useful principle growing out of hundreds of studies of growth is that if an experimental factor capable of producing a difference in growth is introduced, either artificially or naturally, a child tends to resume his own normal rate of growth as soon as the factor disappears or is removed.

To support this view Olson cites a study on head sizes of premature and mature infants. Is this kind of extrapolation, which

I have found often in the literature of child development, sensible when considering the mental growth of children?

The resumption of the normal rate of growth after "deprivation" or "extra stimulation" is "convergence." Olson cites examples of convergence from endocrine therapy and from attempts to stimulate progress in arithmetic and reading. Progress is made during "treatment," but when special attention is stopped, the children resume their previous pattern. Millard (6) presents a striking example of convergence. A girl was given special tutoring in spelling and made phenomenal gains. After the tutoring stopped, she drifted back to the level of her ascending spelling curve.

The convergence notion is evidently not widely held. Thompson (20) cites considerable evidence which appears not to agree. Olson (12) goes to considerable pains to refute the work which presumably showed that special tutoring helped slow readers to become better readers. He says: "Many studies (on remedial reading) of the foregoing types have been reported, but they fail to randomize or control persistence and industry." Herein lie two of the most crucial aspects in the development of mental attributes. Can they be "randomized"? Are they not often determined by the complexities of the teacher-pupil relationship to such an extent that they defy measurement? Those who have been taught by at least one teacher with the power to engender persistence and industry acquire the knowledge that displacement is real and that convergence can be overcome.

Developmental Theory in Education. Although I disagree strongly with many of Olson's views on education, I favor his continuous application to studies of growth through the last two decades. I also favor his recent attempt at presentation of a developmental theory (14) in such a complex field of knowledge. Unfortunately, I do not understand his type of theory, and I question if it is really a theory. The pattern presented by Werkmeister (22) as exemplifying physical theory is not present. Nor is the pattern—facts A, B; deduction 1; fact C; deduction 2; fact D; deduction 3—such as is found in the theory of evolution (4) present.

This absence of a clear pattern may be a sign of developments to follow. Confusion at the beginning seems to be a normal step in the growth of theories. For examples of this see the *Harvard Case Histories in Experimental Science,* especially the one by Nash (10) on *The Atomic-Molecular Theory* in which Dalton's early difficulties are discussed.

Olson (14) first defines growth, maturation, and development. He then presents five "developmental equations" as follows:

1. Maturation $\times$ Nurture $=$ Development

He says that equation 1 is too simple if thought of only as a factor system.

2. Maturation $\times$ Zero nurture $=$ Zero achievement
3. Variable maturation $\times$ Constant supply nurture $=$ Variable achievement
4. Constant maturation $\times$ Variable supply nurture $=$ Variable achievement

Equations 1 through 4 are clearly too simple an answer, for there appears to be evidence for "differential uptake." This results in an enhancement effect, because the differentials, once established in achievement, in turn so modify the organism as to make it more selective, permitting more rapid uptake in some and less rapid in others. In effect, then, the constant supply is surely a myth, since children seek a larger or smaller supply from what is available, as in the following equation:

5. Variable maturation $\times$ Differential uptake of nurture $=$ Enhanced variable achievement

Next Olson presents "The Nature of the Evidence." He says: "There is much evidence to support the general theory back of the writing of such equations as those preceding." What can he mean by this? I had presumed that the equations were possibly the postulates of the theory. Does the theory lie behind these, or is the evidence what lies behind them?

He next describes growth ages briefly and then presents a graph in which the organismic age curves of three groups of boys are compared to their reading curves. The boys were separated into three groups on the basis of their reading scores at age eleven: fast, intermediate, and slow readers. The organismic age curve and the reading age curve of the fast readers are above the other curves from age six to eleven. Except for ages seven to eight the two curves for the intermediate readers are between the curves for slow readers and fast readers. Both curves for the slow readers are below the others except at age six, where the slow readers are slightly better at reading than the intermediate. On the basis of the graph Olson argues in support of equation 5 above.

From this he moves to a model which consists of three approximately parallel lines extending diagonally across a growth age—chronological age plot. The curves represent rapid, average, and slow growth "according to the equation Maturation $\times$ Nurture = Development." Concerning this model Olson says:

We can now set up a series of concepts involving known facts surrounding the model. These are of varying degrees of generalization, and each should be preceded by the qualification "other things being equal." The model is based on the assumption that the growth represented by the curves represents a composite according to the equation Maturation $\times$ Nurture = Development. Viewed alone it appears as a relatively static model with much stability and continuity. Injected into a social field, however, the children represented become dynamic in the sense of relationship to other individuals and to meeting the requirements of each situation.

What general theory can be built around the model in the illustration?

Principles of Human Development

Concepts that will stand the test of universality, of experiment, and of prediction are hard to come by in a field governed by multiple causation. When stated, such concepts are limited in the sense that other postulates may in part account for the phenomenon. There is always something of an indeterminant character when variable individuals experience variable nurture.

The following postulate comes close to having generality: "For all achievements which increase with chronological age, the rapidly growing child will yield the achievement earlier, and the slowly growing child will achieve the status later than the average child of a given age."

From such a postulate one can predict in advance the individual differences that will exist, the factors that must be observed in an adequate experimental design, and the constant errors which must be allowed for or adjusted. We can predict in advance the results of many types of experiment. With such a postulate a person can predict, as an average trend at least, many of the types of data that can be secured in a classroom group or even in physiological experiments. The basic evidence needed for the predictions is a fairly accurate account of age change. For example, knowing that emotional outbursts decrease in number and severity with age, we can predict that a child showing such outbursts will have many characteristics of the slowly growing child. Some of the objective findings on associations with the model furnish a basis for more general theory.

Associations with the Model

Here are some operational associations and deductions from the model. It should be noted that the effects are not only in the model as constructed, but also in the matrix of all the associated factors that go into the loading of the model. The differences shown have important associations with socioeconomic status, social acceptability, responsibility, levels of interests, reaction to frustration, age of accomplishment of developmental tasks, and many valued traits of character and personality. The differences also run in families and are remarkably resistant to planned change, although reflecting changes in design over the years.

More specifically, *A* [the top curve] as contrasted with *C* [the bottom curve] will be higher in social age, will be advanced in interests, and will be superior in social status in the group. *C*, contrasted with *A*, will have more behavior problems, whether checked by self, teacher, parent, or associates. Child *A* as contrasted with Child *C* will be characterized by more active, seeking behavior in general, including motivation for achievement. His appetite and interest in food will be greater, although calories per unit of body weight will be less in accord with the age trend.

The associates of *A* will be more like *A* than they are like *C,* and similarly, the associates of *C* will be more like *C* than like *A*. The rationalization of the association may be in terms of social status, interest, values, levels of development, or comparable skills of achieving or performing.

Some examples of the significance of the associations for other systematic approaches can be illustrated.

The headings of the sections that follow are: The Model and Psychoanalytic Theory, The Model and Frustration-Aggression Theory, The Model and Theories of Intelligence, Reconciliation of Explanatory Theories, Individual Predictions versus Explanatory Principles, The Task of Education, and Seeking, Self-Selection, and Pacing.

What I find in Olson's theory is not what I understand as theory in science, but rather a number of generalizations by simple enumeration, some tentative hypotheses, some vague ideas, and some discussions on related topics. Some of the generalizations seem to me to be those that the percipient and thoughtful teacher would arrive at after two or three years of teaching.

Nowhere is my study of growth age patterns or of this theory do I find a good discussion of the large middle group of average students. The slow and the fast can be recognized, but the only mention of the middle group is the paper by Hughes (5).

On the basis of understanding derived from growth theory and from other "concepts of values and directions," Olson makes many recommendations about pedagogy. One of these is that "absolute standards" are not good. Possibly this is a good decision when considering the children at the high and low levels, but what about the large group in the center? Were not the so-called absolute standards arrived at by the teachers who had had long experience with children? Are not the so-called absolute standards the standards that were found to be achievable by this large central group of children?

Seeking, self-selection, and pacing are also recommended by Olson on the basis of his theory of growth. These recommendations are made on the ground that "The idea that there exists a 'wisdom of the body' that enables children to make wise choices in matters educational has led to direct demonstrations and a whole theory of curriculum and method in education." The paper (23) cited in Olson's book as a demonstration of the working of this idea showed the self-selection group to be a little better in a few attributes than the group taught in the traditional manner. The differences were not so great that I would be convinced until I saw the results of many more experiments.

In support of his views on seeking and self-selection Olson (14) resorts once to a biological analogy, twice to infant growth, and once to the activities of preschool children. Are these a sound basis for making decisions about the management of schools? Why does he not present growth age curves which would permit me to compare children schooled in a traditional way with those schooled under the "wisdom of the body" idea? Ample evidence of this sort would do much to convert the "wisdom of the body" idea from a weak analogy with a biological concept into an educational hypothesis.

Olson says that in order to be sure the seeking activity of the student is satisfied to the full, the teacher must be sure to provide the materials at the right time. This activity of the teacher is called pacing. Pacing also "refers to the attitude which expects from the child only that which he can yield at his stage of maturity."

Some students of child development appear not to be impressed by what they have seen of the permissive treatment of children in schools which presumably gains support from the above ideas. Their views contrast strongly with the ideas of "wisdom of the body" and of seeking and pacing. Breckenridge and Vincent (3) say:

It is in order to build a secure sense of being needed and useful that children should learn to work. Our recent emphasis upon protecting children from child labor, our urgent planning to fill children's time with happiness and play, our progressive education emphasis upon making learning quick and easy through projects and easily motivated activities—all this has resulted in depriving children of the opportunity to learn to work for the sheer sake of fulfilling necessary obligations and responsibilities.

3. *Criteria for the Application of Scientific Concepts to Humans*

The headlong rush to apply new facts and new concepts in the field of education has brought disrepute to professional education in the eyes of most scholars and in the eyes of many citizens. During the last few decades we have seen, for example, the theory of identical elements and a strongly narrowed concept of utility used as the bases for discarding the classics, foreign language, mathematics, and science from the school curricula and from the curriculum of individual students. We have seen the loose and unstudied concept of life adjustment used as a basis for inserting trivia into the regular school hours. Possibly the concept of development is destined to be used as a basis for the support of more trivia. I hope not, because it may develop into a concept of real worth if treated with scholarly rigor, criticism, and imagination.

We have seen the concept of interest in relation to learning perverted into a concept of whim and caprice to such an extent that lack of interest is constantly used by students as a "reason" for not studying. We have seen a concept of integration of knowledge used as the basis for disrupting pedagogical and learning efficiency. This has been done by creating core courses, activity programs, practical courses, community studies, and the like in lieu of the study of traditional bodies of knowledge. The traditional bodies of knowledge exist because there are inherent in them patterns of multiple reasoned relationships that give the best order and greatest simplicity so far achieved. They exist also because they are the most economical way of learning something of the real breadth and depth of human experience. To disrupt this order at the teaching level is to take from the teacher variety, order, and simplicity in presentation; and to take from the student a wealth of opportunities to explore and rediscover the reasoned pathways which were the great achievements of the master minds.

Since man, even though mistaken in his views, will always strive to apply concepts to better the lot of man, how can he avoid the misapplication of concepts? In those areas whose concepts derive from science, this question can be answered in part. Before a concept is applied we should know well the internal structure of the concept and the facts it interrelates. The concept should have withstood the buffetings of scholarly criticism by virtue of its intellectual integrity. And the concept should have been explored long enough and thoroughly enough so that we are aware of several of its major limitations. If the concept is to be taught to prospective teachers who will be expected to apply it, then the limitations should be well enough worked out so they can be taught with efficiency and clarity. These criteria for the application of concepts to humans are severe for persons who seem to prefer immediate utility to understanding; yet, in the long run, the criteria will contribute much to both utility and understanding.

NOTES

1. J. T. Bonner, *Morphogenesis, An Essay on Development* (Princeton: Princeton University Press, 1952).
2. W. Braun, "Studies on Population Changes in Bacteria and Their Relation to Some General Biological Problems," *American Naturalist*, LXXXVI (1952), 355-371.
3. M. E. Breckenridge, and E. L. Vincent, *Child Development, Physical and Psychological Growth Through the School Years* (3rd ed.; Philadephia: W. B. Saunders Company, 1955).
4. G. de Beer, "The Darwin-Wallace Centenary," *Endeavour*, XVII (1958), 61-76.
5. B. O. Hughes, "Variability Among and Within Individuals in Relation to Education," *Merrill-Palmer Quarterly*, I (1957), 167-187.
6. W. A. Ketcham, "Growth Patterns for Gifted Chidren," *Merrill-Palmer Quarterly*, I (1957), 188-197.
7. E. Mechem, "Affectivity and Growth in Children," *Child Development*, XIV (1943), 91-115.
8. C. V. Millard, *Child Growth and Development* (Boston: D. C. Heath and Company, 1951).

9. J. Monod, "The Growth of Bacterial Cultures," *Annual Review of Microbiology,* III (1949), 371-394.
10. L. K. Nash, "The Atomic-Molecular Theory," Case 4, *Harvard Case Histories in Experimental Science* (Cambridge: Harvard University Press, 1950).
11. W. C. Olson, "Meaning of Growth," in C. V. Millard, ed., *Child Growth in an Era of Conflict,* Fifteenth Yearbook, Michigan Education Association and Department of Elementary School Principals (Lansing, 1944).
12. W. C. Olson, *Child Development* (Boston: D. C. Heath and Company, 1949).
13. W. C. Olson, "Achievement as Development," *International Review of Education,* III (1957), 135-142.
14. W. C. Olson, "Developmental Theory in Education," in D. B. Harris, ed., *The Concept of Development* (Minneapolis: University of Minnesota Press, 1957).
15. W. C. Olson, and B. O. Hughes, "The Concept of Organismic Age," *Journal of Educational Research,* XXXV (1942), 525-527.
16. W. C. Olson, and B. O. Hughes, "Growth of the Child as a Whole," in R. G. Barker, J. S. Kounin, and H. F. Wright, *Child Behavior and Development* (New York: McGraw-Hill Book Company, 1943).
17. D. A. Sholl, "Regularities in Growth Curves, Including Rhythms and Allometry," in E. J. Boell, ed., *Dynamics of Growth Processes,* Soc. for the Study of Development and Growth (Princeton: Princeton University Press, 1954).
18. J. C. Sullivan, "Effect of Teacher Pressure," in C. V. Millard, ed., *Child Growth and Development in an Era of Conflict,* Fifteenth Yearbook, Michigan Education Association and Department of Elementary School Principals (Lansing, 1944).
19. D'Arcy W. Thompson, *On Growth and Form* (Cambridge: Cambridge University Press, 1948).
20. G. G. Thompson, *Child Psychology* (Boston: Houghton Mifflin Company, 1952).
21. L. von Bertalanffy, "Quantitative Laws in Metabolism and Growth," *Quarterly Review of Biology,* XXXII (1957), 217-231.
22. W. H. Werkmeister, *The Basis and Structure of Knowledge* (New York: Harper and Brothers, 1948).
23. J. W. Wrightstone, "Evaluation of the Experiment with the Activity Program in the New York City Elementary Schools," *Journal of Educational Research,* XXXVIII (1944), 252-257.

10

The Psychopathology of Scientism

LUDWIG VON BERTALANFFY

1. *The Epistemological Basis*

Scientism and its epistemological root, positivism, either in the original form given to it by Comte and his contemporaries or as modern logical positivism, are not an invention of the scientists. As Hayek[1] has admirably stated:

From Francis Bacon . . . to August Comte, and the "physicalists" of our own day, the claims for the exclusive virtues of the specific methods employed by the natural sciences were mostly advanced by men whose right to speak on behalf of the scientists were not above suspicion . . . The enthusiasm for physicism (it is now called physicalism) and the use of "physical language," the attempt to "unify science" and to make it the basis of morals . . . the desire to organize the work of others, particularly by editing a great encyclopedia and the wish to plan life in general on scientific lines are all present [in Saint-Simon's philosophy].

The present writer feels entitled to some criticism because he himself came from the Vienna Circle, having been a pupil of its founder, M. Schlick. The criticism proffered by Hayek may be supplemented by stating the fact that scientific research rarely follows the rigid commandments of the positivists. Many scientific developments started with "metaphysical" problems which, according to logical positivism, should have been discarded as pseudo problems at the beginning, the theory of the atom, starting with the wild speculations of Democritus and Lucretius, being an example. Even mechanics, the prototype of exact science, was freed from metaphysics and theology only slowly in a period extending from Kepler to Lagrange. Kepler himself derived his laws, not from solid principles of scientific research, but from unbridled neoplatonic speculations. Physical notions like "force" or "cause" were quite anthropomorphic in the beginning, and it took a long development until they were "deanthropomorphized" and became concepts in the sense of exact science and mathematical description of nature.

It is therefore no wonder that the biological, behavioral, and social sciences also began with vitalistic, philosophical, and metaphysical notions and have only slowly reached a state where they can deal with problems according to the modern standards of science.

In truth, of course, science essentially is a symbolic system created in such a way as to describe certain aspects of experience. What cannot be confirmed by experience is by this very fact outside the field of science; but this is not a recent discovery. On the other hand, explanation of and confirmation by experience is a highly technical matter and not only much more than, but very different from, "reduction to observable thing-predicates." Science does not "reduce" to "observation predicates" and "protocol sentences," but to highly technical terms like π-mesons, the space-time continuum, the nucleoprotein helix, the expanding or steady-state universe, and the rest, with the laws applying to such entities—things connected with naive experience only by way of a formidable mathematical and logical machine.

A consequence of this is that science mirrors only certain aspects of experience, to the exclusion of others. What we call scientific experience is a small sector of experience, and not only or necessarily the exclusive and best one. It is chosen for a certain purpose, namely, theoretical description and practical control of nature. What is called "an observed fact" is a certain aspect isolated from the stream of experience for certain intellectual pursuits.

Hence, not only vernacular language, but even science contains a cultural and linguistic bias. For example, the thinking in terms of "substances" and "attributes" is connected with the subject-attribute syntax of Indo-Germanic languages, as Benjamin Whorf has emphasized. This, in turn, colors our scientific world picture. An excellent example is the notion and theory of ether, introduced because there should be something that "oscillates," and so is the substratum of electromagnetic waves. Only slowly is this bias of language and culture-bound categories eliminated in the process of the deanthropomorphization of science,[2] achieved, in this particular instance, by the theory of relativity.

For similar reasons, our physics is concerned with so-called primary qualities, which are conveniently treated with our sort of mathematics. Secondary qualities are eliminated in the physical world picture even though they are not less "real" in immediate experience. It is quite conceivable that intelligent beings with other biological and cultural categories of understanding would develop forms of mathematics (i.e., deductive systems) quite different from our "science of quantities," and consequently other forms of "physics." Even within our own biases, unorthodox branches of mathematics, such as mathematical logic, topology, and group theory, show the possibility of such developments, being concerned with "order" (a tremendous problem in biology, psychology, etc.) rather than "measurable quantities."

As opposed to positivism, a sounder view appears to be what may be called perspectivism.[3] Cultural efforts from science to the arts are different symbolic universes elaborated to catch certain aspects of reality, whatever the latter term may mean. The scientific world picture is one of these perspectives, most useful for constructing a theoretical world view as well as for technological control of nature, but not the only one possible, nor one exhausting reality.

2. *Scientism in Theory and Practice*

In his classical essay, Hayek [4] characterized scientism by three basic concepts:

1. Objectivism, i.e., the contention that the methods of natural science are the only way of knowledge and that all phenomena must be ultimately expressed in "physical language";

2. Collectivism, i.e., what we may call the application of personificative fictions (Vaihinger) to social phenomena, treating them as if they were concrete, organism-like objects and wholes;

3. Historicism, i.e., the contention following from this point of view that laws of social and historical events can be discovered which are similar in structure to the laws in natural science.

Thus scientism, according to Hayek, is the misapplication of the method of natural science in realms where it does not belong.

Hayek's study was written in the early forties. At the time of writing, scientism was largely a theoretical problem and offered a utopian program. Today, it has become a fact and hence poses before us practical problems of paramount importance. It is, therefore, proposed to start the present study where Hayek left off.[5]

Condorcet,[6] writing before the French Revolution, contended that man and human society should be studied with the methods of the natural sciences and in the way we study the societies of beavers and bees. Condorcet's postulate and prophecy were fulfilled with a vengeance. We do not only theoretically describe man and society in this way in recent developments of the behavioral sciences. We also make human society ever more resemble that of beavers and bees.

In rereading Hayek's study, one can see immediately some basic changes which have occurred since the 1940's.

For example, Hayek [7] noted "scarcity of capital" as the "most fundamental economic fact." Today in America the most fundamental economic fact appears to be "Ending is better than mending," [8] that is, to keep an economy of abundance going by artificial means such as hidden persuaders, psychological obsolescence,[9] and the like.

In the earlier technological age, Ostwald's "energetic imperative" to use energy so as to achieve maximum effect with minimum energy-expense was a fair statement of the aims of physical engineering. Modern psychological engineering is essentially based upon the principle of waste, of which any chromium-laden, overpowered, long-finned, once-a-year traded-in car is an example.

Again, the "dislike which our whole generation shows for all commercial activities" and for the "merchant" [10] is now countered by the cultural emphasis on the salesman in prestige and in monetary reward.

A final quote from Hayek's book may be interesting: "Not only the ancient languages were reduced to a minimum and in practice almost entirely neglected, even the instruction in literature, drama, and history was very inferior, and moral and religious instruction, of course, completely absent." [11] This reads like an excerpt from an editorial published in the post-Sputnik debate on American education. As a matter of fact, it is a description of the school reform of 1795 in revolutionary France shortly after the Reign of Terror.

Hayek was well aware that scientism leads to "conscious planning of social phenomena." However, at this time he could refer only to political and social engineering and, in particular, economic planning,[12] which latter he analyzed in his *The Road to Serfdom*. Since he wrote his study the new development of "human engineering" has emerged. The phenomena of "mass man," "organization man," "hidden persuaders," baby's education and sexual intercourse directed by how-to-do books available at the corner drugstore, and a variety of others, are all corollaries to this theme. The criticism against scientism does not appear to be any longer that it is a misapplication of science in fields where it does not belong; rather, in recent years scientists have become only too competent in behavioral and social science and in their technological application. The following discussion suggests a few consequences arising from this fact. The scientistic credo can roughly be summarized as follows:

Our knowledge of the laws of physics is excellent, and consequently our technological control of inanimate nature is almost without limit. Our knowledge of biological laws is not so far advanced, but it is sufficient to allow a large amount of biological technology in modern medicine and applied biology. Our knowledge of the laws of human behavior and of society is still undeveloped. Consequently, human and sociological technology lag behind physical and biological technology. If we had a well-developed science of human behavior and society and a corresponding technology, this would mean the way out of the personal, sociological, and political problems of our time.

3. Scientism and Science

It seems, however, that the scientistic attitude is apt to lead to the destruction of a free society and of science itself. We shall start with a few considerations regarding the second aspect.

Science in the European tradition was a calling elected by a minority of gifted individuals. Today it is becoming a job among others, and much less profitable than those of the used-car dealer or fashion model.[13] The lack of prestige as well as of financial reward for the scientist, and particularly the so-called basic scientist, conceivably leads to a negative selection and hence a progressive decrease in the stature of the individuals engaged in it.

Connected with this is the often complained of, but never acted upon, overemphasis on applied as compared to basic science. Virtually all the achievements of technology were an upshot of basic research unconcerned with practical applications. Hertz's electromagnetic experiments eventually leading to radio and television, the highly speculative theory of the atom leading to atomic bombs, Mendel's experimentation in his cloister garden leading to a reform of agriculture are well-known examples. If, however, the applied scientist in atomic energy, electronics, or medicine commands considerably higher earnings and prestige than the physicist, chemist, or biologist, we may expect fewer new discoveries and ideas in science. Eventually further progress in technology will frustrate itself when the store of basic science is technologically exhausted and bases for new developments fail to be added.

Connected with this is the "mechanization" and "organization" of science. Science in the old tradition first formulated a problem and then looked for machinery necessary for its investigation, often by way of improvisation; and in the last decades in Europe a tiny budget has been the most important limiting factor. Today the tendency is widely reversed. First there is a complicated and expensive machine; then let's think what we are going to do with it. Accordingly, funds for buildings, apparatus, technical help, etc., are nearly unlimited; funds for brains are very hard to find.

Similar considerations apply to "organization" in science. Here we find the mystical belief in the "group" or "team" as a means of unprecedented scientific progress. A group of specialists trained in the same or different fields is an excellent instrument for certain well-definable research development purposes; namely, to elaborate and test a given research or technological program, say, to find the best shape for an ICBM or to test thousands of chemicals to discover whether one of them will prove to be a cure for cancer.

The group, however, is singularly ineffective in inaugurating new scientific developments. Hardly one example is known in the history of science where a "team" has established new principles.[14] History rather shows that major advances and breakthroughs in science have resulted from the often capricious and irrational brain waves of gifted individuals which only subsequently were proved, formalized, and systematized in the accredited ways of science, usually (and quite legitimately) encountering considerable resistance on the part of the profession at the beginning.

Although it is possible to pool capable individuals, their work, and the results obtained, the expectation that a scientific team is more creative than the sum of its members rests on the metaphysical belief that a social group has a "mind" or "spirit" excelling that of the component individuals. There is no foundation for, and many facts against, such a belief.

These and other factors lead to a progressive levelling in science —a phenomenon which is by no means a new discovery, but well-known and a matter of grave concern to its leaders.

These developments further lead to the decay of what is known as academic freedom.[15] The present discussion is not concerned with such limitations of scientific communication as may be necessary for reasons of national security, but solely with infringement in matters without political implication.

Established over many centuries, the freedom of thought, research, and communication has been an unshakeable basis of modern science. Encroachments on this freedom, such as Galileo's trial before the Roman Inquisition, are abhorrent examples even after centuries have gone by. Academic freedom remained unhampered even if a scientist were in violent opposition to the ruling political system. For example, during the time of blackest reaction after the Congress of Vienna, the expulsion of seven professors from the University of Goettingen because of their political views caused an outcry of horror all over Germany and Europe. Virchow, founder of pathological anatomy, fought at the barricades in the revolution of 1848 and consequently was suspended by the University of Berlin, which, as are all European universities, was a governmental institution. However, after two weeks public opinion forced the government to reinstate him. After six months he became head of the first department of pathological anatomy in history, later to become the famous *Geheimrat,* medical pope of Germany, and leader of the opposition against Bismarck.[16]

Control of responsible investigators by innumerable committees, administrative authorities, financial agencies, journals, etc., was unknown up to recent times. It would deserve serious study whether the "space lag," the "missile gap," and many other much discussed "lags" and "gaps" are not connected with the several factors mentioned.

These are various aspects of what Riesman called the "other-directedness" of modern man, including the scientist. It leads to distrust in personal responsibility, dominance of the "group," encroachment on academic freedom and the bureaucratization of science which hardly provide a "climate for basic research." [17]

4. Scientism and Society

Oswald Spengler has become a sort of bogey among modern scientific philosophers and historians, and his *Decline of the West* [18] a paragon of ill-founded and objectionable speculation. The present writer does not quite share this opinion and does not feel compelled to change the views he expressed thirty-five years ago.[19] He agrees that Spengler's intuitive method, his presumptuous attitude, errors in fact and in interpretation are subject to serious criticism.

However, stripped of the poetic embroidery (which forms part of the fascination of Spengler's work compared to the verbose tediousness in much recent philosophy), Spengler's doctrine is simply an attempt to explain history by way of a theoretical model. That he arrived at this conception in an objectionable, intuitive, and romantic way proves as little against it as Kepler's laws are disproved by the historical fact that Kepler found them, not by way of what we consider sound scientific method, but rather by fantastic neoplatonic speculations.

Spengler's model has to be judged by the same criteria that apply to any model in science. It will be found that this model is objectionable in many respects, but also that it has explanatory and predictive value. This is not a contradiction, but a property shared by many models even in the more orthodox branches of science.

Some objections to Spengler are apparent.

1. The basic question is whether a limited number of cultures past and present (eight with Spengler, some twenty with Toynbee) at all allows generalizations or supposed laws of history. This essentially corresponds with Hayek's criticism of the "historicism" of the scientistic attitude, and with Rickert's distinction between the "nomothetic" method of natural science and the "ideographic" method of history.

2. Another objection is against the comparison of "cultures" with "organisms." Trivially, an individual organism circumscribed in space and time is different from a social group consisting of individual conscious persons. However, communities, be they biological or social, can be considered, if not as "superorganisms," then as "systems," that is, collectives of elements standing in interaction, and laws of social systems are in order, as evidenced by mathematical biology, economics, social sciences, etc.[20] This is not a scientistic misuse so long as theoretically the limitations of such

models and consequent over-all laws are borne in mind, and so long as practically they are not used as a tool to make human community into a "society of beavers or bees."

3. Even if the organismic analogy were accepted, Spengler's assumption of a rigid life-span and timetable of cultural development cannot be maintained; even legitimate organisms, animals and plants, of the same species vary greatly in this respect. Toynbee has justly abandoned this Spenglerian assumption. The frills of Toynbee's doctrine, such as the theory of challenge and response and his eschatological views, are hardly less gratuitous (and much less dramatic) than Spengler's metaphysical romanticism.

4. Spengler's contention that cultures are "organisms" unconnected with each other is patently incorrect. The survival and inheritance by newer cultures of what has been achieved in the past is obvious. Our Western civilization, in particular, patently differs from previous ones in its global character as compared to the geographic limitations of the former.

These basic objections as well as factual criticism in detail have to be taken for granted. However, the criterion of verification of any model in science is whether predictions derived from it are confirmed by experience. Irrespective of the defects of Spengler's method and model, many derivations from it appear to be disquietingly correct. This does not imply a predestined doom, but rather a warning signal; much in the same way as, with respect to a human individual, the life-span is not predestined, and illness terminating it may be controlled by timely diagnosis and therapeutic measures.

Spengler's "Decline" stems, of course, from Nietzsche's concept of nihilism, that is, the devaluation of traditional values. Spengler himself described the phenomenon as a Time of Trouble, internecine wars, dictatorships, formation of an uprooted fellaheen society, and progressing statism. Toynbee [21] similarly speaks of a Time of Troubles and redoubtable Universal States. Ortega y Gasset [22] calls the same phenomenon "the Uprise of the Masses," emphasizing demographic pressure as its cause. David Riesman [23] speaks of the "other-directed crowd" of our time compared to the "inner-directedness" of other periods. W. H. Whyte [24] describes the conformity achieved by "Organization Man" and the modern "deification of the organization"; Boulding [25] similarly identifies the problems posed by the "Organizational Revolution." Hoffer's [26] "True Believer" is craving for authority at any price in order to fill his emotional vacuum. Each of these descriptions may be objectionable; but it seems there is a basic phenomenon labelled in different ways.

Apparently, "scientism" plays a predominant role in this development. Superficially, the scientistic character of Western "civilization" (the term used in the technical sense proposed by Spengler) is caused by a prevalence of science and technology unparalleled in past cultures. The machine, instead of saving labor, becomes man's master, making him an automaton and small wheel in the great mechanism. However, the problem has become much more subtle in America and parts of Europe. Automation and related developments tend to save man from becoming a slave of the machine and will undoubtedly do so even more in the future. The problem appears to be shifting from physical to psychological technology, making the basic question: Is a scientifically controlled society desirable? In Hayek's terms, "collectivism" now is not a theoretical, but a practical, issue; the fictitious entities characteristic of the scientistic approach have become more "real" and powerful than in any other period.

Conditioned-reflex methods, "hidden persuaders," "brainwashing," subliminal motivation, and allied techniques form the basis of psychological coercion and control unknown in previous history.

Hayek has made it clear that this problem was recognized by early positivists: Comte already foresaw, even though he derided, a "despotism founded on science." [27]

Absolutism, authoritarianism, and demagogues are phenomena ubiquitous in history. However, coercion imposed from outside, be it ever so ruthless, necessarily breeds rebels, nonconformists, and heretics, as they have existed in all times of history. Dictators can be disposed of and, as a matter of historical record, usually come to a bad end. Only coercion from inside and by psychological means can impose total control. Replacing old-fashioned rhetoric and appeal to limited numbers, modern psychological techniques have made this method scientific, all-inclusive, and nearly infallible.

It appears to matter little whether this totalitarianism is essentially benevolent, as in Huxley's *Brave New World,* or malevolent, as in Orwell's *1984;* or, speaking in realistic and nonutopian terms, whether hidden persuaders are employed democratically to promote a washing machine or a politician, or autocratically to ensure the reign of a dictator. For it is more than probable that methods used for inconsequential advertising can and will be employed for the deification of the state, the nation, its leader, or for global war as those in charge desire.

There is a neologism which was introduced after the war, namely, "genocide," meaning, according to the Oxford dictionary, "extermination of a race." I submit that a similar term, "menticide," [28] be adopted, meaning extermination of the individual mind. As a matter of fact, extermination of a race is hard to achieve. The scars in the body social heal rapidly, owing to its regenerative capacity. Thus, in spite of the large-scale genocide of the last World War, the Malthusian problem of an overpopulated planet becomes more menacing every day.

Menticide, in contrast, is irreversible and irreparable. It is the stultification of the human race, its progressive reduction to automatons or morons by mass media and psychological techniques.

At this point, the psychiatric and criminological question arises: Why, at a time when the "greatest happiness of the greatest number" with respect to material comfort is achieved as never before in history, is society beset with an equally unprecedented menace of mental disorder and criminality?

The orthodox and, at first, plausible answer is that the heavy and manifold stresses imposed in our complicated society are responsible. Nevertheless, the theory is demonstrably untrue. For example, World War II, the stress of which certainly was extreme, as it endangered not only social amenities and values, but biological survival, did not lead to an increase of either neuroses [29] or psychoses.[30] On the other hand, under conditions of economic opulence unparalleled in history one out of twenty Americans is doomed to become mentally ill, and more than half of the hospital population are mental cases.[31] It would appear that mental disorder, in the form both of mental illness and delinquency, is the reverse of, and the price society has to pay for, scientifically granted comfort and conformity.

The hypothesis can well be defended (and is in no way new) that not the stress, but rather the emptiness, of life is one decisive factor in the increase of mental disorder.[32] One may say that "nihilism," [33] the breakdown of a symbolic universe of values, and the conflicts between Riesman's other-directedness and individual resistance may lead to conflicts manifest in mental disorders. One may also say that the rootlessness of modern man (what Spengler called the fellaheen) is apt to lead to deradication neurosis, a well-known psychiatric disturbance. Again, the defense mechanisms manifest in neurosis and psychosis [34] may become active, not because outside stress is intolerable, but rather because the psychophysical organism is weakened, its immanent activity reduced; and inner emptiness and outer enforcement combine to create the conditions for mental illness. Well-known laboratory experiments with sensory deprivation,[35] prisoner's psychosis, and related phenomena tend to support such hypotheses. This is not the place to discuss the merits or shortcomings of these particular formulations. What they amount to is that "culture," among many other things, is an important psychohygienic factor.

Similar considerations apply to criminality. Juvenile delinquency, for example, is easily explainable under conditions of poverty, devastation, broken homes, and the like. But it is a disturbing phenomenon that the rate of juvenile delinquency is lower in poor Italy than in the wealthy United States. As a psychiatrist expressed it, before a Senate Committee:

It is our distinct impression that particularly crimes of violence have increased tremendously, that such . . . acts of seemingly unmotivated violence, as you see them in wolf-packs and such, are really almost a novel phenomena. That form of gang organization, of violence for violence's sake is something new that has been added . . . and there is an increased toleration of brutality and violence, even of the so-called normal adolescent or person.[36]

Apparently when there is an eruption against boredom and the emptiness of life, crime is one outlet, not in the form of crime for want or of passion, but for the fun of it. The classical Leopold-Loeb case characteristically stands at about the beginning of this era.

Conclusion

The diagnosis of the ills of our society appears clear enough. The therapy we do not know, and the present author does not belong to the world-saviors who have invented the nostrum for curing humanity.

In view of the question of scientism, its basic defect can readily be summarized. It is the mistaken belief that science, scientific method, and technology with its achievements for human comfort cover the whole of human experience and fulfillment. This patently not being the case, and nothing else filling the vacuum, the scientistic disappointment is the necessary consequence. An intellectual vacuum being left, it is no wonder that our time of technology and scientism is also the time of pseudo religions and primitive superstitions. This is true for the pseudo religions invented by the founders of positivism and scientism, Comte and Saint-Simon, as well as for astrology, nationalism, the various ways of escapism, semi-Christian sects, and others, of our time. Even traditional religions become pseudo religions when, as stated by Billy Graham,[37]

The church in this country has the highest membership it has ever had, but the country also has the highest crime and divorce rate and the greatest increase in juvenile delinquency in history.

Or else, as Aldous Huxley has foreseen, the greatest happiness of the greatest number in a scientistic *Brave New World* can be maintained by doping. This is largely borne out by this period's subsistence on tranquilizers and allied psychotropic drugs.[38]

It is worthwhile to note that the error of scientism was committed by the positivists from Bacon to Comte to our time, but was not shared by the founders of pragmatism. William James' *Varieties of Religious Experience* is an everlasting document in this respect.

Scientism did not recognize, and helped actively to suppress, an enormous and all-important part of human experience. Thus, it made "Organization Man" into a society of "beavers and bees." [39] This is a consequence of the fact that scientism cannot provide a basis for the uniqueness of human individuality and values. In a reappraisal of the latter will be the clue to the future.

NOTES

1. F. A. Hayek, *The Counter-Revolution of Science* (Glencoe: Free Press, 1952), pp. 14 and 123.
2. L. von Bertalanffy, "Philosophy of Science in Scientific Education," *Scientific Monthly,* LXXVII (1953), 233-239.
3. L. von Bertalanffy, "An Essay on the Relativity of Categories," *Philosophy of Science,* XXII (1953), 243-263.
4. Hayek, *op. cit.*
5. The present paper was prepared before reading A. Huxley's *Brave New World Revisited* (New York: Harper, 1958), where many similar reflections can be found.
6. Hayek, *op. cit.,* p. 108.
7. *Ibid.,* p. 97.
8. A. Huxley, *Brave New World* (New York: Harper, 1932).
9. H. O. Packard, *The Hidden Persuaders* (New York: McKay, 1957).
10. Hayek, *op. cit.,* p. 96.
11. *Ibid.,* pp. 109 f.
12. *Ibid.,* pp. 94 ff.
13. Since documentation of this point was desired, the writer refers to a discussion in *Time* magazine (March 24, 1958).
14. Cf. T. J. (editorial), "Two Heads Better Than One?" *Science,* CXXVII (1958), 933.
15. Cf. P. I. Lazarsfeld and W. Thielens, Jr., *The Academic Mind: Social Scientists in a Time of Crisis* (1959).
16. E. H. Ackerknecht, *Rudolph Virchow, Doctor, Statesman, Anthropologist* (Madison: University of Wisconsin Press, 1953).
17. D. W. Bronk, *"The Climate for Basic Research"* (Presentation at Symposium: The Structure of Science, Wistar Institute, Philadelphia, April 17-18, 1959).

18. O. Spengler, *Der Untergang des Abendlandes* (Rev. ed.; Muenchen: Beck, 1922).
19. L. von Bertalanffy, "Einfuehrung in Spengler's Werk," *Literaturblatt der Koelnischen Zeitung* (May, 1924).
20. Cf., for example: *General Systems. Yearbooks of the Society for General Systems Research,* ed. by L. von Bertalanffy and A. Rapaport (Ann Arbor: University of Michigan, 1956 *et. seq.*).
21. A. J. Toynbee, *A Study of History* (abridged ed.; New York and London: Oxford University Press, 1947).
22. J. Ortega y Gasset, *The Revolt of the Masses* (New York: Norton & Co., 1932).
23. D. Riesman, *The Lonely Crowd* (New Haven: Yale University Press, 1950).
24. W. H. Whyte, *The Organization Man* (New York: Simon & Schuster, 1956).
25. K. E. Boulding, *The Organizational Revolution* (New York: Harper, 1953).
26. E. Hoffer, *The True Believer* (New York: Harper, 1951).
27. Hayek, *op. cit.,* pp. 139, 183, 200, and *passim.*
28. The term was introduced and similarly explained by J. A. M. Meerloo, "Pavlovian Strategy as a Weapon of Menticide," *American Journal of Psychiatry,* CX (1954), 809-813.
29. M. K. Opler, *Culture, Psychiatry and Human Values* (Springfield, Ill.: Thomas, 1956), pp. 67 f.
30. F. Llavero, "Bemerkungen zu einigen Grundfragen der Psychiatrie," etc., *Der Nervenarzt,* XXVIII (1957), 419-421.
31. Cf., for example: M. Gorman, *Every Other Bed* (World Publ., 1956). According to R. Fein, *Economics of Mental Illness* (New York: Basic Books, 1958), the costs per year for care of the mentally ill in the United States are estimated to exceed 1.7 billion dollars, indirect costs adding to some 2.7 billion dollars. "It has been shown that where services for the mentally ill are relatively highly developed, psychiatric cases account for almost half the total number of patients occupying hospital beds; moreover, it was estimated in one country that about one-third of all hospital outpatients attended for reasons that were largely psychological." (*The Mental Health Programme of the World Health Organization, 1949-1957.* Geneva: WHO Int/ Ment/5.)
32. Cf. L. von Bertalanffy, "Some Biological Considerations on the Problem of Mental Illness," *Bulletin Menninger Clinic,* XXIII (1959), 41-51.
33. L. von Bertalanffy, "Human Values in a Changing World," *New Knowledge in Human Values,* edited by A. H. Maslow (New York: Harper, 1959), pp. 65-74.
34. K. Menninger, with H. Ellenberger, P. Pruyser and M. Mayman, "The Unitary Concept of Mental Illness," *Bulletin Menninger Clinic,* XXII (1958), 4-12.
35. Cf., for example, D. Bindra in J. H. Tanner and B. Inhelder, ed., *Discussions on Child Development,* II (London: Tavistock, 1957).
36. F. J. Hacker, in *Juvenile Delinquency* (Hearings before the Subcommit-

tee . . . U. S. Senate, Pursuant S. Res. 62; Washington: U. S. Printing Office, June 15-18, 1955), p. 99.

37. *Los Angeles Times,* June 5, 1958.

38. It is estimated that in 1956, 48 million prescriptions for tranquilizers were filled in the United States at a cost of approximately $200 million.

39. It is perhaps no accident that the late Professor Kinsey originally was an entomologist, studying insect societies. K. Menninger, "One View of the Kinsey Report" (*GP, VIII* [December, 1953], 67-72), justly notes "Kinsey's compulsion to force human sexual behavior into a zoological frame of reference." As stated by Menninger, from this he derives the identification of the "normal" with the "statistically frequent." The "Volunteer Error in the Kinsey Study," tested by A. H. Maslow and J. M. Sakoda, *Journal of Abnormal and Social Psychology,* XLVII, 259-262, probably is responsible for the difference between the clinicians' experience and the Kinsey data as stated by Menninger.

11

Social Science Versus the Obsession of "Scientism"

ROBERT STRAUSZ-HUPÉ

I

A discussion of the scientific study of man and society calls for answers to the following questions: First, what properties pertaining to man and society are the proper subjects of scientific inquiry? What are the appropriate scientific methods for obtaining valid insights into the social process? And what precisely can these scientific methods and the insights which they vouchsafe tell us about the future development of society and about possible alternatives among which we are free to choose?

The idea that human society can be studied as methodically as any object in nature engaged the disinterested and scientific curiosity of the Greeks. In his history, Herodotus set out to study all branches of humanity irrespective of race and cultural level. He takes people as he finds them, held together by nothing but space and time. Herodotus, by his superior impartiality, looks, so to speak, from outside in. In his thought, the phenomenon of universal humanity is as susceptible to objective investigation as is the course of celestial bodies or the consistency of earth and water. Of religious experience, Herodotus does not speak. For Herodotus, the unity of mankind consists of identities or similarities of behavior, and not of a superior meaning derived from a unitary faith and fate.

This is not the place to assess how successful Herodotus was in keeping metaphysics out of his universal history and to what extent his value judgments did infiltrate into his superior impartiality. What matters here is his conception of secular historiography and his methodical separation of consciousness and its object, of man-observing and man-observed. Two thousand years after Herodotus the problem of objectivity was still to trouble social scientists.

The question of objectivity in the exploration of social phenomena can be stated as follows: What is it that we can know about other men, irrespective of the uniqueness of our personality, which at once embraces the experience of mankind throughout the ages and is kin to all men living and dead, and yet is biologically finite and cast in the mold of a unique and more or less transitory society, i.e., irrespective of the insoluble dilemma: the brotherhood of man and the terrible isolation of mortal man? As long as humanism and the social sciences walked hand in hand, social scientists saw no need of dispensing with the common bond of humanity as the datum point of their investigations. They knew (or believed they knew) other men because they themselves thought and felt like the subject of their investigations; they knew (or believed they knew) what made society go around because they themselves were members of that society, observers, so to speak, in the hands of their own observation. The link between the social sciences and the humanities was broken by the impact of science upon society as well as upon political and social philosophy.

With the efflorescence, about a hundred and fifty years ago, of the natural sciences, there began a new phase in the long quest of the social sciences for objectivity, for reality. Social scientists now attempted to equate social processes with natural processes and consequently to apply the methodology of the natural sciences to their universe of discourse. It has been overlooked for a long time how much the popularity and political influence of positivism and materialism owed to circumstance and coincidence rather than to the aptness of their respective scientific apparatus. Not a few leaders of these schools of thought and their sectarian offspring, such as, for example, Saint-Simon, Comte, Häckel, and Pareto, were intellectuals who had been attracted to the natural sciences, had failed to make their mark in pure or applied science, and found their way into the social sciences, prophets in another land. F. A. Hayek, in his *Counter-Revolution of Science,* traced the influence upon nineteenth-century sociology and political science of Auguste Comte, an engineer who, instead of practicing his craft, theorized on social engineering. He fathered a long line of mechanistic utopias of society, pedantic, insensitive, and inhuman. There was not then—and there is not now—a sustained and fruitful participation by natural scientists in the pursuit of political and social studies. There was then—and there is now—a lively traffic between their least competent colleagues, many of whom made their living as literary popularizers of science, and social scientists.

The methods of the natural sciences were introduced into the social sciences in a haphazard way and often by hands far from highly skilled in either branch of learning. It is not surprising that not a few natural scientists came to look down upon their colleagues at the other end of the academic edifice. At the same time, the impact of science upon society not only brought about those many and profound changes which make up the story of progress, but also altered significantly the status relationship of academic disciplines. The physicist and the chemist, not the sociologist and the economist, have become the symbolic figures of the age. The response of the social sciences to the plight of academic, if not social, inferiority was to embrace all the more fervently the scientific methodology *tout court,* namely, the methodology of the natural sciences. To be sure, there were "objective" arguments in favor of chucking out the old tools and importing techniques that had so fabulously enriched human knowledge and, in the bargain, given man such vast powers over nature. But the prestige factor stood—and still stands—for much. Science is not only a pursuit; it is also a distinctive posture that commands popular deference far beyond its own domain.

II

The observations above should not be taken as implying the rejection of the methods of the natural sciences as wholly irrelevant or inapplicable to the study of social phenomena. Scientific method is applicable to all fields of study. It is, however, conceivable, and highly probable, that the specific methods of the natural sciences do not, and cannot, encompass the range of social phenomena and will, in some crucial respects, produce results that are as meaningless scientifically as they are harmful humanly and socially. In brief, the social sciences cannot be expected to do for society what the natural sciences have done for nature until they have developed their own (and not somebody else's) methodology and defined their proper data and criteria of truth, the truth that it is theirs to seek.

As theory, pure science is concerned with the reduction of diversity to identity and thus to order. Practical scientific research is concerned with simplification. It is tempting to apply these methods to the theory and practice of politics. Indeed, it can be argued that a centralized authority bent on making plans for an entire society must, because of the bewildering complexity of the data, proceed as does the scientific investigator who arbitrarily reduces the variables of his problem in order to make it manageable. This is the proper laboratory procedure.

But when applied to the problems of human society, the process of simplification, pushed to its logical conclusion, must lead, in theory, to the deletion of those unique and imponderable factors —nuances, if you will—which endow life with zest, flavor, and creativity, and, in practice, to the repression of diversity and thus to tyranny. Indeed, not a few modern dictatorships have sought to derive the warrant for their authority from the alleged precepts of science and to contrive a more or less successful synthesis of official ideologies and modern science. National socialism, although it did not profess to be a "science," rewarded handsomely those academic toadies who brought "scientific" proof for Hitler's bizarre and spiteful theories on genetics. Marxian socialism does profess to be a science. It has found, in the dominant philosophy of the scientific community, monism, a powerful intellectual *and* political ally. Nowadays scientific pretension rather than the profession of ethical beliefs screens the power urge. This tendency has led to a progressive devaluation of political ideologies and the rise of the universal ideology of the age, scientism. Scientism has swept all before it, and all the political ideologies of our times purport to be scientific. They are, in fact, scientistic. The problem of totalitarianism is the reduction of human diversity to uniformity. It is quite natural that all totalitarian philosophies appeal to the precedents of laboratory procedure, for this procedure bestows respectability upon the ironing out of individual idiosyncrasies.

To simplify reality is to abstract. The scientist, confronted by the data of experience, prescinds from a problem those aspects which are not susceptible to measurement and to causal explanation. His purpose is to explain the phenomenon in terms of causation, not of purpose, intention, and values.[1] Pragmatically, such arbitrary abstraction is justified. The progress of modern science has been due to its rigorous confinement to the measurable aspects of elements of experience which are contained in a causal system. But science does not encompass nor does it profess to encompass all human experience. Science seeks to approximate the truth about the world only within the limitations of specific and rigorously defined contexts. No true scientist will claim more; no educated layman should expect more. Yet the vulgarization of science—scientism—has led many people, including not a few scientists who have lost sight of the philosophical foundations of their craft, to assert that science holds the key to *all* problems of human experience and that those problems that cannot be dealt with by simplification or abstraction are either trivial problems or no problems at all.

The blight of scientism has spread in all sectors of modern life. It has made its most consequential and dangerous inroads in the field of politics. In the arsenal of demagoguery, scientism is the most powerful secret ideological weapon. The demand of the political market for scientific rationalization is great; great are the rewards of the political scientist who will supply it. Thus, for example, complex international problems can be swept conveniently under the rug by reducing international relations to economic equations: by assisting the underdeveloped countries economically, the giver wins, if not their good will, then at least a measure of toleration and, in the bargain, fosters the growth of democracy, which, it is alleged, is correlated closely with the rise of average standards of living. By ignoring unwieldy cultural factors and deep-seated antagonisms to Western peoples and values, one simplifies the problem of, let us say, India's place in what is called euphemistically the "free world": the West, by adding just the right amount of investment capital to India's government-directed economic development, can secure the survival, in India, of parliamentary government and, in world politics, assist India in becoming a counterweight to Red China. Proposals for such a Western "policy" toward India are loaded with eye-filling and vigorously formulated statistics. The trouble with this neat solution —which, in the context of scientific economics, is perfectly plausible—is that the soul of India is not the soul of America, that Indians cannot be equated with Chinese on the basis of per capita economic productivity, and that, strictly speaking, India is *not* a nation.

III

Since the social sciences are concerned with human action, an explanation of data can hardly be satisfying and valid unless it relates "objective" social phenomena to human purpose, intention, and values. This approach is understandably at odds with that of the natural scientist. It is also at odds with the idea of a centrally planned and, therefore, centrally controlled society. The obstacle to centralized, "scientific" planning is individual idiosyncrasy; i.e., individual purpose, intention, and values. The most expeditious way around this obstacle is to assert that individual purpose, intention, and values are scientifically irrelevant or trivial and impervious to measurement and, therefore, should be left out of account. Likewise, it is argued that historical institutions, because they are the traditional repository of purpose, intention, and values, are not proper fields of scientific inquiry. In sum, so the "scientific" proposition runs, the social scientist should not concern himself with what institutions *are,* but with their operation, not with what men *are,* but with their behavior as members of the group.

I do not propose here to examine the position of various schools of behaviorism on what we know about man and society and the relevancy of their findings for the social and "policy" sciences. The behaviorists disagree among themselves on methods of measurement and, more important still, the meaningfulness of the insights produced by experiment. They appear agreed, however, on the rejection of consciousness as a means for gaining insight into psychological phenomena and on explaining human phenomena by the measurement of observed behavior and in terms of a causal system in which human consciousness is not a factor.[2] For the present purpose it suffices that, in this country, it is via behaviorist psychology that the methods of the natural sciences exert their strongest influence upon the social sciences. Let us now examine briefly the implications of the banishment of consciousness—introspection—and the reliance on measurement of behavior as the most important, if not the sole, means for obtaining valid insights in social processes.

To begin with, it should be obvious that, from the point of view of the social sciences, human consciousness—introspection—would have to be invented if it did not exist. Thus, for example, the operation of the market would be inconceivable without introspection. Not only in the market place but also in the daily exchanges of communal life we act on the assumption that other men think as we do, and, therefore, will act as we will act. In the overwhelming majority of instances of daily life it is introspection, and not our observation of other men's behavior, that guides our decisions and triggers our action. The argument that our actions are merely conditioned reflexes and are not engendered by the workings of our consciousness poses an intriguing language problem; it does not add the slightest whiff of an operable concept to our theoretical framework. The fact is that we do assume that we know the other fellow will behave in a manner which is given to us by introspection. We may be wrong in this assumption. But we act on it. And this assumption thus becomes a scientific datum of the social sciences. The circumstance that the data of the social sciences consist of opinions true *and* false calls for a discrete methodology which, although in many respects kindred to the methodologies of the natural sciences, must still stand upon its own feet and stake out its own domain.[3]

Social scientists who infer patterns of human conduct from introspection, and thus rely upon their own consciousness rather than on the no less ambiguous appearance of "behavior," are plainly making use of empirical facts. The progress of modern economics would have been inconceivable without recourse to introspective experience. "Anthropomorphism, rightly scorned in the natural sciences as prescientific metaphysics, is justified in economics because economics is about human action." [4] Statistics has its place in the social sciences as it has in any field of scientific inquiry. The question here is one of available data and of the susceptibility of available data to measurement rather than one of methodology. Obviously, it would be intellectually satisfying if, for example, political behavior could be measured in such a way that the causal system of politics could be explained mathematically. As it is, the statistical tools are powerful, while the available data are either scarce or dubious. Especially in politics a great many more data will have to be collected before their accumulated weight can engage profitably the generous capacity of statistical mathematics. In this country cooperative research, heavily endowed with zeal, faith in calculating machines, and tax-free funds, has produced a vast literature on the regularities and irregularities of the political animal. But it is doubtful that this earnest effort has produced deeper insights than, let us say, Parkinson's more entertaining investigations, which led him to deduce his famous law.[5] To be sure, given the prevalent preoccupation with data-gathering and grinding the data thus gathered into statistical contrivances, some progress will be made. But progress in this field will not render measurable what is nonmetrical, i.e., what by its very nature is unknowable through numbers.

It can be argued that reliance on behavioral analogies has led to an alarming atrophy of the powers of introspection. Thus, for example, not a few Western statesmen are prone to act on the assumption that, because a communist leader *behaves* on certain occasions as such leaders are wont to do, he will prove a predictable and manageable quantity in every world political equation. Mr. Mikoyan eats and dresses as we do, smiles at more or less corny jokes, and, intermittently, kisses babies before the camera and cherishes peace and the middle-class ideal of business as usual. Since the average Soviet citizen displays a well-documented interest in electrical refrigerators and cars, the Soviet rulers will seek to satisfy their demand for semidurable goods, cut down on military hardware, and settle down to the *status quo*— just as our statesmen would do were they in the Soviets' shoes. These clichés reflect all that is most shallow in reliance on both behavioral analogy and introspective analogy. Our "statesman," because he has abandoned an ethical position to empiricism, is smitten with deafness to the voice of intuition and with blindness to observable facts: he understands anything except the inwardness of political conduct.

IV

The aesthetical element of experience is not susceptible to measurement. Yet there is an intimate relation between aesthetics and politics, between aesthetics and economics, and between aesthetics and morals. Artistic creativity and prevailing tastes in painting, the plastic arts, literature, and music are indices of social stability and national power. These indices cannot be expressed in numbers. Yet are they less relevant than, let us say, indices of coal, steel, and uranium production? In brief, social scientists must be concerned with man and his fate, man and his idiosyncrasies.[6] Social scientists, too, are men. At the present stage of imperfection, there is but faint hope that we will be able to deduce from the variety of experience mathematical laws and constants.

It is unscientific—or shall we say "scientistic"—to insist upon applying the methods of the natural sciences categorically to the fields of sociology, economics, and politics. The attempt to do so not only does not advance research, but stultifies it. Yet without a

vigorous advance in the systematic scholarly techniques for analyzing and solving social problems, the increasing bewilderment of
modern men will elude rational treatment, and the concrete result
of so much well-meaning effort and ink spilt will be merely another nail—a rusty theoretical one—in the coffin of the old order
—the good and the bad of it—and not the establishment of a presumably better order. At no time in human history has there been
a more crying need for bringing the unsentimental scholarly outlook to bear upon politics than now.

There is just a faint chance that we can do so before the destructive forces which now impinge upon the political and social structure of the Western world have done their work. We can discern
now on the intellectual horizon the rise, albeit faint, of a new
constellation: the growing awareness of policy-makers of the need
for a genuinely theoretical—not pseudoscientific—approach to politics and the progress toward the development of a pure political
theory, based on a firm grasp of human nature. In a way, the
bumptiousness of the scientific claims advanced by diverse "scientistic" ideologies and their dismal, sometimes bloody failures to
redeem these claims have cleared the decks for the advent of the
true science of politics. The need for such a science of politics is
not a mere matter of academic concern. What is at stake is, in the
most literal sense, the survival of our civilization.

In one of its deepest meanings, the world crisis is a dispute
about political organization. Regardless of the historical roots of
the present conflict and of the contending philosophical concepts,
all existing states are confronted by the need for reorganization.
Without such reorganization, the purpose, intentions, and values
of our society are untranslatable into those actions which must be
taken in order to defend it against the dangers from without and
the eroding forces from within. Such reorganization may have to
bear on the fundamentals of the political structure; or it may call
for the realignment of existing institutions; or the existing institutions, sound as they may be, may require operational improvements.

Whenever men talk politics, they argue, as a matter of course,
about personalities, the management of public institutions, the

usefulness or obsolescence of existing establishments, and the re-form of political and administrative machinery or the creation of new machinery. The discussion of personalities slips easily into emotive terms, and there is, in politics, a proper place for emotion. Management and organizational structure, however, can be discussed meaningfully only upon the identification of problems, the assembly of relevant facts, and the analysis of possible solutions. It is one of the most significant symptoms of the world crisis that our knowledge of public problems is either vague or generalized. At best, the usefulness of our institutions is assessed in impressionistic terms and, more often than not, the stated purpose of the institution, as, for example, the French Chamber of Deputies under the Fourth Republic, is confused with its performance. Public interest centers upon the generalized theory of an institution rather than upon its reality, not to speak of its "organizational yield." Hence, improvements are mostly guided by intuitive judgments and accomplished by accident.

The problem of reorganization is threefold. All societies require, although in different degrees, reorganization in order to achieve good government under modern conditions of technological change, economic development, demographic growth, psychological understanding, and human freedom. Most existing social and political organizations represent some kind of compromise between traditional institutional concepts and the satisfaction of the power urge. Neither the institutions nor their management satisfies the requirements of efficient organization. Efficient organization is not tantamount to good government. Organizational efficiency and political ethics are, however, interdependent variables. Good government is a *contradictio in adjecto* without consideration of purpose, intention, and values. "Good" government seeks to maximize the "organizational yield" of public institutions.

Secondly, the various national or subnational societies have broken out of their historic isolation. During the last hundred years, nations and civilizations have become increasingly interdependent. There is little doubt that this interdependence will continue to grow unless adverse economic and military developments intervene. Consequently, it is necessary to find organizational forms which will provide for the effective collaboration between different societies that are dependent upon one another but lack the commensurate psychological cohesion. This international "growing together" requires a deepened understanding of institutional similarities and differences. Such understanding can be derived only from sure methods of comparison. The actual process of "growing together" requires guidance, hence the need for a theory of institutional synthesis. In the absence of such a theory, peoples will not be able to determine which institution should be abandoned, enlarged, taken over, reformed or developed jointly, and the process of "growing together" might be reversed into a disorderly and dangerous melee.

Thirdly, the global ideological conflict would not be global except for the circumstance that all members of humanity now have become interrelated and can communicate virtually instantly with one another. The leading societies are in disagreement about the ways by which the world society is to be organized. This disagreement is rendered acute by the fact that the contending arguments are almost entirely irrational. Each contending ideology has its own solution. We believe that our solution is the better one, and, for diverse reasons, it probably is. But if actual events can supply us guidance, we have not developed the methodgy for presenting our arguments so effectively and rationally that they will invite acceptance by all men—and, incidentally, considered and serene acceptance by those who now accept them somewhat hesitantly on faith. We hold strong opinions about political organization, but, unfortunately, those notions are convincing only to ourselves and to people who "think as we do." We cannot prove that we are right, for—among other reasons—we have failed to work out our self-evident criteria.

V

The purpose of political-organizational schemes, at least in so far as they are stated to the public, is to achieve a higher degree of freedom. The precise meaning of the term "freedom" is subject to argument. This argument will continue as long as political society exists, remains articulate, and is capable of disagreement. Freedom is an undefined abstraction which refers to many different and often incongruous situations. It is in the nature of a synoptic description, like the term "health," except that it refers to a far larger number of elements. In much the same way as a dying man still has healthy organs, freedom is never completely extinguished in all human areas. Just as the disease of a vital organ terminates health, so nonfreedom or too little freedom denotes the lack of freedom as such. Thus, freedom is not merely a matter of degrees, but also of quality.

Whenever we speak of "freedom," we really imply "more" or "less" freedom. Thus, we are dealing with a notion which is inherently measurable, or which, in any case, contains many measurable elements. It is possible to measure freedom.[7] Keeping in mind the distinction between the basic types of freedom, we would then have to measure:

   (1) the legal constraints imposed upon an individual's freedom of action;
   (2) the capabilities at the individual's disposal and rates of change of constraints and capabilities;
   (3) the utilization of these capabilities both in terms of *de facto* use and of responsible behavior;
   (4) the human results of such capabilities utilized.

Freedom is far broader than simple political rights, however important those may be. It can be considered independently of specific aspects of political organization, as it must be if it is indeed a structural element of society as a whole. But, in addition to paying attention to the intents, causes, modes, and limits of individual behavior, we also must know the *results* of such action. It is, after all, not the institution which counts, but its yield. Once we know the yield, we possess a yardstick for evaluating organizational and institutional structure and performance. How much freedom did the institution produce? And at what price? This is the heart of the matter.

VI

I have dwelt on the hypothetical example of the "measurement of freedom" because it seems to me as being characteristic of the problems—the real problems—which are the concern of the political scientist. It illustrates the need for a theory and a methodology (including a sociometry that does not plagiarize methods of measurement devised for an inanimate *ordre de grandeur*). The science of politics is as yet poorly armed for dealing meaningfully with problems that are incontestably its own and, more importantly, matter crucially to all peoples here and now.

Formal democracy is an essential prerequisite, but not the fulfillment of freedom. Dictatorships do receive popular support. Our wonderment at this incontrovertible fact is nourished by the assumption that dictatorships violate all aspirations to freedom, while democracy satisfies them all. This is not so.

Dictatorship has many advantages. As a rule, it has a sense of direction and mission. Dictatorship is served by genuine dedication. Dictatorship suffers less than does democracy from anomy in decision-making. Under dictatorship, most people are less bored, regardless of the fact that bustling dedication may not serve a good cause and that social zest is kept alive at the cost of individual privacy.

No doubt the overcommitment to formal democracy and to the satisfaction of predominantly material interests has impeded the progress of liberty. The free world has been talking about rights, equality of men and peoples, the welfare of large numbers, and economic security. All these things are important. But we have not talked about obligation and discipline, emotional security, wise and ethical choices, happiness, and creativity.

Democracy has yielded all too easily to the depreciation of its currency. It has been content to "adjust" too many of its values and institutions to mundane pressures and intellectual fashions. It has been easy, therefore, for the exponents of various naturalistic philosophies and psychologies to conceive of democratic institutions as empty of moral purpose, as mere stables of the human animal. We should have tried, and we now must try, to build liberty for the moral person. Perhaps it is unfair to say that we have neglected to preoccupy ourselves with the human problem in its true dimension. Our bodies are better cared for than they ever were, but our minds are anguished and our creative powers stifled. Freedom cannot be won and preserved like a jar of marmalade. Freedom, in its deepest meaning, is a creative process. The free world has still a positive mission.

It is the task of the science of politics under freedom to develop the disciplines and to fashion the tools of creative freedom. Scientism has devoured a goodly portion of democracy's intellectual and moral patrimony. The science of politics has to replace much that has been lost to the academic hosts of the scientistic fury. Perhaps the very challenge of the times—a mortal challenge—will call forth, in society as a whole, recuperative forces and, in the halls of social science, a responsible and competent concern with the search for truth.

NOTES

1. Aldous Huxley, *Science, Liberty and Peace* (New York, 1959), pp. 32-35.
2. Edna Heidebreder, *Seven Psychologies* (New York, 1933), pp. 263-270.
3. F. A. Hayek, *The Counter-Revolution of Science* (Glencoe, Ill., 1952), p. 34.
4. Leland B. Yeager, "Measurement as Scientific Method in Economics," *The American Journal of Economics and Sociology*, XVI, No. 4, 344-345.
5. C. Northcote Parkinson, *Parkinson's Law or the Pursuit of Progress* (London, 1958).
6. For a perceptive critique of social "laws" and the meaningfulness of correlation of social "variables," see Kenneth Boulding, *The Organizational Revolution* (New York, 1953), 76-77, and Ruth Benedict, "Social Stratification and Political Power," in R. Bendix and S. M. Lipset, eds., *Class, Status and Power* (Glencoe, Ill., 1956), p. 608.
7. I am indebted to Stefan T. Possony for a concise statement of the problem of "measuring" freedom in his mimeographed *The Meaning and Measurement of Freedom,* Foreign Policy Research Institute (University of Pennsylvania, 1957).

Editor's Comment

Some critics will question the possibility of measuring freedom; others will perhaps accept it, but wonder about this new "scientism"—the measurement of values that ought not to be subject to yardsticks. However, there are indeed fairly simple ways of measuring freedom that will not degrade the entity being measured. For instance, we have statistics at our disposal recording year after year how many individuals, families, and people in various occupations, choose freedom—they leave from behind the Iron Curtain. We have such data for East Germany, Hungary, Red China, Tibet, and other areas where individuals make a choice from among relative degrees of freedom—such as, for example, between the not-quite-so-oppressive communism in Tito's Yugoslavia and their opportunity to escape into Italy.

Moreover, we can measure in meaningful units, if we want to, the time persons have to spend in offices of the authorities in order to get permission to migrate, to leave a country, to change occupation or residence. All these important segments of a man's daily life are related to freedom. American readers may not be able to see their importance at once because they yet know so few controls over their personal lives. All we meant here is that just as well as the UN can study the degrees of censorship of the press in various countries on a comparative basis, we might try to get similar data for other areas of human freedom, not just the journalist's.

H. Schoeck.

12

Social Science As Autonomous Activity

HENRY S. KARIEL

This essay * seeks to delineate an approach to understanding human society. Those who partake in this approach are persuaded that, far from trying to construct some specific social order or learning how to fit men into it, they prefer public policies which will provide the conditions for the unimpeded pursuit of happiness. They duly respect the various opinions and interests of individual men. Yet their work indicates that more is involved, for it contains uneasily coexisting elements—an on-duty scientific one and an off-duty moralistic one. Both elements embody values. To the extent that these values are in conflict and press on to victory, both social science and liberal-democratic institutions are threatened, for they require one another. Survival of neither seems likely if either an unqualified science or an unqualified moralism triumphs. If it could be shown that liberal-democratic theory is unrelated to the work pursued and therefore fails to confine the scientific quest, while, at the same time, much of social science is impelled to reach out so as to incorporate liberal-democratic insti-

*While responsibility for the ideas here set forth is fully mine, I have benefited from discussions with three members of the Society of Fellows, Harvard University: George Kateb, Peter M. Ray, and Franklin M. Fisher. I am also grateful to the *Western Political Quarterly* for permission to draw on my article, "The New Order of Mary Parker Follett," published September, 1955.

tutions, it may be obvious why today it is far less pertinent to restate professed moral sentiments than to retrace some of the value
assumptions which give meaning, coherence, and prestige to research.

I

The research here specifically focused on is concerned, in
brief, with the construction and the testing of abstract concep-
tional systems composed of neutral terms which are seen as
capable, at least in principle, of relating every effective variable.
Postulating all social forces to be in a state of natural balance
within a self-rectifying and self-sufficient order, it is committed to
a norm which allows reference to existing communities. As an instrumental science, it is believed to be able to determine how
whatever is variable might be economically moved toward the
norm. Because it systematically functionalizes human goals, the
only norms which restrain it are, ideally, the agreed-upon rules of
social science. This capsule characterization begs for elaboration.

What is becoming increasingly clear is that a traditional emphasis of social science on distinguishing between the degrees of excellence of social institutions, historical regimes, public policies, or
individual doctrines is being replaced by a stress on the formulation of an architectonic descriptive theory of social *behavior*.[1] This
stress, one not without antecedents in the history of ideas, is manifest in a concern for the progressive refinement of operational
methods. Identified by an array of vague labels which significantly
suggest the convergence of various disciplines—labels such as functionalism, sociometry, operationalism, equilibrium analysis, topo-
logical psychology, social field theory, social geometry, homeostatic
model construction, or even sociopsychobiology—truly synthetic
knowledge is being earnestly pursued and, so it would appear, re-
spectably endowed.

Such a body of knowledge is to give formal expression to relationships between sensed phenomena. These phenomena, connected by a network of logical or quantitative notations, are not

examined for their intrinsic merits. They are kept from becoming the *object* of discourse. The aim is not the disclosure and objectification of equivocal meanings and values, but, on the contrary, their systematic elimination. The remaining theoretical structure, deliberately removed from experience, is to constitute a positive natural science of society.

The obstacles to its formulation, it is conceded, seem insuperable because they have been so firmly built into the mind of Western man that even as he attempts to reflect upon them they stand in his way. The very character of thought and language allows for misleading distinctions between value-attributing subject and passive object, between substance and function. These distinctions are believed to keep thought from becoming objective, permitting it to correspond, not to the structure of the forces at large in the world, but to the ever-varying desires of individuals.[2] The need, therefore, is to escape the prison of a language incorporating values, to cease using quality-ascribing adjectives which intriguingly hint at the existence of essentials, and to center at last on dynamic processes. It becomes important to extinguish symbols useful only when the channels of communication are not clear, when redundancies are required to catch our attention or overcome noises on the line. The residual system will embrace all meaningful facts of social life, living up to Galileo's great vision:

Philosophy is written in that vast book which stands ever open before our eyes, I mean the universe; but it cannot be read until we have learnt the language and become familiar with the character in which it is written. It is written in mathematical language, and the letters are triangles, circles and other geometrical figures, without which means it is humanly impossible to comprehend a single word.[3]

This geometric design, once apprehended in its fullness, cannot be defiled by historical change. As an absolute, it will be radically unhistorical, compressing past and future into a timeless frame. Thus, in psychology, to introduce but one example, the informed will repress all dramatic language and shift to a functional interpretation of personality. As M. Brewster Smith has authoritatively written,[4]

Modern psychology, historical or otherwise, is in fact overwhelmingly functional. The dominant strain is oriented toward a model of the organism as a self-regulating system and falls naturally into the use of terms like homeostasis, equilibrium and adjustment; while the marginal influence of Gestalt theory leads to parallel emphasis on the field determination of phenomenal properties or behavior tendencies.

Formerly, when the emphasis had been on habits, traits, change, and action, only the historical approach would do. Today, according to Smith, it is fruitful to transcend specific histories, to lay bare a scheme defining the individual's nonhistorical, extemporaneous behavioral dispositions. Such a scheme—one claimed not merely for a strain of psychology—will be a perfect accounting system. It will fully take care of all contingencies, clearly showing that perception of miracle, novelty, or accident must be a symptom of faulty vision or a function of an uncontrolled body of impulses. It is backed by the notion that everything scientifically significant is attached, determined, and at hand. Though much meaningful data may remain hidden until duly approached, all of it is emphatically present, more or less deeply embedded in the present state of man's development. Through the proper method it might be made to yield truthful correlations—correlations which have held in the past as they must surely hold in the future. The real can thus be forced to disclose itself as the ideal while, simultaneously, the ideal can be forced to disclose itself as the real.

II

Of course, social scientists are not conspiring to found a state which, however unrealized, they believe to be woven into the nature of things. To borrow a phrase from American public law, they are merely engaged in parallel action. They labor as if set to actualize a holistic system of elementary relations. And they rest whenever their approach dissolves the peculiarities they encounter, revealing them to be congruent and organized. They are satisfied to the extent that they establish a necessary connection between society and nature. They know that a concern with an unrealizable world must irresponsibly devitalize the scientific activity of developing hypotheses which deal successfully with men in motion.

It may seem, deceptively, that their activity will cause human values to be shunned, that the norms so obviously present in the social field under investigation will be disregarded. Yet, in fact, values will be given their credit when shown to be functions of an efficacious system, one which is at once empirically describable and susceptible to an objective ordering. This is the case even though at present there are no satisfactory quantitative terms to designate degrees of functionality without postulating value predicates. But while it is true, as David Easton has seen,[5] that it has not yet been possible "to reduce the complex power relations of society to the necessary numerical quantities, and [that] there is little prospect that in the foreseeable future it will be in a position to do so," the ideal remains. A genuinely neutral model should connect values with the *real* substructure of social forces, group pressures, and individual drives. Values cherished because man has exercised his reason in the light of his knowledge of the past are not autonomous determinants; they can gain the status of such determinants only when recognized as ideologies, as verbal structures tied to more fundamental data. Thus values must be identified with the substructure of behavior, with the real determinants of thought and action. Human ideals must not be set off from facts, but be equated with them, losing their distinctive qualities. Or, more accurately, they must be exhibited in a new setting which makes it clear that they had actually never merited distinction in the first place. In this framework they will be stabilized because realized. Their new setting will provide full correlations, excepting nothing from its grasp, necessarily handling all meaningful behavior, including the norms and purposes which nonscientific preconceptions respect as incommensurable, unstable, and variable.

The job for social science then becomes, as a matter of course, one of reducing existing instabilities and variations. In this way, the significant facts about social structures will be revealed. Theo-

dore M. Newcomb has sympathetically reviewed what this is likely
to imply, for example, for psychology:

> There is no harder lesson for the psychologist to learn, probably, than
> that of viewing persons as functionaries in a group structure rather
> than as psychological organisms—i.e., as parts rather than as wholes,
> and as parts which, within limits, are interchangeable.
>
> Once this lesson is learned, however, the facts of social structure
> become available; a social system is seen as made up of differentiated
> parts, the orderly relationships among which, rather than the personal
> identity of which, become the major object of concern.[6]

Far more broadly, Hannah Arendt, noting the implications of
functionalizing the purposive, dramatic content of intellectual categories, has shown how it has become possible, for example, to
identify Hitler and Jesus because functionally their roles were
indistinguishable.[7] Such linking of variables becomes essential to
a science intent on dealing with all components of a social field as
role-playing functionaries so as to make society explicable. Full
explication requires treating society as a system whose parts, in
theory if not in momentarily stubborn fact, "make sense," all being
duly related, complementing and balancing one another.

On the basis of this assumption of the natural harmony of structural components, the quest for knowledge may proceed. By the
traditional method of (1) postulating a hypothesis which might
economically relate variables, (2) following through by making deductions, (3) checking whether the hypothesis corresponds to sense
experience, and (4) accepting, amending, or rejecting the hypothesis—by this method reality may be known.[8] Hypotheses, assuredly,
may have to be reversed by "factual reality." Yet, it should be
noted, only after agreement is reached as to what is meant by
"facts" do facts actually have the final say: facts, it is held, must be
so constituted as to leave manifest traces before they can be given a
voice. The social scientist's hypotheses—devised to lead him to uni-
formities of behavior—will permit rational, scientific control only
of such facts as take their place in his conceptual order of uni-
formly related, coexisting parts. His very approach is designed to

permit nothing capricious, unique, or dysfunctional to slip through. When his postulational system makes for the appropriate discriminations, it is a pure theory, one through which it is possible to discern all the dynamically interacting facts of social reality. Thus, the concern of social science is inescapably with the potencies and the actualities of reality. It is, to use Nietzsche's apt phrase, concerned with "quantities of will," with power—its extent and its use.

III

The theory giving integrity to such concerns is not, of course, to be confused with any concrete society. It is merely an analytical model. Nevertheless, it is believed to identify the character of natural conditions, the impetus immanent in historical processes. While it may appear that no particular process is thus valued over any other, a formal valuation does emerge. The notion that "a dysfunction is a condition, or state of affairs that (1) results from the operation (including in the term operation mere persistence) of a structure of a given unit through time and (2) lessens the adaptation or adjustment to the unit's setting, thus making for the lack of persistence of the unit as defined of which the structure concerned is a part or aspect" [9]—this notion leaves the underlying respect for integration and balance scarcely in doubt. Sound research must concern itself with the specification of ties which provide for the system's unity, which enable it to cohere and persist. The task of social studies is thus easily defined: it is to identify the social structure and determine what is functional. It is to gain knowledge of the factors which engage what is idle, attract what is distracted, enlist what is weary. It is to search for the conditions of instability, the prerequisites of stability. It is to restore upset balances, resolve conflicts, heal sore spots, and—most important, perhaps—remove blocks to understanding.

To be sure, the knowledge thus accumulated can be used to achieve a nonconservative end. But such an achievement, certainly possible, could not be certified as scientific at a time when the social world is simply assumed to be nothing but a fundamentally closed, boundary-maintaining, and internally harmonious system.

Whether the social scientist intuits universals—assuming the risks of Burckhardt, Spengler, Weber, and Benedict—or determines, more empirically, just what to do in order to ensure a system's perpetuity,[10] he is directed to engage in patterning deviant elements, and this all the more energetically as he identifies knowledge with the realization of an immanent "true state of affairs," with what would spontaneously occur in the social world were all impediments removed.

As long as this approach remained purely formal and analytical, as it did in the relativistic, comparative analyses of Burckhardt and Weber, it also left unsettled just what the specific impediments to the ideal might be. Hence, discussion about them was not foreclosed. But the abridgement of discussion is fostered as a substantive definition of a disequilibrium is implied. It would be more tedious than difficult to show how massively this is the case, with what readiness undesirable deviants are actually being identified: they are widely seen as the conflicts and displacements which have flowered thanks to modern man's complex industrial society. Only a deeply prejudiced person, it is made to appear, will fail to discern that whatever man's twentieth-century opportunities and goods, the present is a painful era of community disruption, complicated politics, and endless factional crises. If this offered diagnosis is far too broad, it is believed to cover so many contemporary relationships that the application of social skills, of knowledge about human relations, becomes imperative indeed. And this knowledge, at its best, is seen as the product of social science.

There being no question regarding what substantively constitutes social delinquencies—the nature of the pathological being virtually self-evident [11]—social science may rightly apply its knowledge and its methods, working to discover how individuals might be moved with speed and efficiency toward the common, healthy goal. It becomes credible to argue that psychologists should

seek to provide a basic science of human thinking, character, skill learning, motives, conduct, etc., which will serve all the sciences of man (e.g., anthropology, sociology, economics, government, education, medicine, etc.) in much the same way and to the same extent that biology now serves the agricultural and medical sciences.[12]

The ends of just government, it may be inferred, are so fixed that the scientist-governor may furnish the means. Moreover, the laws of psychology may be applied precisely as agronomists and physicians apply the laws of biology: to maximize food production and prolong life.

Like the interest of the engineer, that of the social scientist may consequently center on the means to achieve given ends, to treat the diseases of the body politic. Knowing the common good, he will be prepared and subsidized to perfect the devices for gaining consensus on it and to aid in its attainment. Thus, as social therapists and policy scientists will show, in the language of Harold D. Lasswell,[13] a "lively concern . . . for the problem of overcoming the divisive tendencies of modern life and of bringing into existence a more thorough integration of the goals and methods of public and private action," politics itself will become infused by science.

As this infusion proceeds, a convergence of social science disciplines is only to be expected. On the assumption, articulated by John Gillin,[14] that "the social or behavioral sciences could do with a bit more order in their house," integration is being urged. Social scientists are invited to join up and work on an orderly "science of social man"—one which requires, according to Gillin,[15] that social scientists suspend those competitive urges which impel them to distinguish themselves, that they suspend behavior having the "tendency on occasion . . . of cluttering the field with a variety of ostensibly theoretical statements. . . ." It seems that "it must perhaps be remembered that we live in a culture which also values 'cooperation with others' and 'self-discipline.' " Mark A. May, as head of Yale University's Institute of Human Relations, has logically followed this theme through: [16]

Our particular academic culture [May said during a roundtable discussion on "Integration of the Social Sciences"] tends to reward rugged individualism. . . .

I am a strong believer in rewards and punishments. The prescription for getting more integration in the social sciences is to reward heavily all activities that look in that direction, provided that they are solid and sound and promising. It is important, also to reduce the rewards that have been so heavily attached to specialization. . . . The practical application of this theory lies in the hands of those who sit at the controls of the system of rewards and punishments in colleges, universities, foundations, and scientific societies.

IV

United in their aim of constructing and testing a behavioral science, social scientists are induced to engage in operations which are not checked, theoretically, by anything but their own power to be operative. Of course, prescriptions for social health do not countenance every kind of action. Limitations are imposed by the very purposes for which social science techniques are brought to bear on society. The techniques themselves being wholly neutral, they take on the color of the objective for which they are used. The goodness of the objective being granted, implementation may properly proceed.

But the value of the posited objective is itself defined only by its capacity to fulfill a function scientifically determinable. An adequate social science cannot credit human objectives as irreducible, for they are deemed to lie within its own domain of means and are, therefore, considered to be amenable to functionalization. They are understood as instruments of, not as guides to, human aspirations, as tools for survival and mastery. The final test of their validity is the very one that is applied to the constructs of science, with the result that myths, ideals, ideologies, and scientific formulations all acquire identity. To the extent that scientific knowledge of the links between social phenomena is certain and trustworthy, such knowledge becomes knowledge of objectives.

Seemingly a sharp distinction between the scientific formulations which order the world and the world itself remains. But when it is assumed that the ordering formulations are an inherent part of nature, wrested from it by the scientific effort to control emergencies, to conquer chance, and to make life liveable, they retain no independence save that arbitrarily assigned them. They are legitimate only because they happen to be potent, efficient, or instrumental. All structuring of the natural world—including, of course, of the social world, of the behavior and conduct of individual persons—is based on the belief that those scientific constructs which apparently transcend natural behavior cannot justly be distinguished from it. They are but a form of behavior, a kind of factual datum essentially indistinct from those passions which drive men to seek power and satisfy their need systems. To control constructs themselves, to impose a check on science, is to cut into its capacity for experimental action. It is at once unnatural and suicidal, for it delimits science, accepting not its own reason, but one which professes to transcend it. Such adherence to metaphysical dogma would be self-deceptive when not used as a device for deceiving others. Those who wish to rid themselves of deception and act in a spirit of objectivity must exercise their will—presumably their good will.[17] They must impose upon the social flux, set men in motion, interact with their data, learn by doing, verify by testing.

Knowledge of laws defining social relations in their natural, untouched, and untested state is impossible. To be sure, one is frequently compelled to make the attempt to verify hypotheses by conducting tests in an environment smaller than the one for which the hypotheses are hoped to hold true. Or one may project from past or distant situations about which facts are readily available for correlations. These two methods are indeed conventional and serviceable, yielding knowledge sufficiently exact for such practical purposes as navigating through storms, finding oil under the soil, anticipating the demands of consumers, or predicting the choices of voters. Yet, in terms of the ideal of science, both methods are troublesome all the same. The first assumes that identical causes will tend to produce identical effects, that outside the laboratory nothing is likely to intervene and make effects disproportionate to their causes. The well-recognized trouble here is that in human affairs (and not merely in human affairs) some things sometimes do manage to intervene, however minutely, and that consequently—if the truth is to be known and if only the

testable is admitted as truth—the progressive extension of the
laboratory becomes an imperative. Harold D. Lasswell's observations are to the point:[18]

The principal limitation [to the experimental approach] is that many
of the most elegant findings can only be transferred to other laboratories. They cannot be transferred to field situations because there is
no technique of demonstrating in the field the degree in which the
conditions assumed as constant in the laboratory do in fact occur.

For this reason, "bridges need to be built between laboratory
situations and field situations." It becomes a necessary "refinement . . . to take the laboratory design into the field and to apply
it to a whole community context. In such a setting many of the
procedures devised under laboratory conditions take on new
meaning." The field, in effect transformed into laboratory, may
"then be explored more intensively in order to identify the
variables that account for the deviation. This can be done by
applying more laboratory-type measures at the proper spots and
by instituting a program of 'probers,' 'pre-tests,' 'interventions,'
and 'appraisals.' "

The second method, that of extrapolation, may be seen in its
consequences as but a variant of the first, assuming as it does
that variables which coexisted in the past will tend to do so in
the future. The experience, however rare, that they will not, that
even tendencies may be upset, indicates the essential shortcoming,
in terms of the scientific ideal, of a method which is satisfied with
statistical correlations.[19] "The infinite variety of causal sequences
to which every act and event in history is related," Reinhold
Niebuhr has pointed out,[20] "makes almost every correlation of
causes sufficiently plausible to be immune to compelling challenge." The *ideal* of empirical science is exact knowledge on the
basis of which men might act without further consideration of
alternatives, without further study, research, reflection, or debate.
Before the scientist will be justified in claiming that particular
conditions have such objective existence, he must have exercised

full control. Unless he has, his discoveries cannot be the *final* ground for action.

When his formulations are nevertheless accepted as the final ground for action, the assumption must be that his knowledge is complete, that the real problems and their natural, necessary solutions are known. To act on the basis of such knowledge is in fact to order variables in the light of what is conceived as indubitably real or true. Such ordering constitutes the exercise of control. Since it is possible to obtain certain empirical knowledge only of those relations which men have transfused by their will, which men have actually constructed and in which they can ultimately encounter only themselves, empirical science demands the exercise of the will, a grappling with a nature which insists on having its intrinsic properties. It becomes exasperating and challenging to realize that speculative, reflective knowledge of the world, because of the all-pervasiveness of bias, because man is a determined creature, can be only coincidentally accurate. Being so much part of nature, man cannot truly find out what it is. He cannot look upon it with objectivity; he cannot assess it from above; he cannot gain a disinterested view of it.

But by no means does this require him to give up his quest for knowledge. He feels free to reinterpret the quest, to make it become one for survival within nature, one for natural power over the competing forces of life. Thus, the purpose of science becomes a pseudo purpose: control, not in reference to a transcending objective, but for its own sake. Thereby science, equated with spontaneous right action, gains autonomy, a condition not likely to be frowned upon when its ethos is wholly identified with a rationale for liberal-democratic institutions.[21] It becomes self-reliant and self-justifying; it is measured, not against a higher order of reality, not against standards anteceding the conventions· of empirical science, but against an ideal which values the capacity to exercise power, to be effective, to flex one's instruments (including ideologies and myths) for the control of nature, of society, and of man. Thus a genuine science is manipulative knowledge; it is a body of concepts viewed as valid when they yield results in application. Indeed, a true order of being, an objective model of nature, is not one which man gets out of nature, but one which he imputes to it. The main scientific task, therefore, is to make of nature what one will. Objective knowledge being foreclosed—for nature is undeniably obstinate—subjective action takes its place.

In so far as science requires an attitude of radical skepticism toward relations not yet fixed by scientific resolutions, not yet proved valid under ever more controlled conditions, it exacts a pledge for continuous experimentation, every other approach to gain understanding being but second best. While a fringe of human and social nature may always hold out—and will, to that extent, be beyond understanding—testing will permit ever-increasing knowledge and control. The confirming of hypotheses will mean both adding to theoretical insight and reshaping the social world. Indeed, the constructs of science will *make* the social world, since they alone govern and bestow status. It is true that compliance may be hard to exact, that society may not be infinitely pliable, that there are imprecise forces at work which keep men from bending. Yet it is the existence of these very forces which always poses the initial question. For unless these, too, are controlled, every statement about the true nature of social or political things remains tentative. The task, therefore, is to reduce whatever makes management difficult, to concentrate on those slippery factors which, though still ungoverned, must be made amenable to scientific government. As one social scientist has explained,[22]

Having identified to our satisfaction the relevant factors in a situation, the next step [in following a scientific method] is to select those which we can effectively control. The ideal setup is one wherein we can control every factor. At the present state of the social sciences this is a mere dream. For one thing, in social science we are still lacking handles, tongs, pliers or what you will with which to grasp a situational factor for manipulative purposes.

Poorly equipped though it be, science must put everything of significance within its grasp. Potentially nothing can be exempt from the attempt to establish that social theories are valid, that they work, or that, in the language of Hobbes, some sovereign might convert the truth of speculation into the utility of practice. For it is felt that the knowable world contains nothing uncontrollable, that it is devoid of phenomena not susceptible, in principle, to scientific formulation, circumscription, and enclosure.

Yet it should be noted that science's own framework, including the rules of procedure by which it is built up, remains free. Unlike the data it orders, it is incommensurate, introduced to rid the world of what is designated as risky, providential, or fateful. This framework is the potent variable, presumably defining states of power relations with objectivity by giving these relations symbolic or numerical attributes. These attributes, however, must in practice always constitute a normative standard, for departure from them will make a system's survival unlikely: departure will produce lawlessness and decay.

This cannot mean, certainly, that the social scientist, even when bent on the prevention of social conflict and the maintenance of public health, will go out into the world and literally make good. He may be less interested than Hobbes in having his writings fall into the hands of a sovereign. Depending on his temper, on the vitality of a residual tradition, or on prevailing social restraints—all of which are practically impressive, but theoretically irrelevant—he may be satisfied with having experienced his vision. Being patient, he may relax after having communicated it to those who might listen. But when consistently loyal to his position, he will have to fight for its incarnation, stilling whatever voices presume to resist it, aiding whatever resembles it. He must prompt men to realize their destiny, working not only as their prophet but also as their redeemer. Moreover, his labor may be supported by a belief in success for which his eighteenth-century precursors— savants whose almost unified science was ignorant of the mass-manipulating tools of modern technology—could not reasonably hope. Allied with the powers that be and in the name of the consummation of science, he may at last move men toward the full life, toward fulfillment in a historical millennium.[23]

V

Before outlining a few of the possible consequences of the kind of approach to the study of society which has been discussed, it should be useful to summarize three of its crucial assumptions: (1) The only significant order of social reality is the one inherently susceptible to empirical verification, to factor analysis, and physicomathematical reduction; (2) the pursuit of knowledge manifests itself in the enactment of norms which inhere in the pursuit itself; and (3) it is the function of the scientist to master a nature—including man and society—which is devoid of purposes intelligible and communicable by man.

What are these assumptions likely to imply?

If it is held that orders of reality other than those amenable to reduction to functional terms are merely subjective ones, conjectures about social institutions and policies not susceptible to empirical verification tend to be disparaged. Such speculation, considered untrustworthy, is contrasted to that whose objectivity, empirically confirmed, justifies action along lines making for the functionalization of the subject matter of social science. In this process, social science goes to work in the public arena on the basis of decisive assumptions—assumptions posited as if there were no alternatives to them—which those affected by its action do not share in formulating.

To the extent that the research is theory-oriented, all that is involved is constructing frameworks presuming to embrace variables of significance; to the extent that it is oriented toward the solution of practical problems, it seeks to attain and perpetuate the final good of social harmony. Both orientations tend to cooperate in integrating dysfunctional forces, in curing social and individual ills.

Contribution to the body of science requires instituting that state of unity within which all particulars are truly related. This quest is not one for reflective understanding of the nature of the social world, but one for bringing history to its terminus by resolving historical conflicts in practice.

While searching for the final synthesis of the manifold antagonisms man believes himself to be experiencing, the social scientist
may proceed without objective limits. The limits to his action
are the subjective ones of his energy, his inventiveness, his genius.
Seemingly objective schemes of values which presume to restrain the attempt to control variables dissolve into the "real"
forces which give rise to them. Other checks are unduly diverting,
retarding the accumulation of certain knowledge and the realization of ideals. Social scientists are thus free to dominate nature
with indifference to its own purposes, which are unintelligible
because science cannot establish or validate them. They are free
to press knowledge out of an environment which yields what it is
forced to yield by their practical operations, by their thoroughgoing, endless activity. Potentially, the nature of concern to man
is infinitely pliable; its components are infinitely interrelated. The
only scientific challenge to any particular social arrangement must
be on the ground that control is not total. Not all arrangements,
of course, are equally adequate. Experiments, and the theories
they sustain, may be characterized as trivial or important, depending on the degree to which they make control possible, to
which they turn nature to man's use. Nature, it is assumed, serves
its purpose by being exploited. Its purpose, as Nietzsche was the
first to urge wholeheartedly, may be imputed to it by the survival-
facilitating norms creatively framed by the interested scientist.
Denial of this either reflects hidden but analyzable interests or
else is unhealthy and unnatural, clearly not furthering the per-
petuation of life, the satisfaction of needs, or the production of
comfort.

When men are prepared to act consistently on the basis of the
beliefs (1) that a single approach to phenomena is socially fruitful
and desirable, (2) that nothing but science itself need restrain the
progressive unification of the social world, and (3) that whatever
nature—including human nature—may be, it can potentially be
made into anything else, their action is likely to have several
practical effects:

1. *A unification of the social sciences to carry out a concerted
attack on dysfunctional forces, on social and individual disturb-*

ances. This unification requires and justifies identifying science with techniques of manipulation, letting the techniques determine the valid limits of social research, working for an integration of the outlook and resources of social scientists, and penalizing those who resist convergence.

2. *An attempt to spread information about the potency of the models of social science.* Notational systems, it may be made reasonably clear, are efficient implements for action, effective weapons for the maintenance or destruction of power, likely to become ever sharper in application.

3. *A gradual enlargement of the area considered suitable for scientific operations so that ever more tracts of life may be ordered objectively.* The depreciation of two major ideals would follow from this activity: (1) the ideal that agreement should be reached, however temporarily, by a process of political negotiation; (2) the ideal that conflicts should be tentatively settled by means of human—that is, value-ascribing—discourse, by dialectical social philosophy.

As it becomes possible to place goals into a frame within which they may be objectively perceived, within which those value conflicts left inconclusive by parliamentary politics may be settled with finality, thanks to a neutral "administration of things," the ends of life and action are removed from the traditional process of political compromise and dialectical discussion. Such a process must appear increasingly specious, being predicated on the possibility of human rationality, on the conviction that language may be informative and can make genuine knowledge available. When it is held, to the contrary, that language functions merely to secure or prevent action, to maintain or destroy an equilibrium, to create or undermine consensus, parliamentarianism can be only atmospherically useful.

The assumption that knowledge is gained only by language which has operational meaning and that all other language rationalizes the drive for power or serves to sublimate aggressions and extend pleasures leads not only to the devaluation of political settlements, but also to the rejection of artists, mystics, and philosophers as collaborators in the perennial search for final truth.

Their search, it must be held, will inevitably end in a subjective acceptance of personal feelings passed off as "truths," and no more. No doubt, such truths may still be clarified, analyzed, or causally explained. But they cannot be respected and criticized on the merits as long as all standards in reference to which criticism might be made—including, of course, standards created by social scientists—are themselves deemed to be subjective and conventional.

Reason, unable to decide between right and wrong conduct, to assess the various purposes of action, to connect man with truth, can serve only to adjust him to his desires, aiding survival. Law and policy, legislation and politics, therefore, may be understood as the repercussions of interests, not the ever-amendable result of rational discourse. To judge or construct the public order, it is necessary to understand, not the grounds offered for it, but the power alignments which brought it about, its causes rather than its merits. Its sole criterion is its effectiveness. Thus, the formulation of policy, the drafting of constitutions, become a branch of an empirical science to which ethics is logically quite irrelevant. And the application of this science to solve the problems faced by society will naturally require—Lasswell, among others, has stressed this [24]—"the de-emphasizing of much of the traditional baggage of metaphysics and theology." Politics will become increasingly objective and scientific, a calling for the expert technician.

4. *A growing respectability of an elite of social engineers as the procedures by which free societies determine their policy goals make way for methods by which scientific truths are formulated.* A comprehensive value-neutral science must divest itself, as George A. Lundberg has urged,[25] of "the luxury of indignation," "personalistic and moralistic interpretations," and "deeply cherished *ideologies* resembling in form if not in content their theological predecessors." It must disregard "the goals of striving" and, instead, suggest alternatives, state their implications, and develop the most efficient "method of achieving *whatever* ends men want. . . ." Science is not concerned with what, at least in one sense, are ends. These society sets by any procedure it chooses.

Science, however, cannot sanction every procedure which a society might employ: some of them will not aid the realization of ends. The proper procedures, the only ones which guarantee the successful operation and the effective functioning of society, are those which reject the possibility that a value-impregnated expression of an individual may conceivably be true independently of his interests. In accordance with its commitment to a phenomenal reality—and its attendant discrimination against other realms of reality—science must reduce, or repudiate as myth, the belief that ends may be ontological, that values may transcend individual desires. It therefore recognizes (1) that the end for man is quite literally his end—his death, and (2) that the end for science is the assuring of survival, the maintaining of the social and individual equilibrium. Hence, the purpose of science is to keep everything *endlessly* moving. Its credentials are furnished by its power to make society survive; and as society is in fact kept forever on the move—without hitches, deviations, or back talk—its credentials are authenticated.

5. *A drive to fuss ever more intimately with the individual person so that social science may achieve its end.* Having discovered that at the core of man is an abhorrible void, unfulfilled but crying for fulfillment, social scientists are likely to work on that state toward which man's true will aspires. Such work effects a transformation within man himself. Karl Mannheim has elaborated on this:

Functionalism made its first appearance in the field of the natural sciences, and could be described as the technical point of view. It has only recently been transferred to the social sphere. . . .

Once this technical approach was transferred from the natural sciences to human affairs, it was bound to bring about a profound change in man himself. . . . The functional approach no longer regards ideas and moral standards as absolute values, but as products of the social process which can, if necessary, be changed by scientific guidance combined with political practice. . . .

The extension of this doctrine of technical supremacy which I have advocated in this book as one of several approaches to society is in my opinion inevitable. . . .

Progress in the technique of organization is nothing but the application of technical conceptions to the forms of co-operation. A human being, regarded as part of the social machine, is to a certain extent stabilized in his reactions by training and education, and all his recently acquired activities are co-ordinated according to a definite principle of efficiency within an organized framework.[26]

In accordance with this new regard for human beings, man must be appropriately energized and directed. Being a pliable creature, he must be sufficiently softened and compressed to fit into those compartments which might be readily supervised. Within them, he can be guided to lead a secure and satisfying life. This is best done by quieting his prejudices, straightening out his complications, and exposing the irrationality of his diversions. The expeditors of history must trim and neutralize him, eliminating those of his motives which may set him to doing the impractical, frivolous, perilous, or unexpected. They must allow him to experience the positive harm of having his fling, telling his joke, or sitting the next one out. His environment must be so arranged as to make him comfortable. He must be fitted so that he will become the self-renouncing creature he naturally is. Pains must be taken to relieve him of the agony of choice between alternatives, relieve him of that perplexing inner conflict which jeopardizes every civil order.

Those whose calling it is to assume total responsibility for the whole of man—the elite whose historical function it is to terminate history—must purposefully intervene, varying one factor here, another one there, moving man by affecting his behavior, driving him by harnessing his drives, watching always whether his motions and emotions tend more and more to conform to the plotted ideal, whether the myths calculated to galvanize him will induce him to behave as expected, to make his industry correspond to his true interest.

Fortunately, it is never necessary to tamper with man's true will—only with the will's objectively pathological aberrations, with those human urgings which prompt the individual to conceive of himself as selfishly subjective. Only the deviant, not the norm, need be imposed upon, and hence the elite's tax on non-conformity is justified. Its claim to power is legitimate since, to the extent that it is an elite in the service of social science, it will leave normal men alone.

As Tocqueville perceived, such rational leadership is penetrating, but soothing. It is extensive, but gentle. It slowly breeds a contented mass of men—a mass untroubled by the derangements which spring from the reverberations of the playful imagination and free from that irreducible mystery of spirit upon which man, when self-deceived, bases his dignity.

Above this race of men [Tocqueville concluded in his second volume on democracy in America] stands an immense and tutelary power, which takes upon itself alone to secure their gratifications, and to watch over their fate. That power is absolute, minute, regular, provident, and mild. It would be like the authority of a parent, if, like that authority, its object was to prepare men for manhood; but it seeks, on the contrary, to keep them in perpetual childhood: it is well content that the people should rejoice, provided they think of nothing but rejoicing. For their happiness such a government willingly labors, but it chooses to be the sole agent and the only arbiter of that happiness; it provides for their security, foresees and supplies their necessities, facilitates their pleasures, manages their principal concerns, directs their industry, regulates the descent of property, and subdivides their inheritances—what remains, but to spare them all the care of thinking and all the trouble of living?

VI

It should be emphasized that those whose work has been here reflected on would vigorously repudiate the regime projected by Tocqueville. The grounds for this repudiation, namely, the good motives and worthy interests of social scientists, have not, of course, been the subject of this analysis, one which has been concerned instead with some of their assumptions. And these assumptions, to be fully explicit, make for a state which cannot claim to be legitimate. Although the multiplicity of existing appeals to a just order may make it appear impossible to judge any particular one as legitimate, it might, nevertheless, be suggested that these very claims imply that a normative order transcends the existing one. The denial of the reality of such transcending objectives, whether or not incorporated in a method for understanding society, cannot stand when it is tied to the belief that some specific order truly constitutes the incarnation of justice.

Although this is precisely the underlying postulate of part of the work of current social science, its authors have not simply pointed to part of reality and called it good. Yet, even when they have refused to point, the perspective embodied within their research has acted as a pointer for them. While they have not advocated an amoral power state, they have labored so as to produce one by systematically eliminating any rational alternative. They have effectually cancelled unrealized human ideals—except, of course, when they have found them to be operative, to be real, to be other than ideal. Postulating a state within which all alternatives are unified, within which all ideals are one, they have made the ideal and the real synonymous. They have charged their methods to eliminate all tension between experience and aspiration, between fact and value. Yet once they have dispelled this tension, the very notion of justice must become irrelevant. Once they have encouraged existing conditions and normative standards to blend, the very pursuit of knowledge must become an irrational endeavor. Once they have dismissed value systems providing terms by which troubled individuals might assess moving events, historical states, and political action, man's claim to make meaningful distinctions, ascribe values, and exercise his reason must become impertinent.

That they have not been successful in their quest—and who would doubt the significance of their own contributions to a pluralistic liberal society?—is due to a lack of consistency, to a sentimentality which reflects, perhaps, either the afterglow of an older tradition or some pressing humanistic interest quietly bidding for recognition.[27] Their respect for the individual does not arise from the assumptions basic to their methods of inquiry.

When these, rather than their generous sentiments, are followed through, there emerges a model indifferent to justice, indifferent to that indefinable human uniqueness that still makes it reasonable to speak of man's moral freedom and obliges us to keep the institution of politics in good repair.

NOTES

1. *See* Bernard Barber, *Science and the Social Order* (Glencoe: Free Press, 1952), p. 244. Note especially Roy R. Grinker, ed., *Toward a Unified Theory of Human Behavior* (New York: Basic Books, 1956); James G. Miller, "Toward a General Theory for the Behavioral Sciences," in Leonard D. White, ed., *The State of the Social Sciences* (Chicago: University of Chicago Press, 1956), pp. 29-65; and essays by Richard C. Snyder, Marion J. Levy, and Talcott Parsons in Roland Young, ed., *Approaches to the Study of Politics* (Evanston: Northwestern University Press, 1958).

2. "Our bias centers in the subject-predicate bifurcation of our sentence structure, a division which prevents us from formulating a proposition without a substantive either stated or implied, and which compels us to separate the substantive from the verb. . . ." (Laura Thompson, "In Quest of an Heuristic Approach to the Study of Mankind," *Philosophy of Science*, XIII [January, 1946], 53-66, 54.)

3. Galileo, "Il Saggiatore," *Opere*, 180, p. 232; quoted in R. G. Collingwood, *The Idea of Nature* (Oxford: Clarendon, 1945), p. 102.

4. In John Gillin, ed., *For a Science of Social Man* (New York: Macmillan, 1954), pp. 41-42, 44.

5. David Easton, *The Political System* (New York: Knopf, 1953), p. 289.

6. Theodore M. Newcomb, "Sociology and Psychology," in Gillin, ed., *op. cit.*, pp. 227-256, p. 241.

7. *See* Hannah Arendt, "Religion and Politics," *Confluence*, II (September, 1953), 105-126; Arendt also notes the blurring of distinctions resulting from the analysis of Communism as a religion.

8. For a sophisticated discussion of the procedural conventions for determining the correctness of a decision to accept a proposition as part of scientific knowledge, *see* Felix Kaufmann, *Methodology of the Social Sciences* (New York: Oxford University Press, 1944).

9. This definition is from the appendix of Marion J. Levy, Jr., "Some Aspects of 'Structural-Functional' Analysis and Political Science," in Young, ed., *op. cit.*, pp. 52-66.

10. For an illustration, *see* R. K. Merton, *Social Theory and Social Structure* (Glencoe: Free Press, 1949), pp. 79-80.

11. *See* Edwin H. Sutherland, "Social Pathology," *American Journal of Sociology*, L (May, 1945), 429-435, 431.

12. Harvard University Commission to Advise on the Future of Psychology

at Harvard, Alan Gregg, chairman, *The Place of Psychology in an Ideal University* (Cambridge: Harvard University Press, 1947), p. 2.

13. Harold D. Lasswell, "The Policy Orientation," in Daniel Lerner and Harold D. Lasswell, eds., *The Policy Sciences: Recent Developments in Science and Method* (Stanford: Stanford University Press, 1951), pp. 3-15, p. 3.

14. Gillin, *loc. cit.*, p. 6. *See also* John Gillin, "Methods of Approach to the Study of Human Behavior," in F. L. K. Hsu, ed., *Aspects of Culture and Personality* (New York: Abelard-Schuman, 1954), pp. 3-18.

15. "The Forward View," in Gillin, ed., *op. cit.*, pp. 257-276, p. 276.

16. In Louis Wirth, ed., *Eleven Twenty-Six: A Decade of Social Science Research* (Chicago: University of Chicago Press, 1949), pp. 133-134.

17. Yet note the reservations about the presumption of good will as expressed in Arnold M. Rose, *Theory and Method in the Social Sciences* (Minneapolis: University of Minnesota Press, 1954), pp. 184-188.

18. Harold D. Lasswell, "Current Studies of the Decision Process: Automation versus Creativity," *Western Political Quarterly*, VIII (September, 1955), 381-399, 385, 386.

19. Cf. Morris R. Cohen's conclusion that "despite some amateurish philosophizing on the part of some physicists or biologists when they take a vacation from the field of their special competence, the fact is that natural science is never satisfied with empirical statistical correlation but ever seeks to formulate universal laws. . . ." ("Causation and Its Application to History," *Journal of the History of Ideas*, III [January, 1942], 12-29, 18).

20. *Christian Realism and Political Problems* (New York: Scribner's, 1953), p. 83.

21. *See,* for example, Anatol Rapoport, *Science and the Goals of Man* (New York: Harper, 1950).

22. Ernest Greenwood, *Experimental Sociology: A Study in Method* (New York: King's Crown Press, 1945), p. 78.

23. A conclusion as extreme as this is suggested by Eric Voegelin, *The New Science of Politics* (Chicago: University of Chicago Press, 1952), chap. 4. Few have been as explicit on this point as Laura Thompson (*loc. cit.*, pp. 55, 59-60). She maintains that not until social science has re-evaluated its premises in the "light of the new vision of science" and brought its "methods into line with new operational concepts, will a fundamental integration of the sciences of mankind emerge which may place in the hands of man a key to his own salvation." She concludes that, adopting the proper method, social science can help produce an ideal state by revealing what "nature-culture-personality structures" are conducive to it and by answering, among other questions, "How may those that do not fit tailor themselves or be tailored to a new and adequate design?"

24. In Lerner and Lasswell, *op. cit.*, p. 12.

25. "The Future of the Social Sciences," *Scientific Monthly*, LIII (October, 1941), 346-359, 240-244.

26. Karl Mannheim, *Man and Society in an Age of Reconstruction* (New York: Harcourt, Brace, 1951), pp. 240-244.

27. This may be illustrated by William Foote Whyte's *Pattern for Industrial Peace* (New York: Harper, 1951), an account of the relations of Inland Steel Container Company's Chicago plant with its union local of the United Steelworkers of America. Whyte says (pp. vii, 158) that the purpose of his report was "to discover general principles of human relations that might be applied to other cases, that might enable us to predict and control behavior." Yet, interestingly enough, his account somehow succeeds in enriching and enlarging sympathies for men as autonomous ends, suggesting that Whyte was less the single-minded behaviorist than he supposes. Apparently he permitted purposes other than his professed one to select and shape his material: he notes (p. 159), for example, that he "would like people to read this book." The desire to be read, to partake in human discourse, must have called for inclusion of many a nonscientific symbol, making his work valuable and significant in a sense other than intended.

Index of Authors

Index of Subjects